Wandering in the Garden,
Waking from a Dream

CHINESE LITERATURE IN TRANSLATION

Editors
Irving Yucheng Lo
Joseph S. M. Lau
Leo Ou-fan Lee
Eugene Chen Eoyang

Wandering in the Garden, Waking from a Dream

Tales of Taipei Characters

PAI HSIEN-YUNG

Translated by the Author and Patia Yasin
Edited by George Kao

INDIANA UNIVERSITY PRESS
BLOOMINGTON

First Midland Book Edition 1982
Library of Congress Cataloging in Publication Data
Pai, Hsien-yung, 1937–
Wandering in the garden, waking from a dream.
(Chinese literature in translation)
Translation of: Taipei jen.
1. Pai, Hsien-yung, 1937–   —Translations, English.
I. Kao, George.   II. Title.   III. Series.
PL2892.A345A24   895.1'35   81–47165
ISBN 0–253–19981–6   AACR2
ISBN 0–253–20276–0 (pbk.)   1 2 3 4 5 86 85 84 83 82

To the memory of my parents
and the time of endless turmoil and anguish
through which they lived

Raven Gown Alley

By Vermilion Bird Bridge
    the wild grass flowers;
Down Raven Gown Alley
    the setting sun lingers.
Of old, swallows nested
    in the halls of the Wangs and Hsiehs;
Now they fly into the homes
    of commoners.

—Liu Yü-hsi (772–842, T'ang Dynasty)

Early in the fourth century A.D., *barbarian invaders from the north brought the Western Chin Dynasty to an end, seizing and destroying the capitals of Lo-yang and Ch'ang-an. The Imperial Household, the noble families, and numberless commoners fled south across the Yangtze and re-established their capital in Chien-k'ang (modern Nanking). At Chien-k'ang, they carried on the Chin Dynasty, later known as Eastern Chin. Among the most powerful and cultured emigré families in Chien-k'ang were those of Wang Tao and Hsieh An, who lived in Raven Gown Alley by the Vermilion Bird Bridge.*

Contents

Foreword

Readers of this volume, noting that its author lives and works in the United States, may be disposed to see it as somewhat removed from "authentic" Chinese literature. But they would be wrong. Although Pai Hsien-yung has clearly learned from Western as well as Chinese writers, his stories are essentially Chinese—written in Chinese about Chinese society, published in Taiwan, and appreciated by Chinese readers in Taiwan and Hong Kong and around the world. (Some of his stories have also recently been republished in China.) In choosing to practice his art abroad, he is far from alone—Eileen Chang, the distinguished novelist, lives abroad, as do a number of other Chinese writers. To put Pai's fiction, the highest achievement in the contemporary Chinese story, into some peripheral category would be an injustice both to him and to Chinese literature itself.

All of the stories translated here deal, indirectly, with the crucial event in the modern history of China, the civil war and its bitter aftermath. The collection was published as *Taipei jen* (Taipei People) —an ironic title, since all of the subjects are mainlanders who fled to Taiwan after the Nationalist defeat. They come from all over China— the diversity of their dialects, customs, and local loyalties is remarkable in itself—and from all levels of society, from generals to common soldiers, from dancehall hostesses to cooks and nannies. While some, at a fearful cost to their humanity, have suppressed their memories, most cling to, and even live by, their private visions of the past. Taken together, their memories span much of the modern history of China; it is not without reason that the collection has been described as a "history of the Republic."* Pai's fiction shows them confronting

---

* See C. T. Hsia, "Pai Hsien-yung lun," reprinted as Appendix to *Taipei jen* (rev. ed., Taipei, 1977), p. 294. Ou-yang Tzu provides a detailed analysis of the whole collection in her *Wang Hsieh t'ang-ch'ien ti yen-tzu* (Taipei, 1976). Among interpretations in English, note Joseph S. M. Lau, " 'Crowded Hours' Revisited: The Evocation of the Past in *Taipei jen*," *Journal of Asian Studies* 35 (November 1975), pp. 31–48, and Ou-yang Tzu, "The Fictional World of Pai Hsien-yung," *Renditions* 5 (Autumn 1975), pp. 79–88.

their visions, either through the rituals with which the past is normally confronted (anniversaries and funerals) or through sudden, inexplicable events. By contrast, the real Taipei people, the natives of Taipei, serve as little more than elements of the background—a frequently harsh, always disillusioning background—against which the confrontation occurs.

The civil war has been so regularly subjected to polemical interpretation in literature that one's first impulse may be to ask where the author stands. It is an impulse that can safely be ignored. Pai's fiction is blessedly free of that bane of modern Chinese literature— the tendency to subordinate what is humanly true and significant to political ends. With the exception of the characters in "The Eternal 'Snow Beauty,'" a story written in a different mode, Pai's adherents to the lost cause are seen as human figures, above all. Surviving dully in a city of exiles, cut off from the most significant part of their lives, they are observed with pathos as they confront their visions of the past. The confrontation, for all its starkness, stands easily for part of the universal human experience, a part with which Chinese literature has traditionally concerned itself.

Patrick Hanan

Editor's Preface

The stories in this book appeared some fifteen years ago over a period of time in the magazine *Hsien-tai wen hsüeh* (Modern Literature), which Pai Hsien-yung and other young writers founded, edited, and wrote for in Taiwan. Published in book form in 1971 under the title *Taipei jen* (Taipei People),[1] these stories quickly established their author as a writer with a rare combination of artistic sensibilities, technical equipment, and a deeply moral purpose. The book has since won him a large following in Taiwan and Hong Kong and Chinese communities the world over. More recently, Pai's writings have been allowed into mainland China and are read avidly by a fortunate few among the youths of the People's Republic, who are starved for literature not written to the official line.[2]

That *Taipei jen* is a long time reaching the English-reading public must be attributed in part to the difficulties inherent in translation.[3] The title of the book, literally rendered, would in itself be misleading, since Pai is not engaged in writing polemical or topical fiction, nor is he dealing with what is called the "broad masses of the people." What he has given us, through a series of arresting incidents, is an insight into life as endured by a handful of men and women who sought refuge in Taiwan in the 1950s, following the Communist conquest of the mainland. In this context, *"Taipei jen"* may be more accurately rendered as "Taipei characters."

And what characters, in the colloquial sense, they are: from taxi dancers and sing-song girls to high-toned ladies. Venerable generals and elder statesmen, living out their days with memories of heroic exploits in the early days of the Chinese Republic. Scholars, teaching abroad or yearning to do so, while they recall their own student days of patriotic demonstrations. Old soldiers bearing battle-scars from fighting the Japanese invader. Air Force widows, ancient domestics, a proud food-shop proprietress, an aging homosexual movie director. These flotsam and jetsam of the civil war the author parades before us, in language by turns plain and sparkling, sometimes raw, frequently colorful, but always finely tuned to the speech of his motley crew. Like a solitary star in the sky, he fixes a diamond-hard gaze on the Walpurgis Night that is enacted, scene after bizarre scene, in the world below.

Pai Hsien-yung belongs to a remarkable generation of creative writers that grew up in Taiwan, received university education there, and went on to further studies in the United States before producing their mature works. This group, which includes both Taiwanese and the younger members of mainland refugee families, has already given us Chen Jo-hsi, author of *The Execution of Mayor Yin and Other Stories from the Great Proletarian Revolution.*[4] Chen's book, of more recent authorship and subject matter, documents daily life in the People's Republic during the ten harrowing years 1966–76. Pai's Taipei characters fill out an earlier and not unrelated chapter in the "trouble-ridden" history of contemporary China.

Pai writes out of a personal background rich in opportunities and vantage points for observing the people and things around him. He was born in 1937, the year of the Marco Polo Bridge Incident and the outbreak of war, a son of General Pai Ch'ung-hsi, the distinguished military strategist of the 1927 Northern Expedition and the War of Resistance against Japan. In 1951, General Pai retired with his family to Taiwan rather than join the Communist regime. Thus, there are autobiographical overtones to some of these stories, and in all of them we find evidences of a keen eye, of impressions tellingly registered, as the young Hsien-yung traveled with his parents from their native province of Kwangsi to postwar Nanking, Shanghai, and Hong Kong, eventually to settle in Taipei.

In his unflinching look at these individuals, exiles among their own kind, Pai Hsien-yung does not assign any blame or point an accusing finger one way or another. He notes with a high sense of irony their business (and pleasure)-as-usual lifestyle and, not without compassion, their clinging each to a past of real or imagined glory, or rather the past that lives on in them and haunts them. His is not a political nor even a social history, but a history of "the human heart in conflict with itself," in the words of William Faulkner, who wrote about the crippled and the dispossessed of another culture.

There is something to be said for the kind of hurly-burly society that has nurtured creative talent of this caliber. It was the same kind of mixed soil that produced the first fruits of China's modern literature following the May 4th Movement. Pai, with others of his generation, is a spiritual offspring of the Western-oriented Chinese writers of the 1920s and 1930s. But time has passed and circumstances have changed, and Pai is able to display a healthier appreciation of the Chinese cultural heritage and a more serious attitude toward his chosen craft than we see in the earlier writers.

An alumnus of Iowa's famed Writers' Workshop, Pai Hsien-yung presumably has absorbed the lessons of such masters as James and Joyce, Faulkner and Fitzgerald. His recurring theme of innocence in corruption suggests this, and his description of conspicuous consumption, of fancy foods and *hua-tiao* wine, invites comparison with Gatsby's lavish parties. But whether against a backdrop of high life or low, it is the passionate pursuit of a cherished, illusory ideal that brings humanity to his characters. For their meretricious aspirations, so much buffeted by forces beyond their control, the epigraph is equally apt that Fitzgerald wrote out of the ash heaps and the holocaust of his American Dream—"So we beat on, boats against the current, borne back ceaselessly into the past."

About half of the *Taipei jen* material was first collected, along with a couple of the author's earlier pieces, in a 1968 volume that bears the title of its leading story, Yu-yüan ching-meng (Wandering in the Garden, Waking from a Dream).[5] This poetic and evocative phrase is adopted as the title of the present English edition of the complete *Taipei jen* stories because it conveys both the nostalgia for happier days that runs through the entire work and the shock of reality that hits us at every turn.

In many ways the story "Wandering in the Garden" represents Pai Hsien-yung's style at its best, suffused as it is with the modern creative spirit and yet deeply rooted in traditional Chinese life and culture. The Ming dynasty drama *Peony Pavilion* is employed both symbolically and as closely woven strands in the fabric of a poignant tale. The title "Wandering in the Garden, Waking from a Dream" is, in fact, the name of a regional opera of later date based on Scene 10, the dream sequence, of T'ang Hsien-tsu's beloved musical play. The device of dramatic allusion, as Pai himself has pointed out, is often found in Chinese fiction, notably in *The Dream of the Red Chamber*.[6] In that classic novel of frustrated love the heroine overhears snatches of an aria from a rehearsal of *Peony Pavilion* and is awakened to the tragedy of the evanescence of life. The same aria figures in an even more organic fashion in Pai's story. The nouveau riche Madame Tou is giving an elegant dinner party for both old and new friends at her mansion with its beautiful garden in the Taipei suburbs. One of the guests is her old friend Madame Ch'ien, who was renowned in Nanking days for her singing. The music of the opera, mixed with intoxicating wine, calls up memories and old sorrows in Madame Ch'ien with such traumatic effect that she is unable to sing when urged to by the other guests. The words of the aria, Madame Ch'ien's stream-of-consciousness recollection of the past, and her awareness of her immediate surroundings build up to a climax that highlights the thematic unity in all of the "Taipei characters."

This kind of writing, with its brilliantly allusive language, poses an uncommon challenge to the translator. A time-honored dodge in Western popular fiction about the inscrutable Chinese is to simulate their exotic speech the better to lend "authentic flavor" to fanciful concoctions. A translator of Chinese fiction does not enjoy this luxury of license because he has an original text to which he is held accountable. Still, it is legitimate to translate literally from the Chinese for the sake of verisimilitude, and admirable if one can do so without ludicrous results. Sometimes the practice makes for obtrusive affectations —to say "cow's flesh" for "beef," for instance, or "people-as-host" for "democracy." In other cases admittedly picturesque expressions are transplanted from the Chinese, but their meaning is not apparent from the context and must be explained in cumbersome footnotes. Then there is a school of thought at the other extreme that believes in matching Western idioms to the Chinese. People the world over feel and think alike, so the reasoning goes, and for every well-turned Chinese phrase surely there ought to be an English (or American English) counterpart waiting to be uncovered and brought into play. The trouble is that to the extent one succeeds in this exercise he risks lessening for his reader the illusion of a Chinese story.

It is a testimony to the power and attraction of the *Taipei jen* stories that many scholars, both Western and Chinese, have tried their hand at translating them.[7] In this book the translators have been both bold and flexible in their endeavor to reproduce the pungent speech of the assorted characters. They retain the Chinese idiom as much as possible, while adopting American colloquialisms, even slang, that convey the spirit of the original. In "The Last Night of Taipan Chin," the tough-talking dancehall hostess obviously should not be made to speak standard English nor, for that matter, should she be given the spurious accents of a Dragon Lady. The same is true of the matron who narrates "A Touch of Green" and the boss-lady of "Glory's," through whose eyes we follow the love-crazed schoolteacher to his pathetic end. If English is to be their medium of expression, then they must be permitted to talk freely in the idiom and idiosyncrasies of that language.

The role of the editor in such an enterprise is one of mediation: to steer the precious cargo that is the heart of the story between the Scylla and Charbydis of disparate accents and imageries, to help achieve a tone and texture of language at once natural and precise, intelligible in English and faithful to the original, that will move the reader when the original Chinese does and not cause him to laugh in the wrong place. This means ameliorating an occasional verbal gaucherie and eliminating incongruities that might produce the wrong effect, whether these resulted from over-fidelity to the Chinese text or too free a helping of the riches of the polyglot American tongue.

A case in point: when Jolie Chin, the "last of the red-hot mamas" in any language, exclaims her impatience for the long-deferred altar, ". . . just five more years—five more years, mamma mia!" The equivalence here to the Chinese "wo-tê niang!" could scarcely be more exact, but we were constrained to use instead the equally serviceable "Mother of Mercy!"—at some loss, it is true, of comic vehemence —or the resulting ethno-linguistic mix would be too distracting for words!

Or a mere name can trip you up, such as that given the silent movie actor in "A Sky Full of Bright, Twinkling Stars." Shall we translate it straight and call him "Crimson Flame," or simply transliterate the characters "*Chu Yen*," two syllables utterly without meaning to a foreign ear. Our solution is something of a compromise, just as throughout the book personal and place names are sometimes romanized and on occasion colorfully and significantly represented, in the best tradition of the *Red Chamber* translations. For Chu Yen, or "Crimson Flame," could be interpreted further as a pun on Chu Yen for "Rouged Cheeks"—a Chinese symbol for ephemeral youth which has the weight of thousands of years of poetic literature behind it. A double footnote would have been required to unravel the author's intentions in this one name, not to mention a host of others equally intriguing to his Chinese readers. In such instances the translation has got to suffer a little in the interest of readability, leaving something for the classroom lecturer or the future Ph.D. candidate to explore.

In one case, in the story, "Ode to Bygone Days," the translators have adopted a truly innovative approach: they use the dialect of the American South to represent the homespun talk of two old women lamenting the decline of the once-great house in which they served. I have heard Chinese who know the United States well remark that they are reminded of their own way of life by the American South, with its soft accents and mannerly ways and the vestiges of an old culture in which the master-servant relationship played a strong role. With this in mind, the translation device—a kind of conceit, if you will—is not as strange as it may sound; and so I found it judicious to remove only a few of the more jarring regionalisms. Much of the rest of the translation is left in what I would like to call a "universal vernacular," without which these two nannies or any other of the Taipei characters might not be so readily and vividly realized in English.

George Kao

NOTES

1. Ch'en Chung (Morning Bell) Publishing Company, Taipei, 1971.
2. The PRC post-1978 relaxation in cultural activities has made it possible for certain *Taipei jen* stories to be carried in various periodicals, in each case without the author's permission or prior knowledge. These include: "The Eternal 'Snow Beauty'" in *Dangdai* (Contemporary Era) and "Glory's by Blossom Bridge" in *Renmin zhonggou* (People's China), both published in Peking; "Wandering in the Garden, Waking from a Dream" in *Shouhuo* (Harvest), Shanghai; and "Ode to Bygone Days" in *Zuopin* (Literary Works), Canton. The first of these also appears in a volume *Selected*

Stories of Taiwan. In 1981, the Guangsi renmin chuban she brought out *Selected Stories of Pai Hsien-yung*, with a preface by the editor Wang Jin-min which praises the author's literary achievements. Among the twenty stories collected in this volume are all the stories from *Taipei jen* except "A Sky Full of Bright, Twinkling Stars."

3. C. T. Hsia, among the first to hail the outstanding talent of Pai Hsien-hung, included an earlier story in his anthology *Twentieth Century Chinese Stories* (Columbia University Press, New York, 1971). According to Professor Hsia, Pai decided at the time against translating one of his *Taipei jen* stories "because of the difficulties involved in recapturing the richer language of the best of these stories and in making understandable the subtle allusions contained therein." Joseph S. M. Lau, in his perceptive essay " 'Crowded Hours' Revisited: The Evocation of the Past in *Taipei jen*" (*Journal of Asian Studies* 35, no. 1, November 1975), has emphasized native tradition as the wellspring of Pai's strength as an artist, saying that "no translation can do justice to a language so supple, so laden with symbolism, imagery, and allusiveness."

4. Published in the "Chinese Literature in Translation" series by Indiana University Press, as are two other works cited in passing in this preface: Tang Xianzu, *The Peony Pavilion* (*Mudan Ting*), and Cao Xueqin, *The Story of the Stone* (*The Dream of the Red Chamber*).

5. Hsien Jen Chang (Cactus) Publishing Company, Taipei, 1968. In addition to six of the *Taipei jen* stories, this volume contains the story *Tsê-hsien chi,* translated into English by the author and C. T. Hsia under the title "Li T'ung: A Chinese Girl in New York" in Twentieth Century Chinese Stories, and "Hong Kong—1960," translated by the author and published in *Literature East and West 9*, no. 4, December 1965.

6. At an International Conference of "Redologists" held at the University of Wisconsin, Madison, in June 1980, Pai discussed the influence of *The Dream of the Red Chamber* on his story "Wandering in the Garden, Waking From a Dream," particularly with reference to the use of the drama *Peony Pavilion* in both works.

7. Among those published in books are: "One Winter Evening" and "Jung's by the Blossom Bridge," tr. Limin Chu, in *An Anthology of Chinese Literature, Taiwan: 1949–1974*, distributed by University of Washington Press, Seattle; and "Winter Nights," tr. John Kwan-Terry and Stephen Lacey, in *Chinese Stories from Taiwan, 1960–1970*, Columbia University Press, 1976.

Acknowledgments

It was Joseph S. M. Lau of the University of Wisconsin who initiated the project of translating *Wandering in the Garden, Waking from a Dream* into English, and his enthusiasm carried it through the difficult first stages. Special thanks are due Stephen C. Soong of the Chinese University of Hong Kong for his constant support and his astute observations and advice. We would like to thank the following people for generously providing us with their drafts of seven stories for our reference: Dennis Hu, Thomas Gold, Anita Brown, Stephen Cheng, Linda Wang, S. Y. Kao, and Jeanne Kelly. Special thanks are due Katherine Carlitz, Anthony Yu, Diana Granat, and William Lyell, for their kind permission to have their translations edited and incorporated in this volume. Individual acknowledgments are made on the first page of each of the three stories concerned.

Our sincere appreciation to Irma Cavat and Thomas Perry of the University of California at Santa Barbara, who provided us with a wealth of information. To Irving Lo and especially to Leo Lee, who bore our harassments with utmost grace and good humor, heartfelt thanks for their patience in seeing this book through several years to publication.

Words can hardly express our gratitude to George Kao, our editor, whose devotion and ardor have been a never-ending source of reassurance and inspiration to us and whose incomparable skill as an editor has made this translation in its present form possible. For him it has been a labor of love, and his large-hearted sympathy and understanding have made our work a joy.

Pai Hsien-yung
Patia Yasin

Wandering in the Garden,
Waking from a Dream

The Eternal "Snow Beauty"

I

Yin Hsueh-yen somehow never seemed to age. Of those fashionable young men who had been her admirers more than a dozen years ago in Shanghai's Paramount Ballroom, some had grown bald on top and some were graying at the temples; some on coming to Taiwan had been downgraded to the level of "consultants" in the foundries, cement works, or synthetic-fabric factories, while a small number had risen to become bank presidents or top executives in the government. But however the affairs of men fluctuated, Yin Hsueh-yen remained forever Yin Hsueh-yen, the "Snow Beauty" of Shanghai fame. In Taipei, she still wore her white ch'i-p'ao* of "cicada-wing" gauze, smiling as always her faint smile, not allowing so much as a single wrinkle to appear at the corners of her eyes.

Yin Hsueh-yen was genuinely bewitching, though no one could say precisely where her charm lay. She rarely bothered to put on makeup; at most, she might touch her lips with a little Max Factor now and then, so faint as to be barely noticeable. Nor did she care to wear vivid colors. All through the summer, when the weather was burning hot, she dressed entirely in silvery white, looking cool and fresh beyond words. Indeed, she had lovely snow-white skin and a slender figure, with sweet, exquisite eyes set in an oval face, but it

---

* A long gown slit at the sides and with a high collar that came into fashion in the late 1920s. Called ch'i-p'ao (Manchu gown) because it was supposed to have been modelled on the women's dresses of the Manchu banner people.

This story was translated by Katherine Carlitz and Anthony C. Yü and was first published in Renditions 5, Hong Kong, 1975. *It is reprinted here in slightly edited form.*

was not these features that made her so extraordinary. Everyone who had ever set eyes on Yin Hsueh-yen said that, for some mysterious reason, every lift of her hand and every movement of her foot had an alluring charm the world could never match. While a yawn or a frown would have been unbecoming in others, in her it carried another kind of attraction. She spoke little: at crucial moments she might throw in a few words, ever so pleasant and soothing to the ear, in her Soochow-accented Shanghainese. Some patrons who could not afford to have her at their tables came nonetheless to the Paramount just to enjoy her radiant presence and listen to her soft Soochow speech, which seemed to make it all worthwhile. On the dance floor, her head slightly raised, her hips gently swaying, she always danced unhurriedly; even when it was a quick fox-trot, she never let go of herself, displaying the ease and suppleness of a windblown catkin drifting along, free of roots. Yin Hsueh-yen had her own rhythm; she moved to her own beat. No outside disturbance could affect her natural poise.

Inexplicable and innumerable as the Snow Beauty's charms were, one thing added immensely to her mystery. As her fame grew, she found it difficult to avoid the jealousy of her sisters in the profession, who vented their spite by spreading rumors about her horoscope: that it was dominated by an evil curse, that in it the White Tiger Star was ascendant, and that whoever came near her would lose at least his fortune, if not his life. Strangely enough, this well-publicized curse made her doubly attractive to Shanghai's fashionable men about town. Their wealth and leisure prompted them to adventure, to try their luck with this evil star, the queen of the Whangpoo metropolis.*

One of the men who thus tempted fate was Wang Kuei-sheng, scion of the Wang family, kingpins in Shanghai's cotton-yarn industry. Every evening he waited in his brand-new Cadillac at the entrance of the Paramount until Yin Hsueh-yen had finished her rounds at the tables. Then together they would go up to the roof garden on

---

* One of the colloquial names for Shanghai was *Huang-p'u t'an* (Whangpoo Beach), named after the Yangtze tributary on whose muddy banks had sprung up the cosmopolitan city that used to be known to the world as a "paradise for adventurers."

the twenty-fourth floor of the Park Hotel[†] for their exquisite late-night snack. As they gazed at the moon and the bright stars in the sky, Wang Kuei-sheng said that if he could use his family's gold bars to build a ladder to the heavens he would climb up and pluck the crescent moon to pin in Snow Beauty's hair. Yin Hsueh-yen just smiled, without giving him a word, as she extended her dainty orchid-like hand and slowly conveyed the crescent-shaped canapés of black caviar into her mouth.

Wang Kuei-sheng speculated madly, seeking to triple or qua-druple his fortune by any means, so that he could defeat one by one those wealthy suitors hanging around Yin Hsueh-yen, throw a dia-mond and cornelian chain around her neck, and lead her home. In due course, Wang was charged with the serious crime of manipulating the market in collusion with government officials and was found guilty. On the day he was taken from prison and shot, Yin Hsueh-yen can-celled her appearance for the evening as a gesture of mourning.

The one who eventually won the Snow Beauty was Director Hung, chief of a government bureau and one of the hotshots in Shanghai's world of finance. When he had divorced his wife, aban-doned their three children, and met all of Yin Hsueh-yen's conditions, she married him and moved into an elegant Western-style house taken over from the Japanese in the French Concession of Shanghai. In a few months' time, Yin Hsueh-yen burst upon Shanghai's high society like a late-blooming pear tree, completely overshadowing all the other beauties.

She was certainly able to dominate any gathering. At bril-liant parties where the fashionable daughters of wealthy families sat wrapped in their dark sable or red fox, she had only to appear airily in her waist-hugging, high-collared silver fox for all present to feel themselves intoxicated as with the light breeze in March and invol-untarily drawn toward her. In the crowds she seemed a crystalline ice-spirit, her frosty charm a dangerous force. As she glided along with her zephyr step, the sight of her called forth an answering fire in the eyes of those elegant men and women. This, then, was the fa-

---

[†] In Chinese, *Kuo-chi fan-tien* (International Hotel). For the Shanghai streets and business establishments mentioned in this story, we have used their original Western names, rather than translating their Chinese names literally.

mous Snow Beauty: on the dance floor of the Jessfield Nightclub, in
the corridors of the Lyceum Theater, or in the living rooms of the
aristocratic mansions along the Avenue Joffre, leaning against a sofa
or a chair, a faint smile playing at the corners of her mouth, dressed
in silvery white from top to toe, she summoned into her presence a
host of bankers and bankers' assistants, cotton-mill bosses young and
old, and the *nouveaux riches* and their wives.

But Director Hung's horoscope proved in the end no match for
Yin Hsueh-yen's evil sign. In a year he had lost his position; after
two years he was bankrupt; and upon arriving in Taipei, he could not
even land an idle consultant's job. When Yin Hsueh-yen divorced him,
however, she was magnanimous: all she took, aside from her own
possessions, was her famous Shanghai chef and two Soochow maids.

II

Yin Hsueh-yen's new home was in an elegant section of Jen-ai
Road. It was a new Western-style house with a living room spacious
enough to accommodate two or three dinner-party tables. Yin Hsueh-
yen had arranged her house with meticulous care. The living room
was furnished with rosewood tables and chairs. There were several
old-fashioned high-backed sofas heaped with pillows covered in black
silk with playful mandarin duck designs in Hunan embroidery. Sinking down into these sofas and resting against the soft, yielding silk
pillows, her guests felt supremely comfortable. She had made the
room so inviting that, as everyone remarked, once there no one would
want to leave. For mah-jong, there was a special parlor with the tables
and lamps perfectly arranged to suit the needs of the players. For
guests who liked to play *ua-hua*, she had set aside a soundproof room
where they could play and sing to their hearts' content.* In the winter
the rooms were heated and in the summer air-conditioned, so that sitting in Yin Hsueh-yen's house, one could easily forget Taipei's damp
chill or humid heat. The antique vases on the tables were always filled
with fresh flowers, for Yin Hsueh-yen was very particular about
flower arrangement and the finest blooms of the season were regu-

* In this traditional gambling game, which is something like mah-jong, expert
players often chant epigrams and rhymes about the tiles to heighten the spirit of
their play.

larly delivered to her by Rose Florist of Chung-shan Road. All summer, Yin Hsueh-yen's living room was suffused with the sweet, rich fragrance of tuberoses.

Snow Beauty's soon became a gathering place for old friends and new acquaintances. When her old friends came, they spoke of times gone by. In a nostalgic mood they talked of the good old days and poured out their pent-up feelings before Snow Beauty as if she were an eternal symbol of the Paramount days, a living witness to the luxuries of their Shanghai life.

"Baby, look how your godpapa's hair has all turned white!* But you're like an evergreen—you look younger all the time!"

Mr. Wu had been the general manager of a bank in Shanghai and a regular customer at the Paramount. When he arrived in Taipei he became a gentleman of leisure, having obtained a sinecure with an iron works. Whenever he saw Yin Hsueh-yen, he teased her in this half-playful, half-plaintive way. His hair had indeed turned completely white, and he hobbled from severe arthritis. His eyes were inflamed with trachoma; his eye-lashes were caught under his eyelids, and from constant watering, his eye sockets had started to fester, exposing pale pink flesh. In the winter, Yin Hsueh-yen would place the electric heater by his knees and offer him a cup of Iron Kuanyin tea, saying with an indulgent smile:

"Come now, Godpapa. You're stronger than you've ever been!"

And Mr. Wu's feelings were soothed and his confidence restored. He blinked his farsighted eyes with their rotted lashes and, in front of everybody in Yin Hsueh-yen's living room, sang the aria "Seated in the Palace"† in his old, cracked voice:

> "Like to a dragon in the shallows, I!
> Prisoner on the sandy shore."

Snow Beauty enchanted women just as she bewitched her men. The group of women who associated with her had been mutter-

---

* The practice of adopting "godsons" and "goddaughters" is a Chinese custom between families that have been close friends. Such a relationship can range from a pro forma gesture to a more substantive demonstration of affection. Occasionally, a wealthy old man may have a young and attractive single woman for "goddaughter," implying a liaison of an altogether different nature.
† From the popular opera *Ssu-lang t'an mu* (*The Fourth Son Visits his Mother*).

ing about her behind her back since their Shanghai days. When she rose to the height of her prosperity, they said spitefully, "No matter how high you climb, you'll still be nothing but a taxi dancer!" and when her benefactors found themselves in trouble, they sighed, "You can't escape fate; those people should never have gotten mixed up with such an unlucky woman." And yet for more than a dozen years, not one of these ladies could bring herself to part with Yin Hsueh-yen. When they came to Taipei they swarmed around her new home like bees; they were forced to admit that she had a hold on them. Yin Hsueh-yen could always get a twenty-five percent discount at the Hung Hsiang Silk Emporium, and she knew how to pick out the latest brocade shoes at the Little Garden Boutique. She knew, too, everything there was to know about the Shaohsing plays at the Red Chamber Theater. When the opera star Swallow Wu sang her favorite role in "Meng Li Chün," Yin Hsueh-yen could get free seats in the front row. And she knew intimately all the places that sold Nanking and Shanghai snacks in the West Gate district downtown. And so these ladies, under the leadership of Yin Hsueh-yen, toured West Gate, attended Shaohsing plays, ate cassia-flavored dumplings at the "Three-Six-Nine," and momentarily banished from their minds all thought of the unpleasant things that had happened to them during the past ten years or more. A glorious musky fragrance of eternal Shanghai seemed to emanate from Yin Hsueh-yen, and it so intoxicated these middle-aged women in their present reduced circumstances that they began involuntarily to recount the pleasures of eating crab-roe noodles at Shanghai's famed "Five-Fragrance Pavilion." When they became fretful, which they did easily and often, Snow Beauty bestowed on each of them her boundless sympathy, patiently heard out their tales of injustices suffered, and at the right moment spoke a few comforting words to soothe their ruffled tempers.

"So I'm losing! So what? I might as well lose everything! There's that old mule at home with his piles of money—if I don't lose it for him, somebody else will!"

Whenever Mrs. Sung lost at mah-jong, she poured out her resentment to Yin Hsueh-yen. In Taiwan Mrs. Sung had acquired the lumpy figure of a woman in menopause; her weight shot up to one hundred eighty-odd pounds. Bloated and swollen, she would pant if she had to walk too far. She was bitter because her husband, Assistant Manager Sung, was behaving coldly toward her—he had a mistress, and to make matters worse, the competition was a lissome hostess at a girlie restaurant. A dozen or more years earlier Mrs. Sung herself had been quite a belle in Shanghai society, so she particularly lamented the days long gone. Yin Hsueh-yen was naturally the perfect confidante, the only one who really understood Mrs. Sung's suffering and knew how to comfort her during those moments when, unable to bear her grief any longer, she would cover her face and cry.

"There, there, Sister Sung," said Yin Hsueh-yen sympathetically, handing her a hot towel to wipe her face with. "As the saying goes, 'People do not stay in favor a thousand days; flowers do not stay in bloom a hundred days.' Nobody can count on being happy and prosperous a whole lifetime." But Mrs. Sung, rebellious, continued to complain through her sobs:

"I just don't believe my fate should be worse than anybody else's! Look at you, for example—you'll never have to worry; someone will always back you up."

III

And indeed Yin Hsueh-yen did not have to worry: the stream of cars before her house was uninterrupted. Her old friends, of course, considered the place a blissful haven, but even her new friends felt in it a rare attractive force. The house kept its splendor, for Yin Hsueh-yen never let it fall below the impressive standards of the Avenue Joffre in Shanghai. To be sure, some of her guests were no longer fashionable people, but they had their status, they had their style; and when they entered Yin Hsueh-yen's house, they all felt their own importance. Even if a person's title was one that had been abolished well over a dozen years before, the way Yin Hsueh-yen used it in greeting, so warm and cheerful, made it sound like a royal summons that quite restored one's feeling of superiority. As for her new friends, they regarded her house as the ideal place to establish social connections.

What most attracted them was, of course, the Snow Beauty herself. She was an expert hostess, according the perfect reception to every single one of her guests, whatever their age or position. When they entered her living room and sat on those sofas with their black silk pillows, they had a sense of homecoming, of utter contentment. So, whenever a monthly subscription was taken up, the bidding for the subscription money was held at Yin Hsueh-yen's house; birthdays were always celebrated there; and even when there was no special occasion, her friends would find some excuse to have a mah-jong party there. On more than half of the days in the year, Yin Hsueh-yen's house was brilliant wth activity.

Snow Beauty herself rarely participated in the games. On the days of the parties she made the necessary preparations: sometimes two tables, sometimes three. She knew precisely her guests' temperaments and manners at the mah-jong table, so partners were always matched congenially, with never any hurting of feelings. She personally supervised her two neat-looking Soochow maids who stood on the side, ready to wait on the guests. At noon she might serve Ningpo New Year's pudding or stuffed rice dumplings Huchow style; for supper her chef prepared Nanking and Shanghai dishes: gold-and-silver ham,* Imperial Favorite chicken, prawns eaten raw with soya sauce, and crabs marinated in wine. Yin Hsueh-yen herself designed a sort of rotating menu; each day a new and delectable array of dishes materialized. Around midnight the two maids would serve cool towels scented with cologne, and invite the guests to refresh themselves in the heat of battle. Then came the midnight snack of extra-thin noodles in chicken broth. The guests were liberal with their tips, usually leaving two to three thousand dollars on the table. The winners were happy, naturally, but even the losers were relaxed and satisfied. When they had finished eating and playing, Yin Hsueh-yen had taxis waiting for them and saw them off one by one.

When the excitement of the games was at its peak, she would appear in casual attire and drift between the tables light as the breeze. Moving gracefully back and forth on her tour of inspection, clad all in silvery white, she seemed a priestess officiating at prayer and sacrifices on behalf of her warriors.

"Baby, look, your godpapa's about to be cleaned out again!"

Whenever Mr. Wu began to lose, he blinked his festering eyes with their rotted lashes and cried out in a pleading voice to Snow Beauty.

"It's still early, Godpapa—in the next four rounds you're

---

* Ham steamed and simmered with pork shoulder.

bound to make a 'Pure All-of-a-kind,' "* Yin Hsueh-yen said comfortingly to the luckless old man, placing a black silk cushion at his arthritic back.

"Miss Yin, you're my witness; I haven't played a single tile wrong and my luck is still terrible!"

The women also called out regularly from their tables to her for help. Sometimes when Mrs. Sung got fed up with losing she would forget herself and grab the pair of dice and start cursing:

"Damn! Damn! Damn! Shameless things! Let's see how long you can keep crossing me!"

Then Yin Hsueh-yen would go over to offer the women a few sympathetic words. Her words inspired her guests with almost religious awe, and at the mah-jong table, where one's fate was all too often beyond one's control, they all drew on her auspicious words for strength to restore their confidence and reinforce their will to fight. She stood to one side, a gold-tipped Three Nines between her lips, casually blowing smoke rings and watching with condescending sympathy as this crowd of once-mighty men and once-beautiful women, some complacent and some despondent, some aging and some still youthful, fought each other to the death.

IV

Among her new guests was a middle-aged gentleman named Hsu Chuang-t'u, a graduate of Chiao-t'ung University in Shanghai.† Tall, imposing, and robust, he cut a handsome figure in his well-tailored Western clothing. He was one of Taipei's newly-risen industrial magnates. With the industrialization of the city, many new enterprises had sprung up, and the resourceful and quick-witted Hsu with his knowledge of modern business administration had already assumed the management of a large cement concern, though he was barely forty. His wife was a perfect companion, and his two children

---

* In the "New Mah-jong," Shanghai-style, the winning hands were given various fancy names. "Pure All-of-a-kind" is one that scores high, as are the "Garden Full of Flowers" and "Four Happinesses at the Gate" mentioned later in the story.

† Then "the MIT of China," a technological institute famous for its engineering course.

were adorable. Hsu Chuang-t'u was an ambitious, vigorous business-man with a happy home and a career full of promise.

He paid his first visit to the Snow Beauty's house as a guest at the party she gave for Mr. Wu's sixtieth birthday. He was Mr. Wu's nephew, and he came to the party with his uncle. That evening, Yin Hsueh-yen had taken extra care to dress elegantly. She wore a short-sleeved *ch'i-p'ao* of moon-white brocade fastened with a row of large round frogs the color of ivory. On her feet were soft-soled shoes of white satin embroidered at the toes with flesh-tinted begonia petals. To attract good fortune she for once wore a bloodred camellia the size of a winecup at her right temple, and long silver pendants hung from her ears. The living room where the birthday celebration was held had also been arranged to give it a special air of festivity; the tables were decorated with freshly picked tuberoses, and as Hsu entered he was greeted at once by a sweet, penetrating fragrance.

"Baby, I've brought you a most distinguished guest," said Mr. Wu, resplendent in a new silk robe despite his bent back. Laughing, he introduced his nephew to Snow Beauty, saying as he pointed at her:

"Look at this goddaughter of mine! She's so good to me! I'm old and beat and she still throws a birthday party for me. I say to myself: Here I am, without a job, an old forgotten cripple, tortured every day by this damned rheumatism—hell, I may not deserve it, but I'm going to enjoy this party she's giving in my honor. As for my nephew here," he continued, turning to Yin Hsueh-yen, "So young and full of promise, he rarely lets himself go—today he's just joining us old fogies to have some fun. My li'l Baby here is a perfect hostess —I leave Chuang-t'u to you. Take good care of him!"

"Mr. Hsu is here for the first time, and he's your nephew, Godpapa, of course he's a bit special," said the smiling Snow Beauty, the bloodred camellia in her hair quivering vivaciously.

And Hsu Chuang-t'u did indeed receive special treatment. Yin Hsueh-yen sat at his side during the meal and helped him with the food and wine. Leaning toward him, she whispered:

"Mr. Hsu, this is our own chef's specialty—how does it compare with what you find in restaurants?"

At the end of the meal Yin Hsueh-yen herself served him a bowl of almond-flavored ice beancurd, crowned with two bright red cherries. Afterwards, when they settled down to mah-jong, Yin

Hsueh-yen frequently came and stood behind Hsu Chuang-t'u to watch him play. Being unskilled at the game, he often played the wrong tiles, and by the eighth round he had lost half his chips. At one point, when he was about to discard a "plum-flower five-disc," Yin Hsueh-yen leaned forward and stopped him, placing her delicate hand on his.

"Mr. Hsu," she said, "You mustn't let this one go."

Hsu Chuang-t'u won that very game with a "Garden Full of Flowers" and got back at one stroke more than half the chips he had lost. This raised a joking complaint from one of the other guests.

"Miss Yin, why don't you come over here and check *my* tiles! Look, I'm almost broke!"

"This is the first time Mr. Hsu has come here. It would be a shame if we let him go home a loser, wouldn't it?" Hsu turned his head and saw Snow Beauty smiling at him, her silver earrings dangling against her raven hair.

Toward midnight, the room was heavy with the fragrance of tuberose. After the hot *hua-tiao** at dinner and the excitement of his lucky hand, "Garden Full of Flowers," Hsu Chuang-t'u felt a bit tipsy as he was taking his leave.

"Miss Yin, thank you for being my teacher; otherwise I'd have been a complete flop at mah-jong tonight," he said to her gratefully as she walked him to the door. Yin Hsueh-yen looked like the Goddess of Mercy as she stood in the doorway, all in white, her arms folded across her breast.

"It's nothing," she said, brimming with smiles. "You come again some other day, Mr. Hsu. We'll continue our research in mah-jong."

Two days later he did come again—to pursue the mysteries of mah-jong with Snow Beauty.

V

Hsu Chuang-t'u's wife sat in her wicker chair, staring listlessly at the doorway. Her face was growing daily thinner, and her

---

* Literally "Flower Carving," a very mellow, sophisticated rice wine made in Shaohsing, Chekiang Province. It should be drunk heated.

eyes seemed to peer from deeper and deeper caverns. When her god-mother, old Granny Wu, came to see her, she took Mrs. Hsu's hand in alarm.

"Oh, my dear girl!" she cried. "It's only been a month since I've seen you—how can you have lost so much weight?"

Granny Wu was a woman of more than sixty, with a large build and not a single gray hair. Her feet had once been bound, but nevertheless she walked with a quick, sprightly step. She had trav-elled to Mt. Chingcheng in Szechwan for Taoist instruction and had become the disciple of a learned priest from the White Cloud Temple. The priest chose her because of her uncommon gifts and passed his mantle on to her when he ascended to heaven. She now conducted Taoist ceremonies in her Taipei home. In the center of the room she had placed a photograph of her late teacher, under which was draped an eight-foot-square banner of yellow silk. She announced that the spirit of her teacher often appeared to her on this banner and gave her instructions and that, because of this, she was able to foretell the future and avert misfortune. She had many followers, most of them middle-aged women; some of them were quite prominent socially. Although they were financially secure, they nevertheless felt empty at heart, and so on the first and fifteenth of each month they would stop their mah-jong or subscription-bidding and come in groups to Gran-ny Wu's parlor. There they piously chanted, genuflected, and distrib-uted alms to comfort the afflicted in order to find peace for themselves and their families. For those who were seriously ill or worried about family quarrels, Granny Wu was generous with her promises to seek divine help from her departed teacher.

"My dear, you look absolutely wretched!" she said to Mrs. Hsu, measuring the lady carefully with her eyes. Then she shook her head and sighed. Mrs. Hsu could bear it no longer; hanging her head and bursting into tears, she poured her heart out to her foster mother.

"Oh, Godmama, you've seen it all along," she said through her sobs. "We've been married all these years and he's never said a harsh word to me before, much less blown up like that. You know that in everything he does he wants to win—he always says that a man should think more about his business than anything else. We came to Taiwan, and it hasn't been easy these ten years—it's taken such a lot for the cement factory to get going, and finally he's made it. But when I see him drive himself so hard, going to all those social functions for the sake of the business, I just worry myself sick. I really don't care about his business so much as his health. So long as he stays well, it doesn't matter how hard things are on the children and me. But, you wouldn't believe it, this past month he's been a changed man. He's been staying away from home two or three nights in a row! I ask him a question or two and he gets furious and starts throwing dishes. He even gave the children a terrible thrashing the day before yesterday. And now people are telling me he's got some woman outside, somebody who's popular and smart. Oh, Godmama, what does an honest woman like me know about these things? How can I help looking like this?"

"My dear," said Granny Wu with a clap of her hands, "If you hadn't brought it up yourself, I'd never have mentioned it. You know how I hate to gossip. But since you think of me as your own mother, naturally I'm on your side. You know that fat Mrs. Sung—her husband, the manager, took up with some hostess from the Mayflower Bar, and she came running to me, weeping and wailing, asking me to pray to my old teacher for her. So I looked at her husband's horoscope, and sure enough there was trouble in their way. Mrs. Sung made a solemn pledge before the Master's altar, and I recited twelve texts of scripture for her, and then what do you know, her husband came running back obediently! Then I said to her, 'Stop spending all your time with those foxy women! You should be praying and doing good deeds!' Then she told me all about your husband. This Yin Hsueh-yen they call Snow Beauty, what kind of woman do you think she is? If she didn't have a thing or two up her sleeve, how could she have such a hold on people? Even a good, honest man like your Mr. Hsu she's able to get in her clutches. Oh, it's happened many times before—just look at history: Pao-ssu, Ta-chi, Fei-yen, T'ai-chen*— what a bunch of troublemakers! You think they were human? Demons, every one of them! In times of turmoil, they come down to earth and create trouble for people. God knows what this Snow

---

* All *femme fatales* in Chinese history: Pao-ssu, concubine of King Yu of Chou, "the lady who would not laugh"; Ta-chi, favorite of the infamous tyrant, King Chou of the Yin (Shang) Dynasty; Chao Fei-yen, known to be "light-as-a-swallow," evil influence in the life of Emperor Ch'eng of Han; T'ai-chen, or Yang Kuei-fei, whose romance with the T'ang Emperor Ming Huang is the subject of many works of literature.

Beauty Yin was in her previous incarnation! The way I look at it, you had better conjure up something to save your Mr. Hsu from this calamity!"

"Godmama," said Mrs. Hsu, bursting into tears again, "You know my husband isn't really a man without a conscience. Even though he didn't say anything, I know he feels sorry every time he comes home after staying away. Sometimes he just sits by himself, smoking furiously, and I can see the veins in his forehead standing out—he really looks frightening, but I don't dare go and console him, so I just worry myself to death. These last few days, he's been acting as if he's possessed—coming home shouting that everyone in his factory is making trouble for him. He even blew up at his workmen; yesterday he fired several of them. When I told him he shouldn't be too hard on those ignorant people, he started yelling at me, too! He's acting so strangely, not at all like what he used to be. I can't help worrying!"

"That's it exactly!" exclaimed Granny Wu knowingly. "What could he have done to bring this on himself? Give me his horoscope, and I'll look into it."

Mrs. Hsu wrote down the date and hour of her husband's birth and gave them to Granny Wu.

"Godmama," she said, "I'm counting on you."

"Don't worry," said Granny Wu. "My old Master is known to have unlimited powers. He'll help solve all difficulties and problems!"

But her old teacher's powers were not adequate to the task of saving Hsu Chuang-t'u. One day, as Hsu was pounding the table and cursing at one of his workers, the man, mad with rage, stabbed him clean through the chest with a drill.

VI

Mr. Wu served as the chairman of the committee that arranged his nephew's funeral. The constant activity cost him another attack of arthritis, and he hobbled more than ever as he hurried in and out of the Ultimate Bliss Funeral Parlor, supporting himself with a cane. On the day of the funeral, a chapel was erected inside the parlor, and the massed white wreaths and funeral scrolls sent by Hsu Chuang-t'u's relatives and friends went all the way to the front entrance. The banner from Hsu's colleagues at the cement factory bore this eulogy in large characters: "A HERO IS LOST TO US." From nine in the morning on, the funeral guests arrived in an uninterrupted stream. Mrs. Hsu had cried herself into a daze; in her hempen mourning clothes, her two children at her side, she knelt by the altar and thanked the people for coming. Granny Wu had arrived at the head of a team of twelve Taoist priests who, decked out in their robes and carrying ritual dusters, established themselves at the rear of the chapel and proceeded to conduct the sacrificial service for releasing the soul from suffering. A dozen or so Buddhist monks and nuns had also begun chanting the sutras for the dead, praying for deliverance and purification.

By noon the mourners had overflowed the hall. Suddenly a ripple of unrest spread from some point within the eddying crowd, and a respectful hush fell over the guests as they realized that Snow Beauty Yin had entered unseen, like a breath of wind. She was dressed, as ever, all in white, and she wore no makeup. Lightly and gracefully she walked to the reception table, lifted the brush, and signed her name in a single easy flourish. As she made her way unhurriedly to the center of the chapel, the other guests fell back, allowing her to proceed to the altar. Her face wore a grave expression as she stood before Hsu Chuang-t'u's portrait and made three deep bows. The sight stunned all of Hsu's friends and relatives who were present. Some looked startled, others were angry, and the faces of still others were full of doubt and confusion: but all stood as though transfixed by some secret force that none dared challenge. Even though Hsu's violent death had moved some of his wife's family to put the blame on Yin Hsueh-yen, no one had dreamed she would dare show her face in this brazen manner. The tension of the moment rendered them all powerless. After bowing before the altar, Yin Hsueh-yen walked over to Mrs. Hsu, reached out her hand and stroked the two children on the head, and solemnly shook Mrs. Hsu's hand. Then, even as the mourners stared at each other in amazement, Snow Beauty, with her zephyr step, sailed out of the Ultimate Bliss Funeral Parlor. All at once turmoil reigned in the hall. Mrs. Hsu suddenly fell to her knees in a dead faint. Quickly dropping her ritual duster, Granny Wu dashed over and carried Mrs. Hsu to the rear chamber.

In the evening at Yin Hsueh-yen's house a mah-jong party was going on again. Some of the players had fixed themselves up with partners that very day at Hsu Chuang-t'u's funeral. Mr. Wu once again brought two new guests: a Mr. Yu, the new manager of the Southland Cotton Mills, and a Mr. Chou, the director of Great China Enterprises. That evening Mr. Wu's luck was extraordinary: he won a succession of jackpots. He never stopped laughing and shouting, and the tears fell steadily from his inflamed eyes with their rotted lashes. During the twelfth round, he suddenly waved his hands madly and cried out:

"Baby, come here! Come look! I've got 'Four Happinesses at the Gate'! This is a hand that comes once in a lifetime! North, South, East, West—they're all here! Plus a self-drawn final pair! They say this is such a rare hand that winning the Four Happinesses bodes ill for the player. But since I've been down on my luck all my life, winning this hand may well change my fortune for the better. Come, Baby, look at this hand—isn't it lovely? Isn't it fun?"

Laughing and shouting, Mr. Wu scattered the mah-jong tiles about the table. Yin Hsueh-yen came to his side, and very lightly pressing his shoulder, whispered to him smilingly:

"Godpapa, brace yourself and win a few more hands. By and by, when you win from Mr. Yu and Mr. Chou, I'll come share some of your lucky money!"

A Touch of Green

Part One

It was the year we won the war against Japan and moved back to our capital, Nanking. We lived in Ta-fang Alley in East Benevolence Village, one of the housing complexes for the dependents of middle- and lower-rank Air Force men. To think, after enduring all that misery for so many years in a backward province like Szechwan, that we should suddenly return to the "Painted Capital" of Six Dynasties fame! Everywhere we were greeted by relics of ancient splendors and the hustle and bustle of the triumphant moment, everywhere there was an atmosphere of imperial grandeur; our eyes were continually dazzled.

At that time Wei-ch'eng was serving as commanding officer of the Eleventh Group. Two of the squadrons under him had just come back from training in America, so the pilots in his group were rather highly thought of and kept busy with many assignments. Whenever there was an important mission to fly, he'd take the boys out himself. Sometimes, three or four days in a week, I would not get to see so much as the back of his head. Every time he went on a mission he'd take Kuo Chen along. Kuo Chen was his favorite student; even when he was a cadet at the Air Force Academy in Kuanhsien, Szechwan, Wei-ch'eng used to say to me, "That kid is as smart as a whip! He's got a great future ahead of him." Sure enough, in just a few short years, Kuo Chen had worked himself up to squadron leader and got sent off to America for training.

Kuo Chen was an Air Force orphan. His father was a schoolmate of Wei-ch'eng's who was killed in a plane crash when Kuo Chen was very small, and his mother had fallen ill and died soon after.

While he was at the Academy, whenever New Year's and the other festivals rolled around, I'd invite him over to our home for family dinner. Wei-ch'eng and I had nor chick nor child, and when we saw Kuo Chen all by his lonesome we just sort of took him under our wing. In those days he had his head shaved—his scalp looked green and shiny—and he wore the mud-yellow cotton uniform of an Air Force cadet. He was a bright boy—that you could tell from everything he did and from the way he carried himself. But he was still shy with words, just a kid after all. My, it gave me a surprise the day he got back from America and came rushing over to our home in Nanking! He saluted me smartly and called me "Shih-niang."* I simply couldn't believe my eyes. He was all dressed up in an American-style gabardine uniform, a leather jacket with a fur collar, and a belt buckled tight with his Ray-Ban goggles-case fastened to it. He wore his high-peaked cap with the brim pulled down to just above his eyebrows; he had let his hair grow; it was black and shiny, brushed back neatly over his ears. Only a couple of years. Who would have expected Kuo Chen to turn out to be such a dashing young officer!

"Well, well, young man!" I said to him with a laugh. "You must have brought back some good news this time, huh?"

"Oh, nothing special, Shih-niang. I just saved up a few hundred dollars U.S., that's all."

"Aha! Enough to get yourself a wife with!" I chuckled.

"That's right, Shih-niang!" He grinned. "As a matter of fact, I'm looking around right now."

Our young pilots practically stole the whole show in postwar Nanking. No matter where you went, you were bound to run into some cocky flyboy parading around with a fashionably dressed girl on his arm. Romance was in the air—every pilot who was single talked about falling in love. Every month we'd get wedding invitations from some of Wei-ch'eng's students. But it was more than a year since Kuo Chen was back from America, and I hadn't gotten the good word from him yet. Oh, once in a while he'd bring some stylish young lady or other to our house to sample my famous dish, carp

---

* Literally *teacher-mother*, a term of affection and esteem used by students to address the wife of their teacher. The commonly used term for teacher is *lao-shih* (old or *venerable teacher*).

cooked in bean sauce. Afterwards, though, when I asked him what was what, he'd just shake his head and laugh.

"Nothing of the kind, Shih-niang. I'm just having fun."

Then, one day, he came running and told me the good news: This time it was serious. He'd fallen in love with a student at the Ginling Middle School for Girls. Her name was Verdancy Chu.

"Shih-niang," he told me, full of excitement, "I know you'll like her! I want to bring her over to meet you. Shih-niang, I never thought I could be so serious about a girl!"

By this time I must say I understood Kuo Chen pretty well. He was a proud boy; he'd made his mark early, so naturally he thought rather highly of himself. Whenever we talked about his future plans he'd tell me he would never marry unless he found a girl who met his standards in every way. The young ladies he'd brought over before were all extraordinarily pretty, every one of them, but none had measured up to his expectations. I thought to myself, this girl Verdancy must be some kind of fairy maiden sent from Heaven for Kuo Chen to be so smitten.

When I did meet Verdancy, she turned out to be a total surprise. One day Kuo Chen brought her to our house for lunch. She was rather frail, a slip of a girl of eighteen or nineteen. Even though she'd come as a guest she just had on a plain blue cotton frock, neither new nor old, with an ordinary white silk handkerchief tucked under the flap below her collar. She didn't have a permanent; her hair was combed back tidily behind her ears. She wore plain black leather shoes with straps and a pair of cotton ankle-socks, spotlessly white. I gave her a good looking-over: her body hadn't quite filled out yet, she seemed a bit flat-chested, and her complexion was on the pale side. But there was something limpid and graceful about her eyes— it did your heart good to see. When she saw me she kept her head half-lowered bashfully, with a timid air that somehow reached out to you. All during lunch, no matter how hard I tried to get her to talk, she did no more than mumble a word or two in reply. Kuo Chen kept himself busy, though, helping her to food one moment and pouring her tea the next, all the while trying to prod her into making some kind of conversation.

"You see how difficult this young lady is!" Finally Kuo Chen lost patience with Verdancy. "At least she's got something to talk about when she's with me, but the minute she sees people she clams up. Shih-niang is no stranger, and still she acts like she's lost her tongue!"

Kuo Chen was being a little too rough on her, really! Verdancy turned away, her face red with embarrassment.

"That's all right." I felt rather sorry for the girl and stopped Kuo Chen. "This is Miss Chu's first visit; of course she's a little shy. Now don't you pick on her. After lunch why don't you two go for an outing on Lake Hsuanwu? The lotus flowers there are just blooming. It's a gorgeous sight."

Kuo Chen had come on his flashy new motorcycle. When they left after lunch he put Verdancy on the back seat and helped her tie her black silk scarf around her hair; then he leaped into the saddle and started to rev up; he gave me a jaunty wave and was off in a flash, carrying Verdancy with him. She snuggled up against Kuo Chen's back, her scarf flapping high in the wind. From the way he treated her I knew he was serious this time, all right.

One day Wei-ch'eng came home with a frown on his face; the minute he walked in the door he started to fume. "That kid Kuo Chen is getting to be impossible! I didn't expect him to turn out like this."

"What's the matter?" I was astonished; I'd never heard Wei-ch'eng say an unpleasant word about Kuo Chen before.

"Do you have to ask me? Didn't you know he's been running around with a Ginling Middle School girl? He must have lost his head over her! He thinks nothing of breaking into her school any time of the day and trying to get her out, whether she's in class or not. And that's not all! The other day when he was up on a training flight, he actually flew over the Ginling campus and kept circling the school building! All the schoolgirls got excited and stuck their heads out of their classroom windows to see what was going on. The principal himself reported it to our headquarters—now I ask you, what kind of impression does that create for the outfit? One of my pilots carrying on like a lunatic. I'll have to punish him—but good!"

Kuo Chen got a letter of reprimand in his record and was demoted from squadron leader. When I saw him, he tried to explain to me. "Shih-niang, I didn't mean to violate any regulations and get

Lao-shih mad at me. It's Verdancy, she's stolen my heart away. Honest, Shih-niang, when I'm flying up there in the sky, my heart is down here on the ground, following her around. Verdancy's such a sweet kid, maybe a little shy and doesn't mix with people much. Now I've gotten her expelled from school; her folks have wired her from Chungking to come straight home. She'd rather die than go back! She got into a fight with her parents and broke with them. She says she'll follow me to the ends of the earth, no matter what, for the rest of her life! Now she's staying all by herself in a little hotel, and she doesn't know what to do next."

"Oh, you idiot," I sighed, shaking my head. I had no idea even smart people would turn foolish when they fell in love. "Since you two are so mad about each other, why don't you go get married?"

"Shih-niang, that's just what I've come to talk to you about, and to ask you and Lao-shih to preside at the wedding." Kuo Chen beamed.

After Kuo Chen and Verdancy were married, they moved into our East Benevolence Village. Kuo Chen had two weeks' leave to get married; he and Verdancy had planned to go to West Lake on their honeymoon, but just before they were to leave the civil war broke out. Wei-ch'eng and his group were ordered to Manchuria. The morning they were to take off, in the early dawn, Kuo Chen stole into my kitchen. I was just starting a fire to cook Wei-ch'eng his porridge. Kuo Chen, his jacket over his shoulders, his hair all mussed, eyes bloodshot, unshaven, grabbed my hand.

"Shih-niang," he said hoarsely, "This time, no matter what, I've got to rely on you to take care of—"

"I know," I interrupted him. "While you're gone, of course I'm going to look after that little wife of yours."

"Shih-niang—" Kuo Chen was still worrying. "Verdancy's too young; there's a lot she doesn't understand about the way we do things in the Air Force. You've just got to treat her like one of the family, try to get her to learn how to cope."

"All right, all right," I laughed. "Your Shih-niang has been with your Lao-shih all these years; I guess there's nothing in the Air Force I haven't seen. I don't know how many Air Force wives have learned the ropes from me. Verdancy's not dumb. You just leave it to me, and I'll set her straight—all in good time."

After Wei-ch'eng and Kuo Chen and some of the other boys left, I got my housework done and went over to see Verdancy. The housing allotted to them was a neat little bungalow. Before they moved in, Kuo Chen had the place painted spic and span, put up new drapes, and made it an attractive little home. When I walked in, I saw they still had the wedding decorations up in the living room. The table and chairs were piled high with wedding presents in their red and green wrappings, some of the packages not yet opened. The table was surrounded by baskets of flowers; the roses and the gladioli were still fresh; even the phoenix-tail ferns remained green. The wedding scrolls hadn't been taken down yet; on the living-room wall hung a wedding plaque presented by Kuo Chen's schoolmates, an ebony affair with gold inlaid characters:

TOGETHER THROUGH THE YEARS
TILL YOUR HAIR TURNS TO SILVER

Verdancy was in her room; she hadn't heard me when I came in. She was lying on her side, her face buried in the quilt, sobbing. She was still in her bright-colored silk bridal gown; her new permanent was all mussed up, the hair-ends sticking out like a bunch of twigs. She'd rumpled up their silk quilt-cover; on the traditional nuptial bedding embroidered with pairs of mandarin ducks in all the colors of the rainbow there was a tear stain as big as a bowl up near her face. When she heard me come in, she started and sat up; the only word she got out was "Shih-niang," and then all she could do was sob. Her face was pea-green, her eyes swollen, she looked more fragile than ever. I went over to smooth her hair down, and then I wrung out a hot towel and handed it to her. Verdancy took the towel, covered her face with it, and broke down again. Outside the house military trucks and jeeps were loading and hauling off baggage, the ear-shattering clang of iron rods and chains went on and on. One after another the men in the Village were leaving for the front; there was a general commotion—women screaming and children crying. I waited until Verdancy had cried herself out. Then I patted her shoulder.

"Well, these sudden partings—the first time around, it always hits you like this. Don't cook tonight. Come have dinner with me and keep me company."

Once Wei-ch'eng and Kuo Chen were gone, we didn't have the vaguest notion where they were. One day we heard they were sent to the North, the next day they wrote us they'd flown to Central China. Several months passed, and they didn't come home once. During this time Verdancy was with me constantly. Sometimes I showed her how to cook, sometimes I taught her knitting, and once in a while I even taught her to play a little mah-jong.

"Now this little game is a real cure-all," I told her, laughingly. "Whenever you've got something on your mind, just sit down at the table and—Red Dragon, White Dragon!—before you know it, all your worries will be forgotten!"

After she got married Verdancy had become much more outgoing, but she was still a little timid with strangers. Except for coming to my place she didn't make friends with any other families in the Village. I knew practically all their histories, so by and by I started telling Verdancy about them so she'd know something of the kind of life we lived.

"Don't sell these people short," I said to her. "They've all been through a lot. Take Mrs. Chou, for example, the lady who lives in back of you. She's been married four times. Her present husband and the three before him were in the same squadron—they were all good friends to begin with. When one died the next took over, and so on, one by one. Sort of an understanding, you see, so that there was always someone to take care of her. And Mrs. Hsu across the street from you, her husband used to be her younger brother-in-law. The Hsu brothers were both in the Thirteenth Group. The older brother got killed, and the younger brother took his place. To the children by her first husband he's Uncle, and at the same time he's Papa; for a long time they just didn't know what to call him."

"But how can they still talk and laugh like that?" Verdancy looked at me in bewilderment.

"My dear girl!" I laughed. "If they don't laugh, what do you want them to do, cry? If they wanted to cry, they wouldn't have waited till now."

Ever since Kuo Chen left, Verdancy didn't want to go far from the Village; she just stayed close to home every day and waited. Sometimes a whole bunch of us went off to the Confucius Temple District to listen to the singsong girls, but Verdancy wouldn't join us.

She said she was afraid of missing a telephone call from headquarters about Kuo Chen. One day a message came from headquarters: Wei-ch'eng's group was stopping over in Shanghai for a day or so; they might get a chance to make a quick side trip to Nanking. Verdancy was up bright and early, dashing in and out, and she came back from market with two basketfuls of groceries. In the afternoon I passed by her door and saw her in a blue cotton worksuit, an old kerchief around her hair, standing on a stool washing the windows. She was so small that even on tiptoe she couldn't reach the window-tops; she had a big washrag in her hand and was swinging left and right across the windowpane with all her might.

"Verdancy!" I called out, "Kuo Chen isn't going to see the dust way up there!"

Verdancy looked around; her face flushed when she saw me. "I don't know what's happened," she mumbled. "We've only lived in this house a few months and it already looks old and dirty. I just can't get it clean."

In the evening, Verdancy came by to invite me to go with her to the Village gatehouse where the military telephone was, to wait for the phone call. The people on duty at headquarters had promised to call around six or seven to give us any news. Verdancy had washed and changed. She wore an apricot-colored dress of light silk and, as an additional touch, a pale green ribbon in her hair—she even had some lipstick on—all in all she looked very fresh and lovely. At first she was quite gay, talking and laughing with me, but when it got to be a little past six she became tense, her face drawn, and she stopped her chattering. She was knitting and she kept looking up at the telephone on the table. We waited and waited; it was after nine o'clock before the telephone rang. Verdancy leaped up and rushed to the phone, the ball of wool in her lap fell to the floor and rolled all around, but when she got to the table she turned around to me.

"Shih-niang," she said, her voice trembling, "it's the phone."

I went over to answer the phone; the people at headquarters said Wei-ch'eng and his group had stopped for only two hours in Shanghai; they flew on to northern Kiangsu at five in the afternoon. When I relayed the news to Verdancy, she went pale. For a while she stood there stunned, without uttering a sound, her face twitching as she tried not to cry.

"Let's go home," I said to her.

We went back into the Village, Verdancy walking behind me quietly. When we reached my door I said, "Don't feel bad. In their business you never know what's going to happen next."

Verdancy turned her head away and touched her sleeve to her eyes. "I'm not complaining, really." Her voice shook. "It's only, waiting all day, in vain—"

I put my arm around her shoulders and hugged her. "Verdancy, my dear, Shih-niang's got something to tell you; I hope you'll listen. It's not easy to be the wife of a Flying Warrior, you know. Twenty-four long hours a day your heart is trailing up there after him. You can gaze at the sky, and look and look, until your eyes run with blood, but your men up there won't even know. They're just like so many iron birds—one moment they fly to the east, the next moment they fly to the west; you just can't catch them. Since you're married into our Village, Verdancy, please don't mind if I speak frankly to you: you've just got to harden your heart in order to endure the storm and stress that is to come."

Verdancy stared at me through her tears, nodding her head, only half understanding.

"You go home now." I lifted her chin and smiled at her with a sigh. "Go to bed early tonight."

In the winter of the thirty-seventh year of the Republic,* our side began to lose ground everywhere in the civil war. As the battles in the North grew more ominous, quite a few families in our Village got the bad news. Some of the wives took to going to the temples every day to plead with the gods and pester the Bodhisattvas; others went to fortune-tellers to learn what their future would hold; still others went to physiognomists to have their bones felt. I've never believed in all that mumbo-jumbo myself. Whenever I had no word from Wei-ch'eng over a long spell, I'd invite my neighbors in for a game of mah-jong to last through the night and calm myself down. One night, when I was in the middle of a game, that Mrs. Hsu who lived across the way from Verdancy came rushing in and pulled me right out of there; in between gasps she told me headquarters had

* 1948.

just sent word—something terrible had happened to Kuo Chen—it was over Hsuchou—he and his plane were dashed to pieces. When I rushed to Verdancy's house, it was packed with people. Verdancy was slumped backward on a chair, a woman on either side of her, holding her down by the arms; a white towel was tied around her head; on the towel you could see a bloodstain as big as your hand. As soon as I came in everybody started talking at once: A little while before, when Verdancy got the news, she ran right off to the end of the Village, Kuo Chen's uniform in her arms, howling as she ran; she kept yelling she wanted to go search for Kuo Chen. When people tried to stop her, she started kicking and hitting out as though she'd gone mad. The instant she was outside the Village entrance she dashed her head against an iron telephone pole and drove a big hole in her forehead; when she was carried back, she could hardly utter a sound.

I went over to Verdancy, took a bowl of hot ginger broth from somebody, forced a brass spoon between her teeth, and got a couple of spoonfuls down her throat. Her face was like a fish's belly gashed open, splotches of red and white, blood and sweat all over. Her eyes stared wide open, unseeing. She didn't cry, but her pale lips were opening and closing, a shrill, small noise kept coming from her throat, as if somebody had stepped on a blind mole and it was letting out a dying shriek. It wasn't until I had force-fed her the whole bowl of broth that her eyes regained their sight, and gradually, she came to herself.

Verdancy was ill in bed a long time. I moved her to my house and watched over her day and night; there were even times when I was playing mah-jong that I put her where I could keep an eye on her. I was afraid if I let her out of my sight she'd try to cut it all short again. She lay in bed all day, wouldn't talk, and wouldn't eat anything. Every day I had to force her to swallow some soup or something. In a few weeks, she was just skin and bones, her face ashen, her eyes sunk into two big holes. One day after I finished feeding her I sat on her bedside.

"Verdancy, you mustn't let yourself waste away like this and think you're doing it for Kuo Chen. If Kuo Chen is there and knows about it, he won't be able to rest in peace."

Verdancy listened to me; all of a sudden she sat up, shaking; she nodded at me and laughed coldly.

"What does he know? He fell and his body was dashed to pieces; how can he feel now? So much the better for him: bang and he's no more—I died, too, but I can still feel."

As she spoke, her face was distorted, half crying and half laughing, a terrible sight.

After watching over Verdancy for a month or so, I almost broke down myself. Fortunately, just in time her folks came from Chungking. When her old man saw her he didn't say a word, but her mother spat, "Serves her right! Serves her right! I told her not to marry an airman. She wouldn't listen to me—now see what a mess she's in!"

They just carried Verdancy out of the bed as she was, hair all tangled and face unwashed, called a cart and hauled her off, bedding and all. Only a few days after Verdancy had gone, the rest of us, too, started to flee the war and left Nanking.

Part Two

Ever since we came to Taipei years ago I've been living on Changchun Road. By sheer coincidence this housing complex for Air Force families is also called East Benevolence Village, but there's no connection whatever with the one we lived in in Nanking. We've got people living here who've migrated from all over China; as for the people I knew in Nanking, I have no idea where they've ended up. Fortunately, in these years the times have been peaceful, and the days go by easily for me. Our Air Force Recreational Activities are just as good as the ones in the Nanking days—a Peking opera one day, a dance performance the next. Every time they present something novel I like to go to an evening show and join in the fun.

One year, on New Year's Day, the Air Force New Life Club put on an evening of entertainment. People said it was the most elaborate in years. Somebody sent me two tickets, so I went, and took along the Li girl, my neighbor's teen-age daughter. When we arrived at the New Life Club, the program had already been going on for quite a while. There was a whole crowd of people grabbing for tickets in the raffle; in the New Life Hall the band had already struck up the dance music. The place was so packed you could hardly move an inch: men, women, young people mostly, everybody laughing it up—

my, what a racket! In the main hall red and green balloons drifted overhead; some young Air Force men in blue uniforms were popping them right and left with their lighted cigarettes, and the women jumped and shrieked at every opportunity. Being pushed this way and that in that mob of screaming and howling youngsters was enough to make your head spin! It took us some time, me and the Li girl, to work our way into the New Life Hall; we rested ourselves against a pillar and watched the people dancing. That night they had a big band from the Air Force, over twenty members. Quite a few singers, too, coming on one after the other, all snazzily dressed; they'd sing a hit song or two, then come down on the floor and start tripping the light fantastic with their buddies. Just as the band was at its hottest, a striking young woman dressed in a particularly seductive gown went on the stage. The moment she appeared the audience gave a roar of approval, signifying that here we had someone extra special. She stood on stage, her face wreathed in smiles, without the slightest sign of inhibition, and coolly adjusted the microphone. Then she nodded to the bandleader and began to sing.

"Granny Ch'in, what's the name of this song?" asked the Li girl, who is not up on the pop tunes like I am. I usually leave my radio on from the time I get up in the morning until I'm ready for bed.

" 'A Touch of Green,' " I answered.

I know that song well; I hear Radiance Pai singing it all the time on the disc-jockey shows on the radio. Actually, this young woman wasn't bad at all. She sang in the same lazy, sexy style as the popular singer. Mike in one hand, her other hand toying with her elaborate coiffure with an insouciant air, chin up, every word distinct, she purred:

> On East Hill, a touch of green.
> On West Hill, a touch of green.
> If you've got the fancy,
>   your fancy is mine,
> Darling! We two would make
>   a pair so fine —

Leaning backwards slightly, swaying this way and that, she belted out the refrain with a burst of energy that seemed to come from the bottom of her heart:

> Aiya, ai-aiya,
> Darling! We two would make
> a pair so fine —

While the band continued with the song, she put down the mike, took over a pair of maracas from one of the musicians, and was off *chi-chi-cha-cha* into a rumba-step, shaking and shimmying in a manner I would call quite daring. She was dressed in a purple cheong-sam* of see-through gauze, sprinkled with gold sequins, and three-inch stiletto heels; every time she wriggled, all the gold sequins flashed. When she finished her song there was no end to the applause, where-upon she tossed off an encore before coming off the stage to be snatched up by a group of young pilots. I wanted to hear more of the singing, but the Li girl kept after me to go to the raffle in another room. As we were pushing our way through the crowd, somebody caught hold of my arm from behind and cried, "Shih-niang!"

I turned around; I was amazed to see it was the woman who was on the stage a moment ago singing "A Touch of Green"! Ever since I came to Taipei, nobody calls me "Shih-niang" any more; over here I am "Granny Ch'in" to one and all. It was so long since I'd heard anybody address me by that old-fashioned title that for a second it didn't register.

"Shih-niang, it's me, Verdancy Chu," said the woman, all smiles.

I kept staring up and down at her; before I could say anything a bunch of pilots came charging up and started yelling for her to go dance with them. She shooed them away and whispered in my ear, "Please give me your address, Shih-niang. In a day or two I'll have you over to my place for a game of mah-jong. I'm pretty good at the game now; I've had a lot of practice, you know."

Before she turned to leave, she smiled at me and said in a low voice, "Shih-niang, it took me a good long time to recognize you, too, just now."

A long time ago, I saw the Peking opera "Wu Tzu-hsu Escapes through the Chao Pass." In the story, General Wu's hair turns white overnight from anxiety. I remember I used to think that kind of thing

---

* A later, sexier version of the *ch'i-p'ao*. Called *cheongsam* (long gown) in Cantonese, the word has entered the American English vocabulary.

only happens in a play; in real life, how could people's looks change so dramatically? That night at home, as I was washing my face I took a good look in the mirror; I was startled to see my own hair covered with frost, too. No wonder Verdancy Chu didn't recognize me anymore. When we were refugees from the civil war, our only concern was to come out alive; we hardly had time to think of anything else—the days and nights could turn themselves upside down for all we cared. By the time we were evacuated to Hainan Island, Wei-ch'eng had fallen ill and died. Here he had flown in the sky all his life and nothing ever happened to him—it was ironic that he should have kicked off just like that, while sitting in a ship. He had come down with dysentery; there were too many sick people on board and not enough medicine. I watched him letting loose all that muck until his face turned black. The minute he stopped breathing the sailors wrapped him up in a gunnysack and dumped him into the ocean along with a few other bodies. All I heard was a splash, and he was gone. From the day I married Wei-ch'eng I knew I'd have to plan how I was going to claim his body someday. I knew from the start that a man in Wei-ch'eng's line of work wouldn't outlive me. I didn't expect that in the end I wouldn't even be able to claim his remains. Ever since we came to Taiwan I've been so busy with daily living that memories of things that happened on the mainland gradually faded away. To tell you the truth, if I hadn't run into Verdancy Chu at the New Life Club I'm not sure I'd ever have thought about her again.

Two or three days later Verdancy Chu did send a taxicab with a note to bring me over to her house for dinner. She lived in another air force dependents' complex on Hsin-yi Road, Section 4. There were some other guests that night, three young pilots, probably in Taipei on weekend leave from the Taoyuan Air Force Base. They all followed Verdancy Chu's example and started calling me "Shih-niang."

"This is Smarty Liu." Verdancy Chu pointed at a short pasty-faced fellow, puffed out like a loaf of bread. "Shih-niang, just wait until you see him play mah-jong, the way he blows himself up! Then you'll know what I mean."

Liu sidled up to Verdancy Chu. "Big Sister!" he protested with a leer. "Don't tell me I got on your wrong side again today? Not one kind word so far."

Verdancy, chuckling to herself, simply ignored him and pointed at another fellow who was dark and skinny. "This one is a specialist in kid stuff—strictly minor league, Shih-niang, you might as well call him Baby-doctor Wang. In all the time he's played mah-jong with us, he hasn't shown a respectable hand yet. He's our King of the Chicken Game."

Wang laughed out of the side of his mouth. "Don't you go too far, Big Sister! Wait until we get down to the table, Liu and I, we'll flank you left and right and get you squeezed between us. Then we'll see how tough you can be!"

"Oh yeah?" Chin up, Verdancy sneered. "Never mind you two jokers. You can bring on two of your real tough cookies for back-up, and I'll take the lot of you to the cleaners. So help me, I'll see that none of you leave this place till you hock your pants!"

Verdancy was wearing a stylish sack dress. Her arms were bare, and there was a red sweater around her shoulders, the empty sleeves dancing up and down as she walked. Her body had filled out, too! Even her complexion had grown fine and delicate; her face was fashionably painted; her eyes, once so still and limpid, now darted this way and that, sending out coquettish glances. Then she introduced me to a man in his twenties, Young Ku. He was much nicer-looking than the other two, strongly built, with thick eyebrows and a high nose; he seemed to be a much more solid fellow, not such a wise guy. He followed Verdancy around as she took care of the guests, helped her move chairs and tables, taking orders from her, doing all the heavy work.

In a little while we all sat down to the dinner table. Verdancy came in carrying the first course, steamed chicken, a big fat hen, steaming hot, in a large amber porcelain bowl; the minute she laid the bowl down Smarty jumped to his feet and went around behind Young Ku.

"Young man!" he nudged him and yelled. "You'd better hurry and eat a lot of this stuff. Your Big Sister steamed this chicken especially for you—to make you big and strong!" At this, he and Wang let out a squeal of delight. Young Ku laughed, too, but he looked rather embarrassed. Verdancy Chu snatched a service cap from the tea table and hit Smarty Liu over the head with it; Liu covered his head with his arms and fled around the table. Wang picked up a spoon and ladled a helping of chicken broth into his mouth.

"Wow, it sure makes a difference when Young Ku is around!" He smacked his lips and sighed. "Even Big Sister's chicken broth tastes sweet as honey!"

Verdancy Chu tossed the service cap away and doubled over with laughter. "These two gallows-birds!" she swore between her teeth, shaking her finger to Liu and Wang. "First you cop my chicken broth, now you have the nerve to get fresh with me!"

"Aren't Big Sister's chickens all fresh killed?" Liu and Wang broke out laughing at the same time.

"If Shih-niang weren't here today, I'd really give you a piece of my mind!" Verdancy came over and put a hand on my shoulder. "Shih-niang, please don't be offended. I meant to have these young brothers of mine over so you'd be able to go eight rounds of mah-jong. How would I know I've spoiled these little squirts so, when they open their mouths they have no respect for their elders!" She jabbed a forefinger in Liu's forehead. "You, Smarty, you, you're the biggest nuisance of them all!"

She walked into the kitchen. Young Ku followed her to help bring out the food. All through dinner Wang and Liu kept up their wisecracks with Verdancy.

After that, every week or so, Verdancy Chu would pick me up to go to her place. But in all the times I was there she never said one word about the past. When we got together we'd always be busy playing mah-jong. Verdancy told me Young Ku didn't care for any other games, he just liked to fiddle around with the tiles a bit. Whenever he came from Taoyuan to Taipei on leave, Verdancy would go around finding mah-jong partners for him; very often she'd even pull in the boss-lady of the Supreme Fragrance, the general store around the corner of the alley, to make up a foursome. When Young Ku played with us, Verdancy wouldn't join in; she'd pull up a chair, sit behind him, and give him directions. Her legs crossed, one elbow resting on Young Ku's shoulder, she never stopped humming—songs like "Ten Sighs," "Oo, I'm Scared of the Twilight," you name it, she knew them all. Sometimes she'd sit there and hum through the whole evening, no matter how long we were playing.

"Tell me, when did you learn to sing so well, Verdancy?" I couldn't help asking her; I remembered how in the past when she spoke she was afraid to even raise her voice.

"Well, when I first came to Taiwan I couldn't find a job. So I hung around with the Air Force entertainment troupe for quite a number of years, and that's how I learned my trade."

"Granny Ch'in, don't you know?" The boss-lady of the general store laughed. "We all call her 'Superior Radiance Pai.'"

"Now, Boss-lady, you're pulling my leg again," said Verdancy Chu. "You'd better keep your eyes on your game, or else when you get cleaned out you'll be clamoring for an all-night session again."

One day, barely three or four months after I'd met Verdancy, I was buying some marinated delicacies at the East Gate Market on Hsin-yi Road when I ran into the boss-lady doing some shopping for her store.

"Granny Ch'in!" The minute she saw me she caught me by the arm. "Did you hear? That Young Ku, friend of Miss Chu's, was in an accident! Last Saturday! They said it was right there over the Taoyuan Air Base. He was in the air only a few minutes, and then he crashed."

"I didn't know a thing about it!" I said.

The boss-lady hailed a pedicab, and the two of us went over to see Verdancy. All the way there the boss-lady kept up her commentary.

"Now *how* are you going to explain this? Such a *strong, healthy* fellow, and pfft! he's gone. That Young Ku had been *in* and *out* of Miss Chu's for I guess over two years. At first Miss Chu said Young Ku was her godbrother, but the way they kept eyeing each other, it didn't look like it at *all*. Everybody in our alley says Miss Chu has a taste for 'spring chickens,' particuarly those young kids in the Air Force. Can you blame her, though? A man like Young Ku, such a *sweet* temper, listened to *everything* Miss Chu said—where would you find another man like that? I feel *so* sorry for Miss Chu!"

When we arrived at Verdancy's home, we rang the bell for a long time, but nobody answered. After a while we heard Verdancy calling to us through the window, "Shih-niang, Boss-lady, come on in, the door's not locked."

We pushed open the door and walked up to her living room. There was Verdancy, sitting on the windowsill, in pink silk pajamas; she'd rolled up the cuffs of her pants and was painting her toenails with Cutex; her hair was still in curlers.

"I spotted you two right away." She looked up at us and laughed. "The nail polish isn't dry yet, I couldn't put my shoes on to go open the door for you. Sorry to have kept you waiting—you picked the perfect time to come! I've just cooked up a big potful of sweet-and-sour pigs' feet for dinner; I was worried nobody'd show up to help me eat it. Granny Yu across the street is coming over to return my knitting needles, and the four of us'll be just right for a game of mah-jong.

As she was talking, Granny Yu came in. Verdancy jumped down off the windowsill in a hurry and picked up her nail polish. "Boss-lady," she told her neighbor from the general store, "why don't you set the table for me. I'll go into the kitchen and get the food. This is Ladies' Day today—we're all fast on the draw—and after dinner we should be good for at least twenty-four rounds."

I followed Verdancy into the kitchen to give her a hand. She poured the sweet-and-sour pigs' feet out of the pot, set the pot back on the stove, and started to fry a dish of "Granny Ma's beancurd." I stood by her, holding a plate, waiting for her to put the food on it.

"Young Ku got killed; you must have heard about it, Shih-niang?" Verdancy kept stir-frying the beancurd; she didn't even turn her head.

"The boss-lady just told me, a little while ago."

"Young Ku has no relatives here; it's his schoolmates and me who took care of his funeral. Yesterday afternoon I carried his ashes to the Green Lake Air Force Cemetery and buried them."

I stood behind Verdancy, looking at her, without saying anything. Verdancy had no makeup on, but she still looked extraordinarily young and lively; she didn't look at all like a woman on the wrong side of thirty, probably because her cheeks were now full and blooming and her skin smooth and taut. It seemed the years were unable to carve any lines on her face. Though I had many more years behind me than Verdancy, I felt there was no need for me to find something to say to console her. Verdancy gave the beancurd a few deft flips with the spatula and tipped it out of the wok onto my plate; she scooped up a spoonful and put it in my mouth.

"Shih-niang, have a taste of my hot-pepper beancurd," she laughed. "You think it's spicy enough?"

After dinner, Verdancy set up the mah-jong table and brought out the Soochow tiles she reserved for guests. As soon as we sat down to the game, Verdancy made a Grand Three Dragons the very first hand.

"Miss Chu!" protested the boss-lady. "You're so lucky, you should go buy a Patriotic Lottery ticket!"

"You all better look out!" Verdancy laughed. "Today I'll have everything going for me again."

By the time the eighth round began, Verdancy had practically wiped out the three of us; the chips in front of her were piled all the way up to her nose. Verdancy kept laughing and humming her favorite song, "A Touch of Green." Every so often she would sing the words:

> *Aiya, ai-aiya,*
> Darling! If you want to pick flowers,
>   do it while there's time —

New Year's Eve

On New Year's Eve a cold front suddenly invaded Taipei, and by twilight the sky was already dark. The lights in the houses were lit earlier than usual, as if to hurry away what was left of the old year and make ready to welcome the new.

In East Hsin-yi Village at the end of Changchun Road, the chimneys of the bungalows in the military dependents' quarters sent up puffs of smoke; the noise of spatulas and popping oil, together with intermittent chatter and laughter, spilled into the streets. New Year's Eve was gradually approaching its high point—time for the family reunion dinner.

This evening in Major Liu's house, Number 5 East Hsin-yi Village, the lights were burning especially bright. In the living-room window stood a pair of red candles, about a foot tall and as thick as a child's arm. Their flames shot up merrily, casting a glow over the modest living room.

"Brother Lai!* You've come so far to join us for New Year's; why did you have to spend so much money, too? Wine, and chicken, and those huge candles! It's a wonder you managed to carry them all the way here!" Mrs. Liu came into the room, carrying a copper Mongolian hot-pot with burning charcoals crackling and jumping underneath, and with a warm smile greeted the guest seated in the place of honor at the round dinner table. She was a middle-aged woman of about forty, wearing a new black satin dress embroidered with clusters of purple flowers, over which she had put on a blue cotton apron. Her hair was combed into a glossy bun. Except for her finely pencilled

---

* *Ta-ko*, "Elder Brother," here used as a term of respect and friendship.

This story was translated by Diana Granat and was first published in Renditions 5, Hong Kong, 1975. It is reprinted here in slightly edited form.

eyebrows, she wore no makeup. Mrs. Liu spoke the Szechwanese dialect in such a way that her words rolled off her tongue in crisp and distinct syllables.

"You're so right, Sister!" said Lai, slapping his knee. "Those candles sure gave me a lot of trouble." He spoke in a loud, rough voice, with a thick Szechwan accent. "The Tainan Railroad Station was so crowded today you could hardly breathe. Lucky I'm tall; I held the candles high above my head so nobody would break them. I don't get to see you folks more than once a year, so I said to myself, I must spend New Year's Eve with you, and we'll see the old year out together. We'll sit up the whole night through, and having the candles lit up will bring us all joy." He gave a hearty laugh. His swarthy face was covered with liver spots, and when he laughed his wrinkles stood out like so many ripples. His inch-long hair, already frosted to the top, stuck up like the bristles on a tough wire brush. He was unusually big-boned—seated, he was a head taller than the people beside him. He wore a threadbare Sun Yat-sen tunic of dark blue gabardine and underneath it a grass-green sweater, showing cuffs already unravelled and the seams coming apart. He had huge hands, all ten fingers gnarled like the roots of a tree.

"Brother Lai, that's exactly what my wife had in mind," Major Liu put in. "She's even found mah-jong partners for you."

Major Liu was still in uniform. He was a tall, thin man with lean cheeks, his taut, copper-colored skin burnished by the fierce sun and the sea winds. His sideburns had started to turn white, too. When he spoke his accent was all Szechwanese, just like that of his guest.

"I know Brother Lai loves to play a round or two—that's why I kept this pair here." Mrs. Liu set the cooker down in the center of the dinner table and indicated the young man and the girl seated there. "It's not every day that Cousin Li-chu and Yu Hsin can come, either! Only this afternoon Li-chu was on duty at the Military Hospital, and Yu Hsin just came up today from Camp Feng-shan. The two of them had probably planned on a cozy date tonight all by themselves, but I forced them to stay so they could keep Brother Lai company and in a while we'll play Going Round the Garden together."*

"Going Round the Garden—I, Lai Ming-sheng, am an expert

---

* A friendly game of mah-jong for limited stakes. When a player loses all his chips he is allowed to continue playing, but not for money.

at that!" cried Lai Ming-sheng. "Nobody leaves the table till dawn! My dear Miss Li-chu, if you want to bill and coo with our young buddy here, you go right ahead and do it across the table. Just pretend we're not here."

Li-chu blushed, giggling, and Yu Hsin, a little flustered, managed an embarrassed smile. Li-chu was a petite girl with a rosy complexion and sparkling black eyes. You would think she wasn't more than sixteen or seventeen to look at her, but she had been a nurse for two years already at the Military Hospital. Yu Hsin was seated by her side, his body rigidly upright. He was in an American-style uniform of light khaki, freshly starched and sharp-creased, complete with black tie. A shiny gold cadet-school badge was pinned to his collar. His very youthful face, clean-shaven, shone with a fresh radiance, and his newly cut and blown hair lay obediently on his head.

"I want to stay up all night, too," interrupted Major Liu's ten-year-old son, Liu Ying, who was also sitting at the table.

"After dinner you should be off to bed!" Mrs. Liu hollered at the boy. "Staying up all night indeed!"

"Uncle Lai promised to take me out on the street at midnight to shoot off firecrackers." Liu Ying looked toward Lai Ming-sheng and protested anxiously.

"'Attaboy!" laughed Lai, reaching out a huge palm and giving Liu Ying a pat on his glossily-shaven head. "Your Uncle Lai shoots a mean firecracker. In a little while, I'll show you—bang goes a flash bomb in my bare hands!"

He turned to Mrs. Liu. "My dear Sister, don't underestimate this little fellow. He might turn out to be a general one day!"

"A general?" Mrs. Liu snorted. "In this world you're doing all right if you don't starve. I couldn't care less whether or not he becomes a high-ranking official."

"What do you want to be when you grow up, boy?" Lai Ming-sheng asked Liu Ying.

"Commander in Chief of the Army!" Nose in the air, Liu Ying answered in all seriousness.

Everyone at the table burst out laughing, and even Mrs. Liu couldn't help but laugh. Lai Ming-sheng, his face all wrinkled up with laughter, pulled Liu Ying to his bosom.

"Sounds ambitious enough, all right! Good for you, my boy!

When your Uncle Lai was your age, he set his sights even higher."

Mrs. Liu went back in and came out again with several plates of food for the hot-pot: a plate of tripe, one of kidneys, two plates of sliced mutton, and five or six dishes of assorted Szechwanese pickled vegetables in red pepper sauce. She placed a dish of fried peanuts in front of Lai Ming-sheng specially, for him to eat with his wine, and began to pour wine for everyone.

"Brother Lai also brought these bottles of Quemoy *kao-liang*,"* she announced. "Why did you have to bring a whole dozen? Two bottles would have been enough to add to the holiday cheer. We don't have that many drinking men here."

"I didn't buy them, as a matter of fact," Lai Ming-sheng said, indicating the bottles of *kao-liang* on the side table. "They were brought to me as a gift by an old subordinate—an assistant platoon leader on Quemoy—when he returned to Tainan on leave. He still remembered me as his former chief, bless him, but I had forgotten all about him."

"Brother Lai, you are *my* former superior, too. Permit me to drink a toast to you first!" Major Liu stood up and, holding a brimming cup of *kao-liang*, went over to Lai Ming-sheng. Raising his wine cup in both hands, he offered a toast to him.

"Worthy Brother." Lai Ming-sheng stood up suddenly and, pressing Major Liu down onto the chair, spoke in a hoarse voice. "Surely I will drink this cup with you. But it all depends on how we drink. If we're talking as friends and old brothers in arms, it will not be too much if you toast me ten times tonight. But if you drink to me as your former senior officer, I won't touch a drop! In the first place, I've already retired. In the second place, you're an officer now. A major—you can say it's an important rank or not—a major commands several hundred men. As for me, I'm only a kitchen purveyor at the Veterans Hospital. A—what do they call it in the Army? Chief Army Cook!"†

As Lai Ming-sheng spoke he started to laugh out loud; then little Liu Ying let out a yelp and laughed with him. Lai Ming-sheng

---

* A very strong liquor distilled from millet. The best *kao-liang* in Taiwan is made on the island of Quemoy.

† *Huo-fu-t'ou.* Originally designating the chief army cook, the term is also applied to the person in charge of the military kitchen, usually in a deprecatory sense.

gave the boy a pat on his shiny head. "What are you laughing at, kid? Don't you look down on a Chief Army Cook. Your Uncle Lai started out as a Chief Army Cook, and he made his way up to be an officer! . . . So I tell you Brother, a proper major as you are, if you go around calling a cook 'my former superior,' what will people think? It doesn't sound right!"

All this while Major Liu, held captive on the chair by Lai Ming-sheng, was waving his hand in protest. Mrs. Liu took a cup of wine over to Lai Ming-sheng. "Dear Brother Lai, you're wrong," she laughed. "Not only are you two buddies who have been through thick and thin together, but when you were already an officer, he was nothing."

"Me? When Brother Lai was a company commander in Szechwan, I was just an orderly in his company," Major Liu added at once.

"Just what I said! Now, Brother Lai, will you still deny you were his superior? Not only should he offer you a toast, I want to drink to you, too. Here!"

As Mrs. Liu spoke she drank up half the cup. Everyone at the table rose and, addressing Lai Ming-sheng as "Senior Officer," offered him a toast. Protesting vigorously, Lai Ming-sheng made some effort to decline; then he tilted his head back with a laugh and downed his cup of Quemoy *kao-liang*. He sat down, smacked his lips, poached himself some tripe in the hot-pot, and swallowed it as a chaser. Mrs. Liu began refilling everybody's cups.

"What, our young friend!" Lai Ming-sheng exclaimed. "You haven't finished your cup yet?" Just as Mrs. Liu was about to pour Yu Hsin some more, Lai Ming-sheng noticed the young cadet's cup was still half full. He pointed his finger at Yu Hsin as if he had been insulted.

Yu Hsin stood up hurriedly. "Sir," he explained, his face full of chagrin, "I really can't drink—"

"What's that?" Lai Ming-sheng broke in. "That's all very well for ladies, but how can a military man leave his cup undrained? Young friend, when I was your age I gulped *san-hua* and *mao-t'ai** down by the bowl. I would get so drunk I'd fall off my horse, but the next day I would charge into battle and fight like hell. How can you

---

* Both potent grain spirits. *Mao-t'ai* may be more widely known abroad.

be a soldier if you can't even drink? Drink up! Drink up!"

Yu Hsin had to raise his cup and finish what was left. In a moment his youthful face flushed to his eyelids; at once Lai Ming-sheng snatched the bottle out of Mrs. Liu's hands and started to pour lavishly into the young cadet's cup. Yu Hsin, smiling nervously, didn't dare make any comment. Li-chu, seated next to him, looked at Lai Ming-sheng. "Brother Lai," she said with an imploring smile, "he really can't drink. A few days ago he drank a little rice wine and broke out in rashes all over."

"Now, Miss Li-chu, don't you coddle him. How can a few cups of kao-liang harm a sturdy lad? To tell you the truth, I'm pleased as all get-out to see the two of you tonight. Such a fine, handsome couple—by all means, I must drink a double with you!"

Lai Ming-sheng poured himself two cups of kao-liang, took one in each hand and went over to Yu Hsin and Li-chu; Li-chu hurried to her feet.

"Young friend," he said, addressing Yu Hsin, "I shall presume upon my age and give you straight talk. A soldier's solemn duty is of course to serve the country, but marriage is also an important matter and must not be neglected. Look at your major and Mrs. Liu here—aren't they an enviable pair?"

"That'll do, Brother Lai!" Mrs. Liu shouted across the table with a laugh. "It's not enough that you tease the two kids, you have to make fun of us old ones too!"

"You're pretty lucky, my young friend. You wouldn't find another like our Miss Li-chu here even if you searched all over Taipei with a lantern. So you should try to do like your major and love your wife in the days to come. If you ever take advantage of her, I'll be the first to call you to account."

Li-chu had long before turned completely red with embarrassment and lowered her head. Lai Ming-sheng raised the two cups and, having invoked a blessing on Yu Hsin and Li-chu, gulped them down one after the other.

"Take it easy now, Brother Lai, this is Quemoy kao-liang!" Mrs. Liu called from the other side of the table, but Lai Ming-sheng came behind her in a few strides. Waving his long arms, his swarthy face already flushed, he put his head close to her ear. "Sister," he said, "my worthy brother is certainly fortunate in having a wife like you—

he must have done good deeds in his previous life to deserve you. Although I've been an old bachelor all my life, I've seen a lot of husbands and wives. My dear Sister, it's not easy to find a couple like you. Believe me, it's not easy."

Mrs. Liu laughed till she had to bend over the table. She turned around to him. "Brother Lai, just treat me to a good meal and I promise I'll get you a wife. The boss-lady who runs the cigarette stand on our corner—she's one handsome woman! and she's looking for a boss-man. Would you be interested?"

"My hearty thanks to you, Sister," said Lai Ming-sheng with a throaty chortle as he faced Mrs. Liu and bowed, "but I'd rather defer this share of my good fortune till the next life. I won't keep this a secret from you: last year I did itch with a bit of this worldly desire, and look where it's got me! You see, when I retired last year I got more than thirty thousand dollars in separation pay. To rich people that kind of money doesn't mean a damn thing, but I had never held so much cash in my hands in my whole life. At first I thought of going into some small business, but then a guy from my home town came along and wanted to play matchmaker. He said he knew of some mountain woman,* a widow in Hualien, who was looking for a husband. So I went to see for myself and sure enough she was a young woman in her twenties. Didn't look so bad, either. Her family asked for twenty-five thousand, not a penny less. So like a shot I offered up all my retirement pay plus gold rings and bracelets to doll the girl up from head to toe. How was I to know those wild mountain women don't have one ounce of gratitude in them? Three days after we got married, she ran away without leaving so much as a ghost's shadow. And she cleaned me out good and proper, too—even managed to take the worn-out cotton bedding with her."

As Lai Ming-sheng went on, he drained his cup of *kao-liang* without having to be encouraged and wiped his mouth on the back of his hand. Suddenly he leaped behind Yu Hsin. His hands resting on Yu Hsin's shoulders, he took a good look at the young man. "If I could still look like him, that wild woman—she wouldn't want to leave me even if I drove her out!" Everyone laughed at this, and Lai Ming-sheng went on. "Young friend," he said to Yu Hsin, "I don't

---

* A woman of the mountain tribes in Taiwan, often referred to in English as "aborigines."

mean to brag, but in those days when I had my leather shoulder strap and belt on, I bet I looked even smarter than you do."

"You sure cut one hell of a figure in those days," Major Liu echoed, laughing.

"That's right!" Mrs. Liu put in. "Otherwise, how could he have cut his major's boots and gotten away with it?"

"What's 'cutting somebody's boots,' Cousin?" Li-chu asked Mrs. Liu in a soft aside.

"I don't know how to tell you," Mrs. Liu replied giggling; she covered her mouth and kept waving her hand. "You ask your Brother Lai."

Lai Ming-sheng didn't wait for Li-chu to put the question, but edged closer to her, his smiling face all wrinkles. "Miss Li-chu," he said, "tonight the wine makes me bold. You want to hear about 'cutting the boots'? All right, I'll tell you about the year I cut my major's boots. Worthy Brother, do you still remember Pockmarked Li, Li Ch'un-fa?"

"How could I not remember?" replied Major Liu. "That petty warlord Li Ch'un-fa. I got kicked around plenty by that son of a bitch!"

"That bastard sure was a tin-pot warlord!" Lai Ming-sheng undid his collar, rolled up his sleeves, raised his wine cup, and drank with Major Liu. Beads of sweat appeared on his forehead, and his cheeks burned fiery red. He turned to Li-chu and Yu Hsin.

"In the twenty-seventh year of the Republic,* I was captain of a cavalry company in Chengtu. I was with our Fifth Battalion, and we were camped outside the city. Our major had a concubine who, of all things, loved horseback riding. Our major ordered me to let her ride my horse, and he had me follow her around every day, as if he wanted to make sure she didn't break her arse! One day Pockmarked Li went into town. Well, that concubine-lady of his called a couple of women over to her house to play mah-jong; she wanted me to make up a foursome. Halfway through the game, I suddenly felt a heavy weight on my boots, as if something was pressing down on them. When I reached down under the table, I felt this foot in an embroidered shoe sitting dead on top of my boots. As I looked up, our major's concu-

* 1938.

bine-lady, who was sitting all smiles to my right, played me a "White Dragon."* 'Here's a nice juicy piece for you!' she said. After the game, an orderly came to summon me to the inner chamber; the lady had the chicken soup steamed with red dates† all ready and waiting for me. That night I damn well cut off our major's boots!"

Here Lai Ming-sheng stopped dead a moment, then all at once he leaped up and banged his fist on the table. "That bitch!" he snarled. "What a fine juicy piece she turned out to be!"

His banging made the coals under the hot-pot jump. Everyone gave a start at first, then they all burst into a roar of laughter. Giggling, Mrs. Liu fished a big ladleful of kidneys out of the hot-pot and put it in Lai Ming-sheng's dish.

"You know, worthy brother," Lai Ming-sheng said, turning to Major Liu, "That time Li Ch'un-fa thought he would fix me for sure. You remember he had me transferred to Shantung? At that time, there was fierce fighting on the Shantung front. Li Ch'un-fa had gotten suspicious. That son of a bitch, he wanted to send me to an early death at Taierhchuang!"‡

"Sir, did you take part in the Battle of Taierhchuang too?" Yu Hsin blurted out excitedly.

Without answering, Lai Ming-sheng seized a handful of fried peanuts and conveyed them to his mouth, chewing noisily. After a moment he turned to Yu Hsin and snorted, "Tai—erh—chuang. Young man, that name is not to be mentioned lightly!"

"Last week in our lectures on the War of Resistance against Japan the instructor happened to talk about the Battle of Taierhchuang," Yu Hsin hurriedly explained.

"Who is your instructor?"

"Niu Chung-k'ai. He's a fifth-year graduate of Whampoa."

"I know him. Short, fat fellow. Speaks with a Hunan accent. So he's lecturing on Taierhchuang, is he?"

"He just got to the battle where the Japanese Isogai Division attacked Tsaotse," answered Yu Hsin.

---

* Literally "white piece," one of the mah-jong pieces, or "tiles," it has a smooth, ivory-white surface, without any design on it whatever; known to Western players of the game as "White Dragon."
† This dish is traditionally considered an aphrodisiacal tonic.
‡ A town in soutern Shantung Province, scene of a historic battle in April 1938, in the early stages of China's resistance against the Japanese invasion.

"Ah . . ." Lai Ming-sheng nodded his head. Suddenly, stretching and puffing, he pulled open his blue gabardine jacket and lifted his sweater and undershirt, baring his large chest. On the right side of his chest was the vivid imprint of a bloodred scar, shiny, round, the size of a rice bowl. His whole breast had been hewn away; it had caved in, forming a crater. Mrs. Liu turned her head away, laughing, while Li-chu hurriedly covered her mouth with her hand and bent over with laughter.

Lai Ming-sheng pointed to the round scar, every vein in his head standing out, his eyes reddened. "My young friend, I've spent a lifetime in battle, and I've never once been decorated. But this little mark here is rarer than a 'Blue Sky and White Sun' medal. With this on me, I'm qualified to give you a lecture on 'Taierhchuang.' But people who have nothing like this—what do they know, talking about it? You go ask Niu Chung-k'ai for me: How many of our regimental commanders and battalion commanders were lost in that battle? And who were those people? And how did General Huang Ming-chang die? Does he know?" Tucking in his clothes any old way, gesticulating violently, Lai Ming-sheng went on speaking to Yu Hsin. "When the Japs attacked Tsaotse, I was defending the place! The firepower those midgets had was really something! Hundreds of tanks, twenty thousand infantry—double our number! What could we put up against them? Our bodies! My friend, after one night of fighting I don't know how many from our regiment were still left. General Huang Ming-chang was our regimental commander. At daybreak I was riding behind him on patrol. I just saw an explosion flash, and the next minute his head was gone, but his body still sat erect on his horse, hands grasping the reins, galloping. Hell, I didn't have time to blink before I was blown off my horse myself. My horse was hit in the belly by a shell, and I was all tangled up in its guts. The Japs thought I was finished, and our men thought so too. I lay in the pile of dead for two days and two nights without anyone paying any attention to me. Afterwards when our army won and came to collect the corpses, they dug me out. Ah, my friend!" Lai Ming-sheng pointed to the right side of his chest, "that was the shot that blew off half my chest."

"That battle was truly the glory of our National Army!" said Yu Hsin.

"Glory?" Lai Ming-sheng gave a humph. "Young friend, for you people who've never been in battle, 'Glory' is an easy word to say. As for us in the Nationalist Army, it's all right not to mention other battles, but if you bring up *this* battle, my friend, *this* battle—"

Lai Ming-sheng suddenly began to stammer. One hand gesticulating, his face purple with heat and excitement, he seemed to be groping for some heroic words to describe Taierhchuang, but unable to come up with any on the spur of the moment. Suddenly the sound of an explosion outside rent the air, and an intense white light flashed twice across the window. Liu Ying, who had been quiet for a long while, jumped up and ran to the door, shouting, "They're setting off the K'ung-ming lanterns!"*

Major Liu yelled at the boy and reached out to grab him, but he had already skipped out the door, turning his head and calling, "Uncle Lai, shoot firecrackers with me later—you promised!"

"Little devil!" Mrs. Liu scolded him with a laugh. "Let him go. You can't hold him. Brother Lai, quick! While it's hot, taste my dish of 'Ants up a Tree!' "†

Mrs. Liu put a big bowl of rice in front of Lai Ming-sheng. Lai Ming-sheng pushed it aside and pulled the dish of fried peanuts to him again; he poured a cup of Quemoy *kao-liang* and brought it to his mouth. He drank so fast half the liquor spilled, dripping all over him.

"Take it easy, Brother Lai, don't choke," Major Liu persuaded him as he quickly handed Lai Ming-sheng a towel.

"My dear Brother," cried Lai Ming-sheng, striking the table violently with his empty cup and grabbing Major Liu's shoulders. "You think a little Quemoy *kao-liang* on Taiwan could make your big brother drunk? Have you forgotten how many crocks of Kweichow *mao-t'ai* I used to drink on the mainland?"

"We know about your great capacity," Major Liu reassured him.

"Dear Brother." Lai Ming-sheng clutched Major Liu's shoulder strap with both hands, and his large head almost knocked into his

---

* A kind of fireworks that shoots up into the sky trailing a string of firecrackers behind; named after Chu-ke Liang, the superb military strategist of Three Kingdoms fame. K'ung-ming was his courtesy name.

† A Szechwan dish consisting of minced meat sauce served with hot-pepper oil over deep-fried bean threads (pea-starch noodles).

host's face. "You may be a major, you may even wear stars, but if it were not for our friendship I wouldn't have come today, even if you sent an eight-man sedan chair for me!"

"What talk, Brother Lai!" Major Liu hastened to pacify him.

"You know, Brother, what I say is straight talk, every word of it. That little worm Wu Sheng-piao was once my second lieutenant. When I came to Taipei and walked past his door, I wouldn't even give him a look. He's a big wheel now, well, that's his luck, but licking somebody's arse to get ahead is just not for me. Otherwise I wouldn't be a Chief Army Cook now. Last week I just took a little burnt rice from our hospital kitchen to feed the pigs, and the officer-in-charge looked down his nose at me and read me the Riot Act. So I rolled up my sleeves and pointed right at his face and said, 'Officer Yu, let me be frank with you: in the sixteenth year of the Republic,* I, Lai Ming-sheng, was out there carrying pots for the Revolutionary Army on the Northern Expedition to fight Sun Chuan-fang.† So when it comes to kitchen rules, Sir, I have no need of your advice.' You add it up for me, dear Brother—" he counted on his fingers, his head swaying, "I'm the same age as the Republic itself. All these years, through thick and thin, what strange things haven't I experienced? Now what do I care any more? Frankly, dear Brother, the only regret I have is that these old bones of mine have not yet found their way home."

Mrs. Liu went over and planted herself between Lai Ming-sheng and Major Liu. "Brother Lai, you just keep talking away, and you haven't had a bite of this 'Ants up a Tree,' and after I went to all the trouble to fry it nice and hot for you. Even if you should go to a Szechwanese restaurant, I doubt if they can cook this hometown specialty the way I do."

"Dear Sister—" Lai Ming-sheng reached across the table to get at the half-empty bottle of Quemoy *kao-liang*, but Mrs. Liu grabbed it and hugged it to her bosom.

"Brother Lai, if you drink a couple more, you won't be able to stay awake and see the New Year in."

All at once Lai Ming-sheng struggled to his feet and struck his chest a couple of times. "My dear Sister," he declared in a hoarse voice, "you really think too little of me. Although I am getting a little

* 1927.
† One of the warlords of the 1920s, military governor of Kiangsu Province.

advanced in years, this frame of mine is still made of iron. To tell you the truth, I'm retired but I'm still in training. Every morning as soon as they blow the bugle in the barracks next door, I get out of bed. I go through my routine—'Poisonous Snake Shoots out of the Hole,' 'Praying Mantis Waving its Legs,' 'Large Chariot Wheels,' 'Small Chariot Wheels'*—I wonder if those youngsters could match me."

As Lai Ming-sheng spoke he got up from the table, struck a martial pose and started boxing, brandishing his arms and legs. Beads of sweat ran down his bright red face like water; everyone roared. Rocking back and forth with laughter, Mrs. Liu went over to him quickly and, taking hold of him by the arm, half pushing and half pulling, led him to the rear of the house to wash his face. Before leaving the living room, Lai Ming-sheng turned to her. "Now do you see, Sister?" he said. "When we fight our way back to Szechwan one day, your Brother Lai may not be good for much else, but he can still carry eight or ten rice pots for sure!"

His words made those at the table start laughing again. When Lai Ming-sheng had gone inside, Mrs. Liu directed the group to clear the dinner table and place a square mah-jong tabletop on it. She took out the mah-jong set and assigned the task of dividing up the chips to Yu Hsin and Li-chu, while she herself brought the pair of red candles over from the windowsill and set them down on a side table next to the mah-jong table. The candles were already more than half burnt down, leaving tallow drippings on the candlesticks. While Mrs. Liu was scraping off the clinging tallow with a little knife, the sound of vomiting suddenly came from the bathroom. Major Liu ran inside.

"He's drunk." Mrs. Liu shook her head with a sigh, letting the knife fall from her hand to the side table. "I knew it; it's the same every time. He loves to drink and raise a ruckus, but he can't really hold that much."

"Brother Lai looks so funny when he's high," said Li-chu, giggling as she gave Yu Hsin a mischievous look. Yu Hsin laughed with her.

Major Liu came out somewhat later. "He's asleep," he said in a low voice. "He wants me to play a few hands for him; he'll take over later."

---

* Various moves in boxing.

Mrs. Liu mused for a while. Then she let out a yawn and rubbed her temples. "Say, let's forget it. If Brother Lai has gone to sleep, heaven knows what time he'll wake up. I've been busy all day, and I'm tired. Li-chu, Yu Hsin, you two might as well go on out and have a good time. Sorry to have kept you around all evening."

Li-chu stood up promptly. Yu Hsin helped her into her red coat, put on his Army cap and straightened his tie in front of the living-room mirror. Then they said goodbye to Major and Mrs. Liu. As Li-chu and Yu Hsin stepped out into the lane, they saw the children from the military dependents' families in East Hsin-yi Village, all gathered together in the middle of the lane, twenty or thirty of them. They were in a circle, setting off firecrackers. The Lius' boy, Liu Ying, was squatting on the ground, lighting a big pinwheel. A resplendent bloom of light suddenly burst into the air about six or seven feet above the ground, bathing all the laughing young faces in a silvery brightness. In the roar of cheers, each child scrambled to light his own firecracker, and streak after streak of light broke through the dark sky. The sound of firecrackers all around grew louder and more urgent as New Year's Eve drew to an end and another New Year descended on Taipei.

The Last Night of Taipan Chin

As the bright lights went up in West Gate Square, Taipei's busy entertainment district, a staccato of high heels rang on the staircase of the ballroom Nuits de Paris. Taipan Chin in the lead,* a troop of a dozen or so snazzily outfitted taxi dancers came parading up to the second floor. Just as she got to the entrance, Taipan Chin saw T'ung Te-huai, the manager of the Nuits de Paris, come scurrying out, wringing his hands, his face positively yellow with anxiety.

"Taipan Chin!" he yelled at her. "How long do you people take to eat dinner, anyway? Look, it's almost daylight! The guests won't wait; some have left already!"

"So? What's the big hurry? Aren't we here now?" Taipan Chin retorted, turning on the smile. "The girls wanted to pay me their respects; they were falling all over one another drinking toasts with me. How would I dare to turn them down?" Sheathed in a tight-fitting black chiffon cheongsam shot through with gold thread, her sleek black hair in an enormous bun on top of her head, like a Taoist monk's, she fairly glittered with earrings, necklace, bracelets, and hairpins—gold and emerald from head to foot. Her face already glowed from wine; even her eyelids had turned red.

"I can't stop you girls if you want to get soused. But we've got to take care of business too, after all!" T'ung kept on grousing.

Taipan Chin stopped short at the door. She let the chattering

---

* The captain of taxi dancers is called the "taipan." There are men and women taipans; as a rule, women taipans have been taxi dancers themselves. Before 1949, taxi dancers worked in large Shanghai ballrooms, of which the Paramount and the MGM were the most famous. Ballrooms are operated in Taipei today. A patron buys a ticket per "round," usually about half an hour of the taxi dancer's time. The more popular the dancers, the more they go in for table-hopping, so the tickets they take in are called "table-taxi money."

girls file past her into the ballroom. One hand propped against the doorpost, her alligator bag flung over her other shoulder, she pinned the man back with a glance.

"Say, Mister Big Manager," she opened up with a smile that was no smile at all, "Do you really mean to hand me this crock of hot air, or are you only kidding? If you're only kidding, I'll let it pass. If you mean business, then tonight I'm going to hand you *my* bill, and let's you and me settle accounts. So you want to take care of business, huh?" Taipan Chin sniffed. "Don't blame me if I toot my own horn a little: if it weren't for me being around here these past five or six years, me, Jolie Chin, 'the Jade Goddess of Mercy,' your old drawing card, you think the Nuits de Paris would be where it is today? Who's the one who got Little Sweetie, the hottest number over at the Capital, to come join us? And that sister-act, Green Peony and Pink Peony, from the Overseas? Did *you* steer them our way, Mister Big Manager? As for the big spenders that check in here every day, at least half of them are my old buddies. Do you think they come to the Nuits de Paris to shell out their dough just to make you look good, Mister So-and-so? And what's more, you've only paid me till yesterday. *I'm* doing *you* a favor by coming in tonight; by rights I shouldn't have showed up. Now I'm going to tell *you* something: when I, Jolie Chin, first turned pro at the Paramount back in Shanghai, I'm afraid you hadn't seen the inside of a ballroom yet. You should teach *me* how to behave in a ballroom, Mister Big Manager of the Nuits de Paris!"

Having fired off this salvo, without giving T'ung a chance to talk back, Taipan Chin threw open the glass door to the ballroom and stalked in, her three-inch-high heels beating a rapid tattoo on the floor. She was no sooner through the door than from every side the guests began to cheer and beckon her. "Taipan Chin! Taipan Chin!" Without even trying to make out who they were, she tossed them a smile and a couple of waves of her alligator bag and vanished into the dressing room.

Up his mother's! She flung her bag down on the dressing table as she came in. Spitting out a curse, she parked her ass in front of the large mirror. What a cheap creep! Nuits de Paris, Nuits de Paris indeed! It may not sound polite, but even the john at the Paramount must have taken up more room than the Nuits de Paris dance floor!

Why, with a mug like T'ung's you couldn't even have gotten a job scrubbing the toilets at the Paramount. She opened a bottle of Evening in Paris and dashed a few drops over her head and body. As she gazed into the mirror she became lost in thought. This is a hell of a send-off! Tomorrow she's going to be a Boss-Lady herself, but tonight she has to take crap from that stinking deadbeat. Taipan Chin couldn't help shaking her head and letting out a somewhat rueful sigh. Twenty years knocking around in the business and only now she lands herself an angel. She wouldn't say Jolie Chin was so smart.

She still remembered how when Daidai, the Paramount's Lilac Lady, was about to marry old man P'an the Textile King, she had dropped a catty remark or two. "Isn't our little Lilac the sharp one! She's hooked herself a thousand-year-old gold turtle!" Actually, old man P'an had heaped so much attention on Jolie Chin herself he'd spent enough money to build a gold mountain. She was being picky in those days; the man was old, had one hell of a B. O., too, so she booted him over to Daidai. She'd shot her mouth off in front of her sister dancers. "I'm not as desperate for holy matrimony as you gals— all of you ready to grab any old bird with one foot in the grave!" But then one day she'd run into Daidai in Taipei sitting in her husband's silk emporium, the Rich Spring Pavilion, waving a sandalwood fan and looking high and mighty, just like a bona fide Mrs. Bigshot. The former Lilac Lady was now so fullblown the flesh on her upper arms hung down to the counter. "Well, if it isn't our Jade Goddess of Mercy!" she purred. "My dear, are you still out there on the Sea of Bitterness redeeming those poor souls?" What could she say? All she could do was grit her teeth and let that bitch get even with her. You couldn't say it's so sensational, after sticking it out for twenty more years, to end up with a prize like this. Only those jaundice-eyed little tarts like Little Sweetie would come bustling over to drink a toast to congratulate her. "What d'you say, girls? Our big sister's leading the way after all, first to hit the jackpot. This Boss Ch'en must be worth at least ten million, don't you think?"* A while ago when they were celebrating at the Top Marks Restaurant every one of these little whores from the Nuits de Paris was so green-eyed they were practically drooling. To hear them talk about Boss Ch'en, you'd think he

* In NT (New Taiwan) dollars—equivalent to US$250,000. The average exchange rate is NT$40 = US$1.

was God knows what kind of a rare catch. Couldn't blame 'em, though. How can you expect that bunch of little whores to know any better? They'd never seen the big time, those good old days she'd known; they don't know anything about her kind of style. When she was in Shanghai, she had to use her toes, let alone her fingers, to count up the number of big wheels who worshipped at the feet of the Jade Goddess, men who had cozy little fortunes like this here Boss Ch'en. Anyway, it's nowhere near ten million. She'd asked somebody in Singapore to make a thorough investigation: a small rubber factory, two old houses, and his late wife's two kids had already gotten their share. According to her own private estimate, the whole fortune would come up to about three or four million at best. But that's another matter. The thing is, she'd tested him the last month or so; except for his age and being bald on top—and a bit of a penny-pincher —he was a decent guy. How could you blame somebody who left the Toishan countryside and worked his ass off in Southeast Asia all his life if he treated a nickel like it was five bucks? But as soon as he'd bought that $500,000 villa on Yangmingshan he had put it in her name. Really you had to give the old boy credit! A hillbilly, but still willing to throw that kind of money around for her. As for age— Taipan Chin drew herself up to the mirror and grimaced. Suddenly a few crow's feet appeared on her heavily powdered face. Since when does a forty-year-old dame have any right to talk about other people's age? Even to nab a sixty-year-old bird like Ch'en she'd had to pull out all the stops; God knows how much money she'd squandered this past month or so at the Soothing Fragrance Beauty Salon alone. Face-lifting, eyebrow-plucking—there wasn't an inch of skin on her face that hadn't been gone over. Every time she went out with the old bird it was like she was headed for the execution grounds loaded down with chains and shackles; belly fastened, waist secured, falsies front and rear, she was armed with all the trappings, right in the middle of July, too—Taipan Chin gave her belly a couple of good scratches— the prickly heat made her itch like hell all over. And that wasn't all! When old man Ch'en asked her, right to her face, "May I enquire your age, Madam?" she'd had to play the coy ingenue. "Gue – ess!" she mewed. "Thirty?" Up his mother's! Only an old fool could be that blind. Taipan Chin couldn't help chuckling to herself. Thirty-five, she had flimflammed him; he was so startled his mouth popped wide open as if he'd run into a ghost! The way he looked he probably never got close to any woman but that frumpy grandma of a wife of his. The minute he'd clapped eyes on Jolie Chin in Taipei, three of his seven souls had flown right out of his body; he was so bewitched he didn't know whether he was coming or going. Anyway, whatever he had on his mind, he was way over the hill. Taipan Chin drew herself up, breasts cocked. She wouldn't have to lift so much as a finger to keep that old boy in his place.

Taipan Chin opened her bag and fished out a pack of American cigarettes—Camels. She lit one, took a couple of good puffs, and nodded: she'd finally caught on. No wonder all her sworn sisters were out to grab themselves any old bird with one foot in the grave; it had its advantages, sure saved a lot of trouble. Would a younger guy behave so well? Was there a single time Manny Ts'in came ashore when he didn't give her such a workout that afterwards she ached all over? She'd told him frankly: she was pushing forty, six or seven years older than he; where was she gonna get the energy to tangle with him all the time? Sonuvabitch! he said that's exactly what he liked, an older woman! Understanding. Tender. What'd he want, anyway? A mother? Manny did tell her he was just a kid when his mother died; he'd drifted around on the high seas all his life, never been loved by anybody. To tell the truth, he devoted himself to her more than if she were his own mother; no matter what far-off corner of the world he went to, he'd always send her some gift—a cashmere sweater from Hong Kong, an embroidered kimono from Japan, Thai silks, this and that, there was no stopping him; and on top of it all a letter every week—a dozen or so jam-packed pages copied from God alone knows what Compleat Letter-Writer: "Jolie, My Belovéd!"—enough to give you the creeps! Actually, he was a truehearted fellow, he just didn't know how to show his feelings. Once he came back three sheets to the wind, threw his arms around her and burst into tears; a great big hunk of a man like that, and he laid his head on her bosom and cried like a baby. You know why? Truth was, when he was in Japan he got lonely and slept with some Japanese broad; but then he thought he had done Jolie wrong, and he felt bad about it. Really! What *was* all this? What the hell did he take her for, a high school girl gaga over her first love? All excited, he pulled out his bank book for her to look at; he'd saved $70,000 already; just five more years—five years,

Mother of Mercy!—he'd put in five more years as a first mate, then he'd come back to Taipei, buy a house, and make her his old lady. She gave him a sad smile, but she didn't have the heart to tell him that when she was a red-hot number at the Paramount one night of table-taxi money added up to more than that. Five years—five more years, she might as well be his grandma! If it had been ten years ago —Taipan Chin took a good drag on her cigarette, wistfully thinking to herself—if I had met a faithful guy like Manny Ts'in ten years ago, I might have gotten married and called it quits. Ten years ago she still had a pile of loot, and she was still planning to find someone devoted to her, heart and soul, and settle down. Last time when Manny was about to sail she suddenly got it into her head to go see him off at Keelung. The pier was packed with seamen's wives; as soon as the ship pulled away every last one of them started to cry; they were all staring out to sea as if their souls were lost. That gave her a cold shiver inside; now she was about to marry old man Ch'en and she hadn't even sent Manny a letter. He couldn't possibly blame her for cutting off her feelings; could she wait until *her* soul was lost, like those women? A forty-year-old woman can't afford to wait. A forty-year-old woman just hasn't got the time for romancing. A forty-year-old woman—can even make do without a real man. So? what *does* a forty-year-old woman want after all? Taipan Chin stubbed out her cigarette in the ashtray, mulling it over for a while; suddenly she raised her head and grinned maliciously into the mirror. She wants a silk emporium like Lilac Lady's! Twice as big, of course, right across the street from her rival's Rich Spring Pavilion. Right off she would slash her prices by twenty percent; let that loudmouthed, sharp-tongued blimp of a bitch have a real taste of my sting, then she'll know Jolie Chin, the Jade Goddess of Mercy, is not somebody you can trifle with.

"Big Sister—"

The dressing-room door opened, and in walked a young taxi dancer. Taipan Chin was dusting her face with a powder puff; in the mirror, not even turning her head, she saw it was Phoenix. Only six months ago Phoenix Chu had come from Miaoli to Taipei. She used to be a tea-picker; her old man was a drunken bum and her stepmother made life rough for her, so she just had to get out. When she first came to the Nuits de Paris and put on high heels, Phoenix wobbled around as if she were walking on stilts. In less than a week she'd done something to make a guest mad. Manager T'ung really bawled her out; he would have fired her right then and there. Taipan Chin saw the poor girl shaking with fear, cowering in a corner like a little rabbit, unable to utter a word. How she loathed the meanness of that man. She stepped in just to show him up. Thumping her chest, she guaranteed T'ung: if Phoenix wasn't drawing within one month she, Jolie Chin, would pay him from her own pocket. She'd really gone all out to bring Phoenix up, taught her all the tricks of the ballroom trade, did everything to drum up business for her. Phoenix didn't let her down, either; within half a year, although she hadn't quite made it to the top yet, she pulled in over ten table-tickets every night.

"What's up, Hot Number? How many tables you taxi so far?" Phoenix came over and sat down quietly beside Taipan Chin. Earlier that evening at the Top Marks Restaurant Phoenix hadn't said a word; her eyelids were red the whole time. Taipan Chin understood; Phoenix had depended on her all along, naturally she'd feel jittery now she was leaving.

"Big Sister—" Phoenix called again, her voice quavering. Only then did Taipan Chin realize there was something wrong with her. She turned around swiftly and took a good hard look at Phoenix's belly; in a flash she got the message.

"Got stuck, huh?" Taipan Chin coldly inquired. For the past two or three months a student from Hong Kong studying at Taiwan University had shown up every night to give Phoenix a big rush, and that Cantonese kid was some lady-killer, too. The way Taipan Chin saw it, Phoenix was quite smitten. She'd warned her time and time again: those rich young playboys hang around ballrooms, they're just not for real; if things get serious, it's always the taxi dancer who gets burned.

Phoenix just laughed; she didn't own up. So! they'd been up to the old hanky-panky behind her back, had they. Taipan Chin took another look at Phoenix's belly. No wonder the little whore couldn't get it back in shape even with her girdle on.

"Where is he?"

"He's gone back to Hong Kong," Phoenix mumbled, head lowered.

"Did he leave anything behind?" Taipan Chin persisted.

Phoenix shook her head vigorously and said nothing. Suddenly Taipan Chin felt a flare of rage shoot up in her breast. A feather-brained little tart like this, of course she'd be gobbled up in no time. She didn't feel sorry for her; she was furious; all that trouble she'd taken over Phoenix had gone down the drain. Believe me, it hadn't been easy to turn this hayseed into a fetching dancehall flower; you could see she was just about to bloom. Even Chubby Ch'en, the taipan from the International, had scurried over to ask about her price. Taipan Chin had taken Phoenix by the ear. You hold out for another moment, she had hissed at her between clenched teeth. Your day of glory is almost here. Fun's fun, a game's a game. But the number one no-no for a taxi dancer is to get knocked up. Can you name me one guest who isn't a wolf or a dog? No matter how big a star you are, the minute they know you're in trouble they'll run like hell, one after the other, holding their noses as if you were smeared all over with chicken shit.

"Oh?" With an icy smile, Taipan Chin slammed the powder puff down on the dressing table. "Bighearted, aren't you! *He's* got you knocked up, *he's* hauled ass, and *you* didn't even get so much as a hair off his cock!"

"He said he'll send money as soon as he's found a job in Hong Kong." Head lowered, wringing her handkerchief, Phoenix started to sob.

Taipan Chin sprang up and went round to her. "You're still dreaming your mother's fairy-tale dreams!" she spat. "Anybody can see you've let the big fish off the hook! Think you're going to get him back? Since you couldn't catch a man with your cunt tricks, you should have kept your belt fastened tight! Now you've let him plant the seed of disaster in you, and here you come, blowing your nose and spilling your tears all over the place—is there a single reason why I should have any respect for you, tell me? All the things I've taught you—you heard them all right, and then where did they go? So that little squirt did a hit-and-run, huh?" Taipan Chin lunged forward and shouted in Phoenix's ear. "Couldn't you just pick up a bottle of Lysol and gulp it down right in front of his nose?"

"Stuff like that—" Phoenix recoiled, her lips trembling. "I'm afraid of the pain—"

"I see—afraid of the pain, huh!" Taipan Chin couldn't stand

this any more; she jerked Phoenix's chin up with one hand and with the other jabbed her right between the eyebrows. "Afraid of the pain? If you're afraid of the pain, why don't you get your tail back to Miaoli and make like a young lady? Why do you have to hang around a joint like this and let the men grab you and feel your ass? Afraid of the pain? One of these days for sure you'll get your share of it; you'll be on the street selling your wares!"

Covering her face with her hands, Phoenix broke down and cried. Taipan Chin simply ignored her; she lit a cigarette, took a hard drag, and paced around the room a couple of times. All at once she went up to Phoenix.

"Come to my place tomorrow; I'll take you to go get rid of that lump in your belly."

"Oh no—" Phoenix looked up and uttered a cry.

Taipan Chin saw her desperately protect her slightly protruding belly, her face anguished, white as paper. Taken aback, Taipan Chin began to scrutinize her in silence. Phoenix's eyes flashed fiercely, filled with venom, like a young brooding hen pitting her life against somebody out to steal her eggs. She's fallen in love with him, Taipan Chin sighed to herself. If this little tart has really fallen in love with that young punk, there isn't a damn thing you can do about it. These little sluts who don't know the first thing about Life, you can talk till your tongue falls out and they won't hear a word. Even she, herself, the time she was carrying Moon Boy's child, when Momma and Elder Brother grabbed her by the arms and tried to haul her off to get it removed, she'd hugged her belly and rolled all around crying to Heaven and Earth for rescue: Want to cut out the living flesh in her body? Not unless they find a cord and strangle her first. Momma was real cruel; she slipped some powerful herb in the noodles and aborted the already-formed male fetus. In all her life that was the only time she had thought of cutting it short. Swallowing gold, stretching her neck, taking rat poison, jumping into Soochow Creek—ah, fuck it all, she just wasn't gonna die. Every day Momma tried to comfort her. Baby-girl, you're a bright kid; he's a young gentleman from an official family, and an only son, too; would they let you ruin his future? A taxi dancer like you, with a fatherless, nameless by-blow in tow, who'll ever want you? You can't say there wasn't a lot of truth in what Momma said. Once Moon Boy's bigwig of an old man had sent over some bodyguards and kidnapped him from their little nest at Zee-kawei, she knew for sure that never in this life, never in this world would she meet her little love face to face again. But she was still young then; she, too, had a lot of foolish ideas; she wanted to bear her student sweetheart a son and devote her whole life to their little heartbreaker; she'd do it willingly, even if she had to beg in the streets. Who says taxi dancers aren't human? Their hearts can melt, too, especially when they meet up with some smart-looking college boy. Chicks like Phoenix who had just barely gotten their feet wet—how many of them could resist?

"Take it." Taipan Chin pulled a big one-and-a-half-carat diamond off the ring finger of her right hand and tossed it in Phoenix's lap. "It's worth five hundred U. S. dollars, enough for you and that little bastard in your belly to get along on for a year or so. After it's born, there's no need for you to come back to this place either; this kind of life just isn't for you."

As she spoke, she flung open the dressing-room door and stalked off, ignoring Phoenix, who was calling after her. Outside, the floor was already jammed with people; in the air-cooled mist the lights shimmered red and green, the orchestra was playing sultry swing, and couples swayed this way and that, stuck together like twists of salt-water taffy. Taipan Chin was caught by a guest as she passed a table; she turned her head. It was Tycoon Chou, Chairman of the Board of the Great China Textile Company, who came specially to be Little Sweetie's sugar daddy.

"Taipan Chin, *would* you be kind enough to do me a big favor? You see, she's in a rotten mood tonight; I'm afraid she won't come over unless *you* take the trouble to bring her round." Tycoon Chou held on tight to Taipan Chin's arm, an anxious look on his face.

"It all depends on what kind of tip I get from the Chairman of the Board," Taipan Chin smiled.

"Ten tables for the banquet when you and Boss Ch'en get spliced, how about that?"

"You got a deal!" Taipan Chin stuck out her hand, gave Tycoon Chou a big handshake, sauntered off to Little Sweetie's table and sat down beside her.

"After this table, you'd better get over there," she whispered. "He's about lost his soul waiting for you."

"Who cares?" Little Sweetie retorted, not even turning her head as she continued to flirt with the guests. "Is his cabbage greener than anybody else's? Go tell him Mona from the Singapore is waiting for him for a midnight snack."

"Aha. So the grapes have turned sour." Taipan Chin laughed.

"Pugh. Is he worth it?" Her nose in the air, Little Sweetie sniffed. Taipan Chin drew closer to her ear.

"Do it for Big Sister's sake; the gentleman's going to lay on ten banquet tables for me."

"So, you've been wheeling and dealing behind my back," Little Sweetie remarked snidely. "Why don't you go keep him company yourself?"

Taipan Chin didn't say a word; she stared sideways at Little Sweetie; with one swoop she grabbed Little Sweetie's tits. Little Sweetie let out a shriek like a wet cat and tried to pull away; the guests at the table roared. Little Sweetie hollered uncle fast!

"If you insist," she whispered in Taipan Chin's ear. "But you better make it clear to that so-and-so name of Chou that tonight I'm doing him a favor because you asked me; *I* haven't let him off. You've been through it all, Sister Chin; you understand the saying 'Strike while the iron is hot'—'cause when it gets cold, you can't hardly bend it!' "

Taipan Chin leaned back against a pillar and picked her teeth with a toothpick while she watched Little Sweetie, in a sheer gauze cheongsam of pomegranate red, her white, well-rounded arms bare from the shoulders, wiggle saucily over to Tycoon Chou's table. Her whole body flaunted sex. She not only fires up any man who sets eyes on her, she even causes women's hearts to skip a beat. What's more, she's a first-class hard-to-handle bitch, blackhearted and cold-blooded; in all the years she's been in this game she hasn't slipped up once. That guy Chou must have thrown away $200,000 more or less on her, and maybe he hasn't even had a chance to lick her ass yet. That's the perfect material for a top taxi dancer, Taipan Chin thought to herself admiringly. Phoenix, that softy—she's only fit to pick up after Little Sweetie. Although still miles away from the popularity she herself, Jolie Chin, the Jade Goddess of Mercy, enjoyed at the Paramount in Shanghai, you could rank Little Sweetie one of the hottest numbers around the Taipei ballrooms. You count them all in cosmopolitan

Shanghai in those days, but only Joy Wu, the eldest of the "Five Ti-
gresses" at the MGM Ballroom, was any match for Jolie Chin. Everybody said the two of them were the Fairy Princess from Ninth Heaven
and the White Tiger Star incarnate, come to Whangpoo Beach to raise
hell in this human world. Somehow or other she and that striped she-
critter had become sworn sisters; late at night, after the two of them
were done table-taxiing, they'd go over to the Welcome Café and eat
fried spring chicken; they'd compare notes, counting on their fingers
to see who'd cleaned up on more big spenders more mercilessly, more
stylishly. Flouting convention, corrupting morals, what have you, she
had to admit she'd done quite a bit in her time. God knows how many
men had ruined themselves on account of the Jade Goddess of Mercy,
deserted their wives and children, and wrecked their lives. Joy Wu
left that world early and married a businessman, on the quiet. Taipan
Chin had been bewildered then; she'd felt pretty lonesome. After she
got to Taipei she went to Chung Ho Village to look Joy up; who could
ever have imagined that the saber-toothed, claw-flashing she-critter
would have converted into a devout Buddhist matron. Joy had set up
a Buddhist chapel in her house and enshrined two emerald jade Lo-
hans. Her family said she did nothing all year round but eat vege-
tarian and chant sutras; she wouldn't even set foot outside the chapel.
When Joy saw her, she didn't even so much as raise her eyes, just
shook her head and sighed. "Tsk, tsk, Jolie, my dear girl, are you still
out there causing trouble and making a mess of your life?" That sent
a chill through her heart. Well, well, they were smart all right, those
others; as if driven by a ghost, every last one of them caught a husband in time and attained salvation. She, the Jade Goddess of Mercy,
was the only soul left floundering around on the Sea of Iniquity.
Twenty years—gone just like that. Damn it all, she simply wasn't cut
out for Buddahood like Joy. No way *she* could get to the Western
Paradise. Now really! Would she actually set up a Buddhist chapel
like Joy and enshrine an authentic Jade Kuanyin? She'd spent a whole
life in sin, enough to muck up all those nice old Bodhisattvas! She had
made her mind up, her own way: the minute her number was up she
was going to head straight down for the eighteenth floor of Hell and
get to know what it's like climbing the Knife Mountain and diving
into the Boiling Oilpot.

"Taipan Chin—"

Taipan Chin turned; a group of young sprigs who had just taken a table by the orchestra were waving to her and yelling. She knew them, the whole crew of whippersnappers working for foreign companies. They had some dough, and one and all, they thought they were hot shit. Just the same, Taipan Chin grinned and sashayed over.

"Taipan Chin—" Little Ts'ai caught her hand and sniggered. "By tomorrow you'll be Mrs. Bigshot, and Little Horse here says he hasn't even tasted your steamed chicken yet!" They all started to whinny.

"Oh ye-es?" Taipan Chin smiled coyly, landed right in Little Ts'ai's lap and ground it a couple of times, one arm around his neck. "I haven't slaughtered *you* yet, you little spring chicken! Where'm I going to get a chicken to steam for *him*?" Her other hand crept stealthily down and gave his leg such a hard pinch he let out a loud squeal. Just as his hands were about to misbehave, she leaped to her feet and pushed him away, still laughing. "Don't you get fresh with me. Your old flames are here; I don't want them to make fun of me and talk about 'an old cow eating tender grass.' "

A few table-hopping taxi dancers had arrived; in a twinkling they were snapped up by the young sprouts, carried off to the floor and dancing cheek to cheek.

"Hey, cutie, what about *your* old flame?" Just as she was about to walk off, Taipan Chin saw one young man left with no partner.

"I can't dance very well; I just came to watch them," the young man murmured. Taipan Chin paused in spite of herself and gave him a good looking-over. Why, he's a young kid, maybe twenty or so, probably a student at the university, clean and fresh, quite nicely dressed, all right, in a light gray sharkskin suit with a red tie, his whole bearing betraying his greenness. One look and you know this is the first time this tenderfoot has ever strayed into a ballroom. Taipan Chin held out her hand to him with a charming smile.

"Come now, we can't just let you watch for free. Why don't we make this my treat tonight?" And she drew the self-conscious young man out onto the floor.

The orchestra was playing "Little Darling," a slow fox-trot. On stage, the sisters Green Peony and Pink Peony, one in red and one in green, were holding each other round the waist and crooning,

You, oh yes, you,
   you're my little darling.
So why oh why
   must you be
     so cold and unfeeling?

Under the spotlights Taipan Chin, head back a bit, studied the young man carefully. Then she saw how fine his features were; his dark moustache was still soft; his long hair was nicely brushed, with a mild, sweet fragrance of Brylcreem. He didn't dare press up close to her, just barely held her waist, dancing clumsily. After a few steps he stumbled against her high heels, lifted his head in alarm, and with a bashful smile mumbled apologies, his face crimson. Taipan Chin smiled and gave him a loving look. Probably only a tenderfoot who came to a ballroom for the first time would blush like that, come to a ballroom to make whoopee and blush—seems like I always fall for a man who blushes. That night, the first time Moon Boy came to the Paramount and danced with her, he was so shy he couldn't even raise his head; wave after wave of crimson rose to his face. That very night she took him home with her; when she found out he was still a virgin, she held his head close on her bosom and pressed it to her naked breasts; two streams of hot tears welled up and flowed from her eyes. That moment her heart was filled with gratitude and tender love, that she should be rewarded with the virginity of such a shy man. In that instant she felt that all the contamination and abuse she had taken from other men's bodies was washed away by her tears. She had always thought the male body was dirty and ugly and stank; she had gone to bed with many men before; each time she had turned her head away and kept her eyes closed. But that night, after Moon Boy had fallen fast asleep, she got up and kneeled beside the bed; by the light of the moon she gazed entranced at the naked man on the bed. The moonlight shone on his pale chest and fine-drawn waist; it was as if it was the first time she really saw a naked male body; only then did she realize that a woman, too, could be so ecstatically, so passionately enraptured with a man's body, a man's flesh. And as she gently touched her burning cheek to his ice-cool feet, she couldn't help but start to weep silently again.

"I don't know how to do this dance," the young man said. He

stopped, looking at Taipan Chin in embarrassment. The orchestra had just switched to another tune.

Taipan Chin looked at him for a moment; then she broke into a gentle smile.

"Don't you worry, this is a waltz. It's real easy; you just follow me, I ll keep time for you."

She embraced the young man, her cheek close to his ear, and counted softly and tenderly, "One two, three—One two, three—"

A Sea of Bloodred Azaleas

According to Chinese mythology, in ancient times Tu Yü, the king of Shu, had a love affair with the wife of one of his ministers. Ashamed, he fled his kingdom and turned into a tu-chüan, a cuckoo. The cuckoo is said to sing unceasingly through the spring for his tragic love, until he spits blood, which is transformed into tu-chüan flowers, or azaleas.

The Chinese literary tradition also maintains that the singing of the cuckoo evokes homesickness in the exile.

It was on a remote, deserted beach near Keelung that they found Wang Hsiung. His body was swept back in among the rocks and stuck there in a crevice; he never got to drift out to sea after all. When my aunt, my mother's brother's wife, sent me to identify the body, Wang Hsiung had been in the water for days. His whole body had turned black and blue; his belly was so swollen it had burst through his shirt; the fish had been eating at his head and it had turned into rotten pulp with little holes all over, some dark red, some inky black; even the eyes and eyebrows were gone. Even when you were yards away, the stench of the decaying corpse carried on the breeze and nauseated you. If it hadn't been for those gigantic hands of his with their round, stubby fingers, still unaltered, I would never have suspected that the huge monster lying there on the ground could be Wang Hsiung, the manservant at my aunt's house.

The death of Wang Hsiung caused a great stir. That very night, my aunt burned a big wad of paper money in the garden; she squatted on her heels, burning the money and muttering prayers to appease his soul. She said that with a violent death like Wang Hsiung's you never knew if the house would remain peaceful. When I told my aunt that Wang Hsiung's body had already decomposed, Happy, the maid, who was standing nearby, overheard me and let out a shriek of terror. My aunt tried hard to get her to stay, but Happy wouldn't remain another instant; then and there she threw her belongings together and fled back to her home in I-lan. My cousin Little Beauty was the only one we kept in the dark about all this; we never told her, we were afraid it would frighten her. When my aunt and I went to Wang Hsiung's room to collect the things he had left behind, she swore to me that after this lesson she'd never again, not as long as she lived, hire another manservant.

The first time I saw Wang Hsiung was two years ago, in the spring. I had been in the ROTC on Quemoy and had just been transferred back to Taipei to work in an administrative job at Supply Headquarters. My home was in Taichung; my only relatives in Taipei were my aunt and her family. As soon as I had reported for duty, I went to my aunt's to pay them a visit. My uncle had owned a big business; he died young—he had had only one child, my cousin Little Beauty. He left a considerable estate, so my aunt and my cousin had always lived a luxurious life. At that time my aunt had just moved, and now they lived on a half-acre of land, in a huge Western-style house with a garden, on Jen-ai Road, Section 4. The day I went to my aunt's she was in the living room, in the middle of a game of mah-jong; she gave me a casual greeting and told me to go out into the garden and look for Cousin Little Beauty. My mother had told me my aunt watched over Little Beauty like a mother cat; she was still personally spoon-feeding the child at the age of six. Little Beauty was so spoiled that even though she was now in the sixth grade in primary school she still refused to tie her own shoelaces. But she was such an adorable child, with such winsome features, that everyone doted on her. I had never seen any other child with such snow-white skin, and so roly-poly; her face, her eyes, even her nose and mouth were round and cute-looking. When she shook her short hair and giggled, that baby-girl innocence of hers couldn't help but win you over. She was like a jade doll. On the other hand, very few childern had her willful and imperious temperament either. At the least provocation, she'd grab something, no matter how valuable, and dash it to the ground.

Then she'd sit on the floor rubbing her plump legs and cry and cry until her voice was gone; she simply wouldn't stop, and nobody, not even my aunt, could make her come round.

My aunt's garden was very spacious, the new-grown grass, flowers, and trees all carefully tended; in the center of the garden there was a lush green lawn of downy Korean grass; surrounding it were flower beds filled with azalea bushes—many were beginning to bud—all of them would be flaming red when in bloom. The minute I came into the garden, I heard tinkling, rippling laughter that went on and on. When I walked around the grove of banana trees, I was surprised to see Little Beauty astride a large man on all fours who was trotting around the lawn like a beast. Little Beauty was sitting straight up on his back, her plump little hand holding an azalea branch which she swished in the air like a riding crop. She was wearing a red corduroy skirt. Her bare white legs kicked and flailed; her head bobbed up and down; her short hair flopped to and fro; she was so happy she couldn't stop her shrill laughter.

"Cousin! Look at me riding my horsie—" When Little Beauty saw me, she threw away the branch and waved at me with both her hands; then she jumped off over his head and ran to me.

"Young Master-Cousin." The man scrambled to his feet, smiled at me, and murmured the greeting sheepishly.

I hadn't realized he would be such a giant, well over six feet, with an enormous head, his scalp shaved to a green-blue glow, his face swarthy, his whole body gleaming like black bronze. He grinned at me, showing a mouthful of white teeth; he kept rubbing those gigantic hands of his together bashfully; his stubby fingers looked clumsy and somewhat comical. He wore a pair of soldiers' pants washed to a faded white, the knees plastered with mud and grass.

"Cousin!" said Little Beauty, pointing at the man, "Wang Hsiung said he could crawl like that for miles and miles!"

"That was in the war, lo-ong ago-o—" Wang Hsiung hastened to explain; he had the very heavy accent of a native of Hunan.

"Nonsense!" Little Beauty cut him short with a frown. "You *did* say it, that day. You said you would let me ride on your back all the way to school."

Wang Hsiung looked at Little Beauty sheepishly; he seemed unable to get a word out; he even started to blush through his swarthy skin, as if some secret between Little Beauty and him had been revealed.

"Cousin! Let's go look, Wang Hsiung's caught me a whole lot of big green crickets." Little Beauty went running ahead of me, leading me toward the house; after a few steps she stopped, as if she'd suddenly thought of something; she turned around and stretched out her round, white arm at Wang Hsiung.

"Come, Wang Hsiung," she called out.

Hesitating for a moment, Wang Hsiung finally came shuffling up. Little Beauty snatched his dark, brawny arm; hand in hand with him, hopping and leaping about, she ran toward the house. Wang Hsiung lumbered off after her, pulling his colossal body along.

That night, after my aunt finished playing mah-jong she sat around and chatted with me; she told me Wang Hsiung was the manservant she'd just hired. He had been a soldier all his life and was recently discharged. "You simply couldn't find a more honest fellow!" my aunt declared approvingly. "Not a peep out of him all day long, he just buries himself in his work. And you should see the way he takes care of the trees and flowers! Amazing for such an uncouth fellow. He certainly has his own idea of how to go about it." My aunt told me that every single one of the hundred or so azaleas in the garden had been planted by Wang Hsiung with his own hands. Why so many azaleas? "For Little Beauty, of course," my aunt explained with a sigh. "What else? Just because that little imp is crazy about azaleas."

"I've never seen such a thing in all my born days!" Suddenly my aunt laughed behind her hands. "A forty-year-old great big hunk of a man letting a baby-doll of a little girl lead him around by the nose! Why, he caters to her every wish." It's a miracle, my aunt wondered out loud with a shake of her head; the two of them must be fated for each other.

Indeed Little Beauty and Wang Hsiung must have been fated for each other. Every time I went to my aunt's I saw them playing together. Each morning Wang Hsiung would carry Little Beauty to school in his pedicab; in the afternoon he would bring her home. He always polished his pedicab bright and shiny; he had little bamboo sticks topped with woollen balls of rainbow hues, paper-cut phoenixes and little pinwheels stuck all across the handlebar; the vehicle was decorated like an Imperial Palace carriage. Each time Wang Hsiung went out to transport Little Beauty he made himself spic-and-span; even on the hottest days he was always respectably attired. As Little Beauty marched through the gate, chin in the air, hair shaking, haughty as a little princess, Wang Hsiung brought up the rear, holding her schoolbag, his back straight and his face solemn, every inch the Imperial Guard to her Royal Highness. The minute she got home Little Beauty would drag Wang Hsiung out into the garden to play. Wang Hsiung would dream up a hundred little games to delight her. Once I saw him seated by himself under the eaves, at his feet a multicolored pile of glass beads; he was holding a golden thread and stringing the beads with the utmost concentration. As he reached out to catch the glass beads that were rolling in all directions, his gigantic paws looked really clumsy, yet rather engaging. When Little Beauty got home that day and came to the garden, Wang Hsiung decorated her from head to foot with bracelets and necklaces of glass beads. She wore a double-ringed crown on her head and five or six bracelets on each arm; she kicked off her shoes and, barefoot, her skirt tucked up showing her white legs, she had her ankles ringed with several rainbow-colored bangles. She was chanting—*"ee-yah-oo-yah"*—and laughing, her plump pretty arms waving aloft two bouquets of azaleas, and dancing on the lush green lawn the aborigine dance she had learned in school. Wang Hsiung was circling around her, bounding up and down, clapping his hands, his swarthy face flushed crimson, his mouth wide open in a toothy grin. The two of them—one big, one small, one dark, one white—leaping and gamboling, sang and danced against a sea of flaming red azaleas.

During my tour of duty at Supply Headquarters, I'd stay overnight at my aunt's two or three days a week. My aunt wanted me to tutor Little Beauty, because she was going to take the entrance exam for middle school in the summer. As a regular visitor at my aunt's I became better acquainted with Wang Hsiung, and on occasion he'd tell me something about himself. He told me that originally he was a peasant boy from the Hunan countryside; during the Anti-Japanese War a press gang got him and put him in the army. He said he was only eighteen then; one day he was trotting off to town to sell the two baskets of grain on his carrying pole; the minute he stepped outside his village he was taken away.

"I thought I might still get back in a few days," he said with a chuckle. "Who'd have dreamt? Before you know it, so many years have gone and I never made it back to home."

"Young Master-Cousin," Wang Hsiung once asked me, as if something were on his mind, "Can you see the mainland from Quemoy?"

I told him that through a telescope you could practically see people moving on the other side.

"That close up?" He stared at me, disbelieving.

"Why not?" I said. "Very often bodies of people who have died of hunger drift over to our side."

"They come over to look for their kinfolk," he said.

"Those people have died of hunger," I said.

"No, Young Master-Cousin, you don't know." Wang Hsiung stopped me with a wave of his hand. "Down in our Hunan countryside we got zombie-raisers; when people die outside and they got some kinfolk at home they're attached to, you wouldn't believe how fast them zombies run home."

When I was on Quemoy, there were a number of old soldiers in our battalion; they must have been in the army for almost twenty years, but it seemed to me they had still kept a childlike innocence; their joy, anger, sorrow, and happiness were just like the burning sun and sea storms of Quemoy, primitive and direct. Sometimes I'd see a whole lot of them naked in the ocean having a water fight; from time to time one or another of their wrinkled faces would suddenly break into a child's smile, the kind of smile you never see on grownup faces. One night when I was out on patrol, on a rock by the beach near our barracks I found an old soldier sitting there all by himself playing the *erh-hu*.* The moon was bright that night; there was almost no breeze off the ocean; I don't know if it was that pensive posture of his or the mournful sound of his Tartar violin that made me associate his nostalgia with that of those sentries of olden days along the frontier, so profound and ancient.

"Wang Hsiung," I asked him one night when we were sitting

---

* From *Hu-ch'in*, "Tartar violin," a viol of the rebab family, of Central Asian origin. The *erh-hu*, "second *Hu-ch'in*," is the viola to the violin.

outside to cool off, "who is left of your family?" He'd been telling me about his old home in the countryside of Hsiangyin in Hunan.

"Oh, there's my mamma, don't know if she's still alive or not," said Wang Hsiung. "And there's—"

At this point he suddenly became shy and tongue-tied; then, with a lot of hemming and hawing, he told me that before he left home he'd been engaged at an early age; his mother had bought him a little Sissy from the next village.

"She weren't more than ten, only that high—" Wang Hsiung made a gesture with his hand. How that Sissy of his loved to eat and hated to work! His mamma would pick up a broomstick and give her a licking for it; when she got spanked she'd turn and hide herself behind his back. "Sissy was right white and plump, a very silly little gal." Wang Hsiung bared his teeth and started chuckling.

"I've got a nice lot of squid for you!" Happy, the maid, had sneaked up behind Wang Hsiung; abruptly she thrust out a string of barbecued squid and dangled it right in front of Wang Hsiung's face. She had just washed her hair and come out to the garden to cool off. She was a big-breasted female who was particularly fond of wearing skintight clothes, so tight you could see her flesh jiggling around in them. She always painted her face oily white, and pencilled her eyebrows heavily. She would ogle people with her small eyes and purse her lips defiantly, fancying herself very seductive. My aunt said the two of them, Happy and Wang Hsiung, must have their horoscopes crossed in some way; from the first moment Wang Hsiung set foot in the house they were deadly enemies. Whenever Wang Hsiung saw her he would try to avoid her, but Happy took a perverse delight in provoking him, and whenever she made him turn red as a beet she would laugh in his face with great glee.

Wang Hsiung rudely brushed her hand away and growled; he jerked his head away with a frown and wouldn't talk any more. Happy, laughing out loud, threw back her head and lowered the barbecued squid into her mouth; then, tossing her long, dripping-wet hair, she strutted over to the rattan lounge under the banana trees and stretched out on it. The big, round yellow moon had just climbed up over the garden wall and shone on the fat banana leaves till they gleamed. Happy was fanning herself with a large rushleaf fan; she kept slapping at her legs to chase away the mosquitoes. In a shrill voice she began to sing a Taiwanese "sob-tune," "Tossing and Turning till Dawn." Brusquely Wang Hsiung stood up; without so much as turning his head he dragged himself off to the house.

Little Beauty was a bright child, all right; after I'd tutored her for only a few weeks during the summer vacation, she passed the entrance examination without much effort and was admitted to the Provincial Middle School Number Two for Girls. My aunt was so happy she could hardly close her mouth for laughing; as soon as the names of the successful candidates were posted she took Little Beauty to a tailor and had her measured for her school uniform and took her out shopping for her schoolbag and other supplies. The day school started, the whole household was in a dither; my aunt personally packed Little Beauty's schoolbag and ironed her uniform. As Little Beauty marched triumphantly to the front gate dressed in her smart Girl Scout uniform with all the accessories, her cap at a jaunty angle and a brand new black leather schoolbag under her arm, it seemed as if she had changed in the twinkling of an eye from a little girl into a real middle-school student. Wang Hsiung had already wheeled the pedicab to the gate and was waiting there; when Little Beauty emerged, Wang Hsiung looked awestruck and gaped at her, utterly speechless. Little Beauty tossed her schoolbag into the pedicab and nimbly jumped in after it; she waved at us and gave her driver a push, saying:

"Let's go, Wang Hsiung!"

Little Beauty became totally fascinated with her middle-school life. The first few days she simply wouldn't take off her uniform after school; she stood in front of the mirror and kept looking at herself this way and that. Whenever she got the chance, she would pick up her *Far East English Reader* and read aloud in English with great pride. One day she was standing on the stone steps leading to the garden, holding the English reader in her hand; Wang Hsiung was down below, his head raised, listening intently to the young lady read English.

"*I am a girl.*" Little Beauty pointed at her chest; then she pointed at Wang Hsiung.

"*You are a boy.*" Wang Hsiung's mouth hung open, his face full of admiration.

"*I am a student,*" Little Beauty read on; she cast a glance at Wang Hsiung; suddenly she pointed at him and shouted, "*You are a dog!*"

Little Beauty went off into a fit of laughter, giggling and swaying to and fro, her short hair flying in all directions. Wang Hsiung blinked his eyes in bewilderment, totally at a loss; then he opened his mouth and laughed happily with his little mistress.

Three weeks after school started, one Saturday around noon Little Beauty returned home where we were all waiting for her so we could eat lunch together. The girl flung open the living-room door and walked in, her face stormy; Wang Hsiung was following behind with her schoolbag.

"Beginning next week, I don't want Wang Hsiung to take me to school any more!" she said to my aunt the minute she sat down. We were all very surprised; quickly my aunt asked her whatever was the matter.

"Everybody laughs at me!" Little Beauty threw up her head, her face reddened.

"Why should they laugh?" My aunt went over and tried to comfort her; wiping the perspiration from Little Beauty's forehead with her handkerchief, she said gently, "Lots of other people ride to school in pedicabs, don't they?"

Little Beauty pushed my aunt's hands away; suddenly she pointed her finger at Wang Hsiung. "All my schoolmates are talking —they say he looks like a big gorilla!" She glanced at Wang Hsiung; all at once her face was full of disdain. My aunt stared at Wang Hsiung for a moment and burst out laughing. Happy nearly doubled up with laughter, her face buried in her skirt. Holding onto Little Beauty's schoolbag, Wang Hsiung just stood there, completely mortified, his swarthy face turning purple; he stole a glance at Little Beauty, his lips quivering as if he wanted to give her a smile in apology, but the smile just wouldn't come out.

After Little Beauty began riding her bicycle to school she was seldom with Wang Hsiung. She was very active in school and would often invite a whole bunch of schoolmates home to play. One Sunday afternoon Little Beauty brought seven or eight schoolfriends—all twelve- or thirteen-year-old girls—home to play kick-the-shuttlecock in the garden. Little Beauty was a champ at this game; she could kick up to a hundred nonstop. As I was standing on the stone steps watching the little girls, who had their skirts tucked up and were kicking the shuttlecock with great enthusiasm, I saw Wang Hsiung steal out of the banana grove. Beckoning to Little Beauty, he called her in a hushed voice:

"Little Beauty—"

"What are you doing here?" Little Beauty came over, somewhat annoyed.

"See? What I've got for you?" From a brown paper bag Wang Hsiung pulled out a fragile glass bowl with two goldfish swimming around in it. I had once bought a bowl of goldfish for Little Beauty. She was very fond of it and hung it in the window; every day she asked Wang Hsiung to feed the goldfish red worms; later a cat from next door tipped the bowl over, and ate up the fish. Little Beauty cried her heart out; I tried to comfort her and I promised to buy her another bowl, but I'd forgotten all about it.

"Who wants to play with that stuff any more?" said Little Beauty scornfully, her chin in the air.

"It took me a powerful long time to find these two," Wang Hsiung said earnestly.

"I'm going back to play shuttlecock!" Little Beauty turned to run off.

"These here two are phoenix-tails—" Wang Hsiung caught Little Beauty's arm; he held the bowl close to Little Beauty's face to let her see.

"Let go of my arm!" Little Beauty cried out.

"Please, just take a look, Little Beauty—" Wang Hsiung pleaded; he held Little Beauty tight and wouldn't let her go. Little Beauty twisted around and couldn't free herself; her other arm shot up and struck the bowl and crack! the bowl was knocked to the ground and smashed to pieces. Little Beauty flung Wang Hsiung's hand away and ran off without looking back. The water in the bowl was splashed all over the ground, and the two bright red goldfish kept leaping up and down. Wang Hsiung uttered a cry of alarm; he squatted down, his fists clenched, and looked helplessly at the two struggling goldfish, not knowing how to rescue them. The two delicate goldfish gave a couple of final desperate jumps and fell to the ground, inert. His head lowered, Wang Hsiung stared at the two dying fish for a long time; then he picked them up by their tails, laid them in his palms, and holding them carefully, walked out of the garden.

From then on, Wang Hsiung grew more reticent than ever. Whenever he had time, he would retreat into the garden and water the flowers. Every day he would sprinkle every one of the hundred or so azaleas in the garden; early in the morning or late in the afternoon you could see that giant form of his moving back and forth among the flowers, alone. His head bowed, his body slightly stooped, with a long-handled bamboo dipper, one after the other, splash after splash, very slowly, very carefully, he watered those azaleas he had raised with his own hands. No matter who spoke to him, he would ignore them. Sometimes when my aunt called urgently for him, he would just answer in a raspy voice: "Yes, Ma'am," and at once quietly flee back into the garden. Then, the day before it all happened, Happy went into the garden to get water from the faucet to do her washing; Wang Hsiung had already hung a bucket under the tap to get water for the flowers. Happy took Wang Hsiung's half-filled bucket off and set her own washtub under the tap. Wang Hsiung came over; without a word he kicked over the tub and sent the water flying, splashing all over Happy. The maid flared up, her face turned a dark red; she threw back her long hair, one step and she was blocking Wang Hsiung's way to the faucet.

"Nobody's using this water today!" she yelled.

Head in the air, arms akimbo, breasts thrust high, her face sprinkled with beads of water, the hem of her skirt still dripping, she kicked off her wooden clogs and stood in her bare feet confronting Wang Hsiung challengingly. His lips tightened, Wang Hsiung glared at her. Happy looked him up and down; suddenly she broke out laughing, sassy and wild, her whole body trembling.

"Big gorilla!—Big gorilla!—" she shrieked through her laughter.

The words were barely out of her mouth when Wang Hsiung reached out his gigantic hands, seized her by her fleshy shoulders and began to shake her violently, growling and snarling like a mortally wounded beast letting out its howl of fury and anguish. Happy's face twisted in pain; she was probably so shocked that for a moment she couldn't utter a sound. Just as I ran over to stop Wang Hsiung, Happy let out a scream; Wang Hsiung relaxed his grip and Happy picked up her skirts and took to her heels. As she ran she kept massaging her shoulders; not until she was a safe distance away did she turn and spit. "Rot your parents!" she cursed.

Wang Hsiung stood there, motionless, panting heavily, beads of sweat rolling down his face one after the other, his eyes red enough to spit fire. I suddenly saw that Wang Hsiung was a completely changed man. He had stubble all over his face, his unshaven hair had grown an inch, sticking out stiffly, his head looked like a porcupine, and his eyes had sunk way back in, the rings blackened as if he hadn't slept for days. I could hardly believe that in a few days Wang Hsiung could have turned so withered, so savage.

Even so many days after it happened, my aunt still refused to believe it. She said she would never have dreamed an honest fellow like Wang Hsiung would do that kind of thing.

"That damned ghost—" Happy would bury her face in her skirt and burst into tears whenever Wang Hsiung's name was mentioned; she would caress her neck with a look of lingering fear.

That morning when we found Happy, we thought she was dead. She was lying in the garden under the azalea shrubs, unconscious, her skirt ripped to shreds, naked to the waist, her breasts covered with bruises and scratches, a ring of finger-marks around her neck. That same day, Wang Hsiung disappeared. My aunt asked me to distribute the belongings he'd left behind among those old soldiers in my company. Rummaging through his trunk we found a big package of colored beads left over from the time he made bracelets for Little Beauty.

After I was discharged, I went back home to Taichung. It was not until the following spring when I returned to Taipei to look for a job that I visited my aunt's house again. My aunt had been ill in bed for a long time; she looked pale and listless. She said that ever since that unlucky thing had happened in her house she hadn't had a single day of good health; she simply couldn't sleep at night. She struggled to sit up and caught my hand.

"Every night," she said in a hushed voice, "I hear someone watering the garden."

Mother had told me my aunt was a hopeless neurotic—all her

life she loved to talk about ghosts. When I walked out into the garden, I was stunned to see those hundred or so azaleas, one mound piled on another mound, one wave churning up another wave, all exploding in riotous bloom as if a chestful of fresh blood suddenly had shot forth from an unstanchable wound and sprayed the whole garden, leaving marks and stains everywhere, bloodred. I had never seen azaleas bloom with such abandon, and so angrily. Little Beauty and a bunch of girls were playing hide-and-seek in the garden; they cut to and fro through the sea of bloodred azaleas. Peal after peal, with ever-heightening insistence, the little girls' shrill, ringing laughter reverberated through the bright spring day.

Ode to Bygone Days

One winter evening an old woman stopped in front of the main gate of the Li residence in Lane 120 on Nanking East Road. She lifted her head, squinted, and gazed for a long time at the double door of Chinese cypress; the vermilion paint was cracked and falling off, and spots of mould were already showing on it. The old woman's spine was completely bowed, her jagged shoulder blades thrust high, her bony little head wedged in between. The hair on top of her head was thinning, almost gone, leaving only a small salt-and-pepper bun at the back of her neck. She was wrapped in a long, loose black sweater of heavy wool that hung down to her knees. Her body was shriveled to a skeleton; when the wind blew, the clothes around her trembled and rustled. On the crook of her left arm she carried a bundle in a black cotton cloth.

The Li residence was the only old house in the lane; on all sides modern apartment buildings of gray concrete towered over the wooden one-story house, hemming it in. The Li house was quite dilapidated, some of its roof-tiles were broken or missing, and tufts of wild grass sprang out of the crevices in the ragged eaves. There had once been a pair of glass lamps over the gate—but of the one to the right only the rusty iron bracket remained. Nailed to the upper corner of the door was a dark bronze plaque shiny with age, on which the words "LI MANSION," inscribed in the tomb-rubbings style, stood out clearly. The old woman stretched out her scrawny, birdclaw right hand; trembling, she felt the doors, so cracked with the years. She wanted to push the doorbell, but after some hesitation she drew back her hand; head raised, she looked around in bewilderment, then finally she tottered round the house to the back door.

"Mamma Lo—" Standing below the kitchen window the old

woman ventured to call out—she had heard someone turn a faucet on in the kitchen.

Suddenly a head popped out of the dark cavernous window. It was another ancient woman; her dishevelled white hair, still unusually thick and heavy, hung like a mop of white hemp around her face, which was stout and round with liver spots and wrinkles piled on top of each other, the hard, dried-up rind of a grapefruit; the dark pouches under her eyes were so swollen that her eyes became two thin lines; her ears were big and fat, their droopy lobes pierced by gold earrings well worn to a dull reddish glow.

"Second Sister, it's me—Nanny Shun-en." With her face tilted upward between her hunched shoulders, Nanny Shun-en called up in a shrill, tremulous voice.

"Good Lord Almighty!" boomed out Mamma Lo in her hoarse voice. At once there was a rapid thudding of feet, and Nanny Shun-en saw Mamma Lo open the back door and come waddling over to greet her. Mamma Lo was twice as big a body as Nanny Shun-en; she wore a cotton-padded jacket of coarse blue cloth; her paunch stuck out as if she was holding a winnowing basket in front of her; the apron tied around her waist practically reached her feet; as she waddled, her enormous paunch bobbed up and down, and her long apron billowed rhythmically.

"Why, if it isn't Old Sis Shun-en!" The minute Mamma Lo reached Nanny Shun-en, she caught her by her thin, feeble arm and supported her into the kitchen. "My left eyelid's been jumping the whole day long, well now who would've dreamt it was on account of you!"

Mamma Lo set Nanny Shun-en down on a low stool in the kitchen, took her bundle from her, drew up another stool, and sat down facing her. After the two old women were settled, Mamma Lo heaved a deep sigh.

"Old Sis, I thought you was never going to come by here and see us all again."

"Second Sister—" In great agitation Nanny Shun-en waved her bony claws in a gesture to stop Mamma Lo. "How could a upstanding old lady like you say such things?" she said in a plaintive voice. "In all the years since I left this house I haven't spent so much as a single day in good health. I'm old now; I ain't no use no more;

this old body just won't hold up no more. . . ."

"That's right, isn't it, Sis." Mamma Lo took a good look at Nanny Shun-en. "You sure do look poorly, more than you used to a few years back. Is your blood pressure down these days?"

Nanny Shun-en shook her head with a doleful smile. "Just you tell me where on this earth am I going to find that good fortune? All these years down in Tainan I've been laying in my bed; dizzy spells, you see; just couldn't get to my feet. I'm being a heavy burden on Ch'i-sheng and his family, poor souls."

"Now you've just got to count your blessings!" Mamma Lo stretched out her big, plump, work-coarsened hand and patted Nanny Shun-en's shoulder. "Why, you've got yourself a mighty fine, dutiful son to carry you to your last resting place. Now me, I ain't got no son, I ain't got no daughter; when the day comes I don't know where I'll be laying my body down, in the head of a street or in the tail of a alley."

"Second Sister—" Nanny Shun-en held Mamma Lo's plump hand in hers. "Why, you've been in this house for scores of years! Now the day you go to the Western Paradise, would the General and Young Miss begrudge you your casket and your burial clothes?"

Mamma Lo pulled her hand out of Nanny Shun-en's and stared at her, nodding. After a while she let out a deep sigh.

"Old Sis, you have been away a long time; can't blame you noway, I'm afraid you just don't understand how things are with us now. . . ."

Shakily Nanny Shun-en rose to her feet and unwrapped the black cloth bundle on the kitchen stove; in it lay a pyramid of large snow-white eggs.

"Ch'i-sheng's wife has been raising a few dozen Leghorns. I picked these here double-yoke eggs special for the General and Young Miss. Second Sister, would you kindly go and announce me to the General, just tell him Nanny Shun-en's come by to inquire after His Excellency's health?"

"My, these sure are mighty big eggs!" Mamma Lo picked up a couple and held them to her ears and shook them. "You might as well leave them down here a while. The General's feeling right poorly, he's got a upset stomach again. I just been waiting on him to give him his medicine. He's laying down now; it'll be a good long wait for you."

"This time, no matter what it took, I had to come on this journey up here. At my age, you never know if there'll be a next time." Nanny Shun-en sighed.

"You'd have done better to have come to see them a long time ago—" Mamma Lo didn't even turn around. She took an empty biscuit tin from the cupboard and with the utmost care placed the eggs inside it. She picked up a cake of alkali soap, stooped over, and scrubbed away laboriously at the grease and dirt on the stove. Nanny Shun-en stood by the sink next to the stove; soaking in the sink were two washrags black with use; she gave them a few good rubs and wrung them out for Mamma Lo, her thin, feeble arms trembling.

"Second Sister—" Hands gripping the two washrags as if she had suddenly remembered something, Nanny Shun-en called Mamma Lo. "Madame—"

"Huh?" Mamma Lo, cheeks puffed out, panting heavily, was scrubbing the stove so hard it was filled with gray, slimy water.

"Madame—did she leave any last words behind?" Nanny Shun-en asked, her voice hushed.

Mamma Lo stopped, wiped the sweat off her forehead with her apron. She closed her eyes and pondered. "Seems to me I heard the General say that when Madame was carried to the hospital for the operation she woke up just the once; she didn't say but one thing: 'So cold.' Then she didn't say nothing no more."

"That must be why . . ." Nanny Shun-en nodded her head, her face all at once filled with sorrow. Mamma Lo plucked the two washrags out of Nanny Shun-en's hands and swiped at the grimy water on the stove. "Second Sister, do you still call to mind that grand mansion of ours on Cool-Clear Mountain back in Nanking? Wasn't there a powerful lot of peonies in that there garden?"

"Think I don't remember?" Mamma Lo snorted, washrags twirling in the air. "Red ones, purple ones—they bloomed the whole garden round! Was there a single spring in those days Madame didn't give a wine-party for her guests to admire them peonies?"

"It's already three nights one after another, Second Sister." Nanny Shun-en's tremulous voice suddenly turned mournful. "I been dreaming about Madame; she stood right in those peonies there, beckoning to me: 'Nanny Shun-en, Nanny Shun-en, go quickly and bring me my cape; the wind has risen.' Year before last when Madame passed away from this world I was took so ill I didn't know where I was; when she was carried to the mountain to her last home I couldn't even join in for to see her off; all I could do was to burn two paper maids to service our Madame in the Other World; but in my heart I always felt it so bad. These two years since Madame is gone, in this house . . ." Nanny Shun-en's voice was choked.

Mamma Lo flung the two washrags back into the sink. "In this house? Huh!" Arms akimbo, paunch stuck up, she cut Nanny Shun-en short. "Who but this here old too-mean-to-die is here to bear all these burdens? Why, the First Seventh wasn't even over yet,* when that Cassia and Little Wang done run off together; and them two god-damned no-accounts stole the whole of Madame's caseful of jade. Didn't leave nothing at all."

"Lord have mercy! . . ." Her eyes closed, Nanny Shun-en shook her head; her dried, sunken lips smacked in commiseration.

All of a sudden Mamma Lo grabbed her ropy white hair with one hand and with the other snatched up the chopping-knife from the table, and struck the chopping-block ferociously several times. "Day in and day out in this kitchen I struck this block and cursed," she growled. "I cursed them two wolf-hearted, dog-gutted traitors: May Heaven smite them! May Thunder strike them! May the Five Devils tear them into pieces! I was the one who done bought Cassia for Ma-dame, wasn't I. That damned wench, didn't she wear silks and satins and all kinds of fine feathers in this house? And Little Wang. His pappy Wang the orderly before he died begged the General to look after him. They raised him in this house for twenty years. Why! even a hound dog will howl three times when his Master's gone! I want to take a good look at the hearts in them two goddamned no-accounts and see what they are made of!" Nanny Shun-en was muttering as-sent, her eyes closed, her small head nodding up and down.

Mamma Lo laid the chopping-knife down, straightened up and gave the small of her back a few solid whacks with her fist. "It ain't only that Cassia and Little Wang run off, but they done cast this old

---

* The Buddhist funeral service lasts forty-nine days. During the first forty-nine days after death, the soul is undergoing a period of transition before rein-carnation, a period of judgment which determines the next state of the deceased. Sutras are chanted for the dead every seventh day of this period, seven times until the Seventh Seventh Day. It is the family's obligation to observe the proper rites to help the soul overcome the perils of judgment and transition.

woman in the pit. This whole house, inside and out, every little sesame seed of a thing, ain't I the one who lays my hands to it all? Soon as I get to fixing up the inside I have to leave the outside go. Just cleaning this here kitchen alone is enough to break my weary back." Mamma Lo pounded her back again. Nanny Shun-en came over to her and held her plump, calloused hands in hers and raised them.

"I reckon you are the faithful one who has been taking care of them, Second Sister, and when Young Miss goes to wed she surely will take you along to be the Venerable Matriarch of her house."

"My good old lady!" Mamma Lo jerked her hands out of Nanny Shun-en's. "That's a mighty fine thing for Your Ladyship to say, but I regret to tell you that just ain't my fate. Young Miss?" Mamma Lo sniffed, arms akimbo again, paunch stuck back up. "I'm going to tell you the truth, Old Sis. At the very beginning of this year, Young Miss got stuck with some man with a wife to home, and she done got big-bellied; and she and the General had a terrible fight when she told him she was leaving home. The General beat her 'most to death right there, beat her till her face got all swollen up. That gal ain't got no heart at all, she didn't let one tear fall! She told the General, 'Papa, if you allow me I'll go, and if you don't allow me I'll still go; all you have to do is just pretend you never had daughter like me, that's all.' And she walked out and didn't even look back. Just last month I saw her, at the East Gate Market; she was carrying a vegetable basket, with her big belly and her hair every which way. When she saw me, she hung her head, eyelids all reddened, and she called me 'Mamma.' Imagine, a young lady from an official family, the way she looked! I didn't even know where to hide my face."

"Lord have mercy—" Nanny Shun-en again gave out her mournful comment.

"Things here ain't nothing like the way they used to be no more, Old Sis," said Mamma Lo, shaking her white head. "These last two years the General ain't himself no more; soon as Young Miss gone he was so hurt and grieved he wanted to leave home and become a monk in a temple in Keelung. His old followers came by here every day to beg him to change his mind. One day, I saw things had really gone too far, so I walked into the living room; first I ran to Madame's memorial portrait and I got down on my knees before it and knocked my head three times on the floor; then I stood up and spoke to the

General: "Your Excellency, I reckon since I first came into your family with my Lady, it's been over thirty years. I have seen all the glory and splendor of the days of your house. And now, those who have died have died and those who have gone away from home will not return; if but the sight of this broke your servant's heart, how much deeper Your Excellency's grief must be! Young Miss disgraced the family, and Your Excellency wants to renounce the world; I don't dare stop you. But there's just one thing: I'm way past seventy, half of me is already in the grave; Your Excellency, when you're gone and leave Young Master behind all by himself, I'm afraid I cannot shoulder this burden alone.' The General heard me out, then he stamped his foot and fell silent."

"Second Sister," Nanny Shun-en faltered, "what's that you say? Young Master—he done come back from abroad?" She clutched Mamma Lo's arm, her bony, birdclaw hands trembling.

Mamma Lo stared at her for a long moment; she nodded her head. "Old Sis, you poor creature, you truly must have been took so ill you never heard nothing about it."

"Second Sister—" Nanny Shun-en whispered. Mamma Lo didn't pay her any attention; she freed herself, undid her apron and mopped the sweat and grime from her face; then she went over to the rice-vat, poured some water into the pot of washed rice on top of it and set the pot on the coal stove; finally she turned to Nanny Shun-en and spoke to her.

"You're the one who nursed him from a suckling babe at your breast; no matter what, you're the one who wore yourself out for him; now I got to take you to see for yourself."

Mamma Lo helped Nanny Shun-en from the kitchen to the back court. Supporting each other, the two old women made their way with effort along the small stone courtyard path overgrown with moss. On both sides of the path wormwood sprang up as high as a man's waist, fertile, rampant; between the fat, gross stalks wove spiderwebs full of stuck-fast insect bodies. As Mamma Lo walked she swept the encroaching wormwood aside to let Nanny Shun-en pass. When they reached the end of the stone path, Nanny Shun-en was stunned to find, behind the wormwood bushes, seated squarely on a round marble stool, a large fat man; the wormwood leaves and stems rose above his head and hid him from view. A swarm of gnats circled above his head.

He was swaddled in a baggy wool overcoat, old and worn, with all its buttons gone but one. His belly burst through his overcoat like a hempen sandbag overstuffed with sand and mud; his fly was half undone and the string of his drawers was showing. He had taken off his shoes and socks, and his big, plump bare feet, red with cold, were placed neatly together on the muddy ground. His head was big and fat, too; his short hair, parched brown and dried out, was almost gone, exposing his pink, tender scalp; his fleshy cheeks drooped flaccidly—they curved his big mouth, always half-open, downward like a bow. The large fat man was holding a bunch of dandelions already past their bloom; he was playing with them, and their white down was sprinkled all over him.

Mamma Lo helped Nanny Shun-en all the way over to the large fat man. Nanny Shun-en leaned forward and looked at the large fat man intently, for a long time.

"Young Master—" Nanny Shun-en called softly. The large fat man looked up at Nanny Shun-en blankly, his eyes vacant, dull, his face devoid of expression. "Young Master, it's me, it's your Nanny Shun-en." Nanny Shun-en took a step closer and whispered gently in the large fat man's ear. The large fat man turned towards her and stared; suddenly he opened his large mouth and broke into a silly laugh; drool ran from the corner of his mouth onto his lapel. Nanny Shun-en took her handkerchief out of her jacket-flap and stooped to wipe the large fat man's mouth and his coat; as she was wiping him off, she suddenly opened her thin, feeble arms wide and hugged the big head of the large fat man tight to her bosom.

"Young Master, Baby—you can still laugh—and you the one to be pitied the most—if Madame had lived to see this, her heart would have broke right into pieces—"

Nanny Shun-en pressed her withered cheek to the large fat man's balding crown and started to sob.

"This here family, and their ancestral graveyard. The Wind and Water moved against them." Mamma Lo stood by, muttering to herself.

"Young Master, Baby—Young Master, my boy—" Her arms around the large fat man's head, her thin, small body swaying to and fro, eyes closed tight, her dried sunken lips trembling, opening and shutting, Nanny Shun-en let out wail after desolate wail.

A blast of winter evening wind swept through; it set all the tangled, untended wormwood in the courtyard to hissing, lifted Nanny Shun-en's long, loose sweater up and blew it round the large fat man, covering him. Mamma Lo stood among the bushes; her hands clasped around her paunch, eyes narrowed, she looked up at the heavens overcast with gathering evening clouds. The cold wind sent her thick, ropy white hair flying in all directions.

The Dirge of Liang Fu

"The Dirge of Liang Fu" is the title of a burial song in the Music
Bureau collection of the Han Dynasty, named after Liang-fu, a mountain near Mount Tai in present-day Shantung Province. The song is
associated with Chu-ke Liang, the brilliant military strategist and
heroic prime minister of Shu Han during the Three Kingdoms period
(A.D. 220–265), who dedicated his life to the restoration of the House
of Han but died without achieving his goal.

Centuries later, the great T'ang Dynasty poet Tu Fu, an ardent ad-
mirer of Chu-ke Liang, wrote his own "Dirge of Liang Fu," called
"Climbing the Tower."

> When the Flowers touch the high Tower
> > it cuts the Exile to the Heart
> As from this Ascent I look down—
> > so many Catastrophes throughout the Land!—
> With Spring Splendor the Silk River
> > roars forward through Heaven and Earth
> As on Jade Castle Mountain floating Clouds
> > transform the Ancient to This Moment.
>
> The Polar Star, the Imperial Court,
> > shall endure to the last.
> Ye Bandits from the Western Mountains!
> > Invade us not!
> Even that pitiful Hou Chu
> > still retains his Shrine.
> As the Day ends, in vain I sing
> > the Dirge of Liang Fu.
> > > Tu Fu (T'ang Dynasty,
> > > 712–770)

Tu Fu wrote this poem while in exile in Szechwan during the An
Lu-shan rebellion. When he addresses the "Bandits from the Western
Mountains," he is referring to the Turfan tribe from Tibet. The name

of Hou Chu, the second and last ruler of the Kingdom of Shu Han (one of the Three Kingdoms) had become a byword for incompetence and dull-wittedness.

Late one afternoon, in the deep of winter, a black old-model sedan drew up to the gate of the Weng residence in the Taipei suburb of Tien Mu. The car door opened and two men got out: an old gentleman of three score and ten, followed by a middle-aged man of around fifty. The older man was attired in a long black satin gown figured with darker, round designs and shoes of black flannel, and on his head he wore a hat of sable fur. A few strands of white hair were visible beneath his hat, covering his ears, and his cheeks bore a rich growth of silvery beard. He was of majestic stature. As he walked, his long, full beard caught the wind and flared; still his face preserved its grave expression. The middle-aged man behind him was also clad in somber black, in a Western suit and tie. He wore silver-rimmed glasses, and his hair, too, was turning white; his face looked weary and sere. As they neared the main gate, a wizened old aide opened it from the inside and came out to greet them. He was wearing a faded blue Sun Yat-sen tunic; he was well past sixty himself—his hair was completely gone and his back was bent like a bow. He kept nodding to the two gentlemen.

"General, you've returned. Commissioner Lei, how are you, Sir?"

Commissioner Lei returned the old retainer's salute, turned to the old gentleman, and bowed respectfully.

"His Excellency has had a tiring day and would probably wish to rest. I ought to take my leave."

"That's all right." General P'u gave a wave of his hand. "Come in and sit for a while. I still have something to talk to you about." Without turning his head, he walked through the gate with a slow, firm step, Commissioner Lei close behind. Immediately the old aide went back in and closed the main gate after them.

"Lai *Fukuan!*"* the General called.

"Sir!" From force of habit, the old aide quickly stood to atten-

---

* *Fukuan:* a military rank particular to the Chinese army, similar to an aide-de-camp. The *fukuan* is in close personal attendance on a general.

tion, his hands pressed to his sides, but his back was still so bent he couldn't straighten up.

"Make two cups of tea and bring them to my study."

"Yessir, General." Body bowed, Lai *Fukuan* quickly took himself off.

In the inner courtyard there were no trees other than the dense clusters of purple bamboo around the wall. It was late winter, so the stone path was strewn with fallen leaves and sheaths. As His Excellency and the Commissioner went toward the house treading on the crisp, dry leaves, there was a crackling, breaking sound. By the time they entered the study, Lai *Fukuan* had already brought two cups of Iron Kuanyin and set them on the marble-inlaid tea table. He turned to the Commissioner with a bow.

"Commissioner Lei, please have some tea."

Upon entering the room, without removing his hat General P'u went straight to a red sandalwood Grand Minister chair by the tea table and sat down. He picked up the cup of hot tea and warmed his hands around it, blowing back the tea leaves floating on the surface, took a sip, and drew a deep breath. He raised his eyes and, noticing that Commissioner Lei was still standing, motioned him to another Grand Minister chair.

The study was furnished with archaic elegance. On one wall hung the large center-scroll from a triptych, a Ming landscape, "Fisherman-Recluse in Winter Forest," by Wen Cheng-ming. The couplet on the two scrolls on either side, taken from Tu Fu's poem "Climbing the Tower," was written in the vigorous and forceful hand of Cheng Pan-ch'iao.

> With Spring Splendor the Silk River
> roars forward through Heaven and Earth
> As on Jade Castle Mountain floating Clouds
> transform the Ancient to This Moment

On another wall hung a pair of calligraphic scrolls in the tomb-rubbings style of the Han and Wei Dynasties, from the writing-brush of the late Mr. Chan-t'ang.* The first scroll was inscribed: "To Comrade P'u-yuan, for Mutual Encouragement." The second was dated:

---

* The courtesy name of Hu Han-min (1886–1936), a Kuomintang elder statesman and one of the early associates of Dr. Sun Yat-sen.

"On the Eve of the Battle Oath for the Northern Expedition, the Fifteenth Year of the Republic." Recorded thereon was the oft-cited exhortation from the Last Will and Testament of Sun Yat-sen, the Father of the Country:

> The Revolution is not yet accomplished.
> Our Comrades must strive on with all their might!

Against the window on the left stood a large ebony desk with the four treasures of the study arranged on it. A brushstand of Han jade in the shape of a carp; an antique inkstone from the Heavenly Music Pavilion; a carved bamboo brush-holder containing writing brushes of various kinds. The desk was uncluttered save for a well-thumbed set of the multivolume history *Mirror of Government* by Ssu-ma Kuang. Against the window on the right stood an altar table; on it was placed a set of the Diamond Sutra. Next to the Sutra was an old bronze tripod decorated with mythical *t'ao-t'ieh* creatures.* The tripod was heaped with accumulated incense ash, remnants of burnt incense sticks still stuck to its center.

"Your revered teacher—" General P'u had been deep in thought for quite a while before he spoke.

"Yes, Your Excellency." As the old general left his words unfinished, Commissioner Lei spoke up in response.

"Your teacher and I, we were together well over fifty years all told—" The old man again paused, then continued, "I knew very well the kind of man he was."

"Yes, Your Excellency. The deep friendship between you and my mentor is known to us all."

"Ardent yet high-minded—that would be the phrase I'd use to describe your teacher's strengths. Yet ever so often throughout his life that's precisely why he got into trouble. Yes—Meng-yang's character was a little too uncompromising." General P'u gave a sigh and nodded his head.

"Truly, by the way in which he conducted himself, my mentor caused people to look up to him," said Commissioner Lei.

"That's so. But he was a difficult man to work with, though." His Excellency turned and faced the Commissioner. "You were his

---

* *T'ao-t'ieh*: a ravenous beast, all head and no body, often depicted on ancient bronzes.

secretary all these years, of course you know."

"Of course, of course," Commissioner Lei quickly agreed. "When my mentor acted, his orders were weighty as mountains. His word was our command. None dared disobey him."

"All of you used to compare him behind his back to the blazing sun in July—too hot to withstand, isn't that so?" General P'u leaned toward Commissioner Lei with a smile. The Commissioner laughed knowingly; he didn't dare reply. His Excellency removed his sable-fur hat, scratched his white head, and sank into his thoughts again.

"Actually, he was quite lonely in his last years—" the old man murmured to himself.

"Your Excellency?"

"I said—" General P'u turned and raised his voice— "Meng-yang, he was a little too hot-headed. He had accomplished a great deal in his life, but he hurt a lot of people in the process. Only Chung-mo and I were able to talk to him."

"My mentor always held Your Excellency and His Excellency Chung in the highest esteem." The Commissioner bowed respectfully to the General. His Excellency stroked his silvery beard and smiled a little.

"Well, Chung-mo and I really didn't have that much about us to command his respect. However, there's quite a history behind the way we three first got to know each other—I'm afraid even you don't know the whole story."

"I remember my mentor once told me that he, Your Excellency, and His Excellency Chung were all schoolmates at the Szechwan Military Academy."

"That's so. It's a long story, though, if I take you through all the twists and turns . . ." General P'u sighed softly and closed his eyes with a faint smile. Commissioner Lei saw he was lost in thought and did not dare disturb him. He waited a while in silence, then ventured, "If Your Excellency would allow us of the younger generation to hear the story, in the future when it comes to writing my mentor's biography we would have something to go on."

"Hmmm . . ." General P'u mulled it over a bit. "Well then, to start from the beginning: it was the year of Hsin Hai.* Chung-mo and

* 1911.

his wife, Yang Yun-hsiu, had just returned from Japan where they had joined the T'ungmenghui.* They came back with a mission: to rally the revolutionary elements at the Szechwan Military Academy to help with the great Wuchang Uprising. At that time the chief of the Society of Elders and Brothers was none other than Lo Tzu-chou, the 'Eighth Prince.' He was in the vanguard protecting our secret shipment of ammunition into Wuchang. Even though all of us went to the same school, we didn't really know each other; we ended up in the same unit purely by chance. We called ourselves the Dare-to-Die Corps and wore a red mark on our earlobes as a secret sign. Our slogan was: Revolution to Overthrow the Manchus; To Overthrow the Manchus: Revolution! Overnight people of every degree rose to arms; by day and by night, by land and by water they marched into Hupei Province. And let me tell you about Chung-mo's wife, Yang Yun-hsiu —there was a woman of valor and intelligence!" General P'u nodded his head in admiration.

"Indeed, His Excellency Chung's lady was a true heroine!" Commissioner Lei echoed the praise.

"Did you know the day we shipped the ammunition into Wuchang Yang Yun-hsiu disguised herself as a bride and had the dynamite hidden in her bridal sedan chair? Now Meng-yang and I, we wore red turbans and acted as her chair-bearers, and Chung-mo was the bridegroom on horseback in a long gown and vest. We were escorted by a number of Elders-and-Brothers comrades blowing horns and beating gongs, and the whole bunch of us passed right in through the Chengyang Gate. As we entered the city, none of us realized that rumors were already flying everywhere inside the city, that alarms had been raised and unrest and panic reigned among the people. Some comrades in the Literature Society had let the secret slip out, and the Governor-General had ordered arrests throughout the city. Even now the heads of several of our revolutionary comrades hung before the yamen gates. Immediately we received orders from No. 10 Rouge Alley: Unexpected Developments—Coup Moved Up—Midnight To-

---

* Literally, Alliance Society, abbreviated from the Chinese Revolutionary Alliance Society, a precursor of the Kuomintang, organized in 1905 in Japan under the leadership of Sun Yat-sen. This loose-knit federation of anti-Manchu, pro-Republican elements was responsible for many uprisings in the Chinese Empire, and its activities culminated in the successful Wuchang Uprising of 1911 and the establishment of the Republic of China.

night. Signal: Cannon-Fire. Our mission was to blow up the Governor-
General's yamen and rescue those comrades in the prison. We hid in
the house where Yang Yun-hsiu's elder sister lived and awaited our
chance to act. That very night, as if Heaven had willed it, the entire
city was bathed in moonlight. A tragic and solemn sight! We all
changed into battle garb; even Yang Yun-hsiu put on men's clothes.
One and all we downed cups of fiery liquor, while we spoke loftily of
the nation's rise and fall; we couldn't help but feel a surge of exalta-
tion. Your teacher was the most aroused of all. I still remember he
drank till his face was bloodred, and then banged his sabre on the
table and pulled Chung-mo and me outside into the courtyard. There
we swore an oath in blood in the manner of Liu, Kuan, and Chang of
Peach Garden fame.* We vowed to Heaven: 'If we don't kill off the
Manchu oppressors, we shall not return alive!' We promised each
other that from then on we would share and share alike, come prosperity or adversity. At that moment we were indeed ready to die, and
in our pledge the three of us carefully recorded our names and our
respective dates of birth. I was the eldest; Chung-mo was second;
your teacher was the youngest, our Kid Brother. He was barely twenty
then—"

"Oh?" the Commissioner exclaimed. "I haven't been told this
before. To think that Your Excellency, His Excellency Chung, and my
mentor came to know each other in such historic circumstances!"

"Naturally you could not have known." The old general stroked
his beard again and smiled. "This particular relationship was truly a
secret kept among the three of us. That night we waited until it was
barely ten o'clock; then there was a burst of gunfire from the area
around the Engineering Corps in the eastern part of the city. As some
of us still hesitated, your teacher leaped to his feet and cried out,
'They've started the fighting out there! Are we still waiting here to
die?' He grabbed a few hand grenades, seized his sabre and charged
off, and we all stormed out after him. Outside, the crowds were seeth-
ing; flames shot sky-high inside Wuchang City. We fought all night;

* Liu Pei, Kuan Yü, and Chang Fei, heroes of the popular historical novel *Romance of the Three Kingdoms*, who as sworn brothers established the kingdom
of Shu (centered in present-day Szechwan Province) and pledged their lives to
the cause of reunifying the Chinese empire and perpetuating the Han Dynasty.
They were aided in this unsuccessful struggle by the loyal prime minister Chu
ke Liang. (See the title note in this story.)

by dawn the battle was won. The white banners of our revolutionary forces waved everywhere throughout the city. A troop of us marched to the Ch'u Wang Terrace on Snake Mountain to regroup. As we passed the Yellow Crane Tower, your teacher couldn't contain his excitement any longer. In a flash he climbed the tower, tore off his bloodstained white jacket, raised it with a bamboo pole, and stuck it under the eaves. Then he stood on the balustrade, brandishing his sabre, and shouted to us, 'Your Revolutionary Hero Wang Meng-yang is here!' To this day I can still see him. What ebullience! What exuberance!" General P'u laughed and paused for a sip of Iron Kuanyin.

"If Your Excellency hadn't evoked them today, these memories of my mentor's heroic deeds would have remained buried," said Commissioner Lei. "This is properly the stuff of biography."

"By all means." His Excellency P'u nodded his approval. "I'm the only one alive who can testify beyond question to all those heroic acts of your teacher's youth. During the Uprising things happened fast; it started out with just a few hot-blooded youngsters raising a ruckus, and before you knew it there was a Revolution—exactly because of those youngsters' dare-devilry our Republic was born. The next day we issued a circular telegram throughout the country announcing the First Year of the Republic: the 4,609th Year of the Yellow Emperor . . ." The general mused for a while and resumed, "From that time on, through scores of years, the three of us together fought any number of campaigns, east and west, and we were always able to hold fast to our oath 'to share prosperity and adversity.' Later when your teacher became the Commander-in-Chief his rank was higher than either of ours, yet among ourselves Chung-mo and I still called him 'the Kid,' just as we always had." General P'u turned to Commissioner Lei and chuckled. So did the Commissioner. "He, too, from first to last, treated us like his elder brothers. That is why Chung-mo and I were the only ones who could hold him back a little from time to time. I have been a cautious man all my life, and I haven't gotten my fingers burned very often. As to Chung-mo, he was a kindhearted fellow; he didn't like to fight with people. But, to be fair, when it came to talent and a flair for military strategy, I must rank your teacher tops among us all—" General P'u raised his venerable eyebrows and turned his thumb up. "Early on, a long time ago, I had told Chung-mo, just between the two of us, 'Second Brother, in the future I suspect the Kid's the one who's going to make the world sit up and take notice.' Later my prophecy did come true. Your teacher's accomplishments indeed surpassed our own."

"My mentor's genius in military affairs truly compelled admiration," Commissioner Lei declared. "What a pity he was not given the opportunity to exercise it fully."

"Well, you can't really say that." His Excellency P'u stopped Commissioner Lei with a wave of his hand. "In fact, he had a magnificent career. The thing is, your teacher made his mark early—as a result, he was sometimes guilty of overweening pride, which simply wasn't the way to get along. For this you can't lay the blame on Heaven or man; it was his own character that was responsible. Mengyang . . ." The old soldier heaved a heavy sigh. "I'd say he was just a bit too hot-headed and uncompromising." General P'u and the Commissioner sat face to face, each sunk in reflection. After some time the Commissioner sighed gently.

"Still . . . I must say it was quite an occasion today. Amazing how everybody came—even His Excellency Wang Ch'in-chih, His Excellency Li Hsien, and His Excellency Chao Mien. They all came in person to pay their respects."

"Really?" General P'u appeared surprised. "They came, too? I wonder why I didn't see them."

"They came quite early and left after only a short while."

"Oh . . ." the General murmured wistfully, "It's been a good many years since I saw them last. I did notice the memorial scrolls which they presented hanging in the funeral hall. Wang Ch'in-chih's scroll even worked in the couplet

> That thou shouldst have died ere victory
> did crown thine expedition!
> Still do the homeland fathers and elders
> all long for the sight of thy banners.

There had been discord between him and your teacher, and yet this shows he still held your teacher in high esteem."

"That's very true, Your Excellency," the Commissioner hastened to reply.

"I suppose today's memorial service turned out fairly well," General P'u continued. "Although you may say all this is posthumous glory of a kind, such ceremonies should not depart too far from the proprieties. From what I observed, that son of Meng-yang's didn't seem to know the proper way to behave. It must be that after living abroad for so long he doesn't understand our Chinese manners and customs any more."

"Brother Chia-chi has just come back from America. It's understandable that he's a bit unfamiliar with the way we do things here," the Commissioner tried to explain.

"The Memorial Service Committee tried to discuss matters with him; he vetoed every suggestion we made. I was the head of the Committee, and it made things very difficult for me. Since he's a member of the family of the deceased, and the chief mourner as well, it was not for me to make all the decisions. Later he just went too far, it seemed to me, and I had to call him to one side and say to him: 'According to the ancient precepts, grief supersedes all formalities, it is true, but your father was no ordinary man; he had done great deeds for the country. The day of the memorial service the ceremony will be that of a state funeral. Thousands of people from all over will come to pay their last tributes to your father. It isn't just a matter of avoiding public criticism, but if we were remiss in any way during the rites, it would be disrespect to your dead father.' That was as far as I could go in offering advice. From what I observed, he even displayed some signs of annoyance."

"Indeed, Brother Chia-chi is somewhat gauche in such matters," Commissioner Lei agreed.

"There was another thing I discussed openly with him. Meng-yang's first wife passed away early; while Meng-yang lay ill in hospital these past two years it was his second wife who was constantly by his side, attended to his medicines, helped him in and out of bed, and so on. When the family published the obituary they actually left out her name. She came to me and wept and asked me to see that justice was done. Given the close relationship between your teacher and me, I had to do something. But this was their family affair, after all; no matter how you look at it I'm still an outsider. I was in no position to interfere. In the end all I could do was mention the matter tactfully to Meng-yang's son: 'For the sake of your late father, do see that she is taken care of in the days to come.' " General P'u gave a long sigh and said sorrowfully, "To see the way the younger generation behaves nowadays, sometimes it chills one's heart."

"I know. I know," nodded Commissioner Lei in sad agreement. The cup of Iron Kuanyin the old general held in his hands had long since grown cold; he appeared pensive again. Commissioner Lei perceived signs of fatigue on His Excellency's face.

"Your Excellency must be tired. I should be . . ." he suggested.

His Excellency looked up, glanced at the Commissioner, and gazed out the window.

"It's getting rather late already. Look, you might as well stay and join me in a game of *go*. You can leave after dinner."

Without waiting for Commissioner Lei to accept, General P'u went straight to the *go* table and set up the game. The Commissioner came over and sat down. No sooner was His Excellency seated than he looked over at the incense tripod on the altar table; the incense had long since burned out. He stood up again, went to the altar, removed the burnt-out sticks, lit a sheaf of Dragon Saliva incense sticks, and stuck them into the tripod. Soon the heavy scent of Dragon Saliva pervaded the entire room. General P'u and the Commissioner began the match. After two or three moves, the study door suddenly opened and in came a fine-featured boy of eight or nine in a neat khaki school uniform, a steaming bowl of herbal broth in his hands.

"Grandfather, please take your medicine." Carefully he laid the bowl of herbal broth on the tea table. General P'u looked around at the boy, and immediately his face broke into a smile, but he assumed a stern voice.

"Shouldn't you say hello to Uncle Lei at once?"

"Uncle Lei." The boy quickly stood to attention and made a deep bow to the Commissioner.

"This must be Your Excellency's grandson." Smiling, the Commissioner returned the salute.

"My little grandson Hsiao-hsien." The old man pointed to the boy.

"What a smart-looking young fellow!" the Commissioner complimented the boy.

"He's in the third grade at the Elementary School attached to the Women's Normal College," explained His Excellency by way of introduction. "He was born in America—both my son and his wife are there teaching. A few years ago his grandmother had him brought back here. Ever since she passed away, he's stayed with me. When he first came back he couldn't speak a word of Chinese; he'd practically turned into a little foreigner! Now, after he's been studying with me for a while, he's even managed to memorize a few T'ang poems."

"Oh . . . ?" The Commissioner was impressed.

"Can you recite a poem for Uncle Lei?" General P'u stroked his silvery beard.

"Which one should I recite, Grandfather?"

"How many can you still remember?" the General retorted. "Do you still remember 'The Song of Liang-chou' I taught you last week?"

Without the slightest hesitation the boy recited "The Song of Liang-chou" in accents loud and clear, nodding his head in time.

> A fine grape wine,
>   a night-shining cup of jade—
> As I'm about to drink,
>   on horseback the *p'i-p'a*
>   sounds an urgent recall.
> If I lie drunk on the battlefield,
>   you mustn't laugh.
> Since ancient times, pray,
>   how many soldiers
>   have returned alive?

"Splendid! Splendid!" Commissioner Lei cheered. "Such a keen mind at such a tender age. Your Excellency," he turned to General P'u, "If you'll forgive my presumption, in the future this little fellow may well be—as they say—'A fledgling phoenix who sings more sweetly than the parent bird!'"

"You mustn't overpraise him." His Excellency couldn't help a smile of satisfaction. "Run along, now," he told the boy.

After his grandson had left the room, General P'u lifted the bowl of hot herbal broth and took a mouthful or two.

"Has Your Excellency been indisposed lately?" Commissioner Lei interrupted his move to inquire with concern.

"It's nothing, really," replied the General. "Do you recall when your teacher and I fought during the Battle of Lungt'an on the Northern Expedition? I myself got a shrapnel wound."

"Of course, of course, I remember."

"I was still young then, and what did I care? I guess it's caught up with me now that I'm getting on in years; on chilly days my lower back aches and turns stiff. I've had electrotherapy a few times and it didn't do a bit of good, so I went to Dr. Hsi Fu-yi and got a packet of Chinese herbal medicine; it seems to be working all right." General P'u finished the herbal broth and resumed the game. After some twenty moves, one of the Commissioner's corners was besieged; he was completely cut off. He toyed with the *go* pebbles in the bowl and pondered for ten minutes or so before he could lay down another piece.

"Your Excellency—" He looked up and found the old man dozing off, his head bowed. He rose in a hurry, went over and called softly in the General's ear. "Your Excellency—"

"Eh?" General P'u opened his drowsy eyes and murmured, "Is it my move now?"

"Your Excellency must take a rest. I've imposed on you all afternoon. I think I'd better take my leave now. Besides, there are still a lot of things I have to see to over at my mentor's."

General P'u hesitated for a while before he finally stood up.

"Well, all right, why don't you keep today's latest position in mind. The next time you come, we'll finish what's left of the game."

The old general walked his guest as far as the courtyard. The Commissioner tried over and over to stop him, but His Excellency paid no attention and walked straight to the main gate. As he reached the gate he stopped, as if he had thought of something.

"The twenty-fifth of next month is your teacher's 'Seventh Seventh.' "

"Yes, Your Excellency."

"Does your teacher's family plan to observe it at home or in a temple?"

Commissioner Lei looked disconcerted at this question.

"I've discussed the matter with Brother Chia-chi," he said at last. "He told me they've all become converted to Christianity and wouldn't want to perform Buddhist rites."

"Oh . . ." His Excellency nodded his head and thought about

this. "Well, then let's do it this way. We'll invite people in my name on that day to the Temple of Kindly Guidance and have the monks chant the sutras and perform the necessary rites for Meng-yang's departed soul. Next month also happens to be the first anniversary of Chung-mo's death, so we might as well perform the rites for both of them. I think Chung-mo's widow, Yang Yun-hsiu, would want to take part, too."

So saying, General P'u leaned further toward the Commissioner and spoke in his ear. "Your teacher fought in battles his whole life and accumulated a heavy weight of karma for taking lives. On his deathbed he told me in confidence that his conscience often troubled him. I made a vow on his behalf that I would copy a volume of the Diamond Sutra for him, and I've just finished it. On the day of the Seventh Seven, when they perform the Grand Penitential Mass, will be the best time to take it to fulfill his vow."

Lai the aide had the car ready to take the guest home. He opened the car door and stood waiting. As Commissioner Lei stopped to get in, General P'u called him back.

"There was one other thing. Just before he died, your teacher expressed a last wish: In the future when we fight our way back to the homeland, no matter what, his body must be returned to his birthplace. Please tell his heirs that they absolutely must have one of his full-dress uniforms put aside for this purpose and that his medals must be preserved as well. When the time comes to move his body, it is important that his full military regalia be displayed."

"Yes, Your Excellency, certainly, I shall see to it."

"Hmm. . . ." The old man thought some more before concluding, "When your teacher was alive, he always held you in the highest regard. For his remaining affairs, please do your best to take care of them. If the heirs do anything inconsiderate, try to bear with them and don't take it to heart."

"Your Excellency may rest completely assured." Commissioner Lei bowed deeply to General P'u and got into the car.

"Lai *Fukuan*," ordered General P'u, after watching Commissioner Lei drive off, "Time to have dinner served."

"Yessir, General." Lai *Fukuan* snapped to attention as far as his bowed back would permit. He shuffled over to the gate and shut it.

By the time General P'u returned to the courtyard, a wintry evening breeze had come up; the purple bamboos rustled and shivered. In the western sky a dab of the setting sunlight froze, bloodred. The old soldier strolled to a corner of the courtyard and paused. There stood a three-tiered iron flower stand, on which were arranged nine pots of orchids, all superior Pure Hearts. All nine flowerpots were square; they were white porcelain patterned with dragons of Mohammedan blue and were filled with pieces of cold-fir bark. The orchids had already finished blooming; the three or four withered blossoms that still hung on the dried, brown stalks gave out a faint wisp of cold fragrance. Only their sword-blade leaves still stood green and shining. General P'u stood in contemplation before the sparse orchids for a long time, his hands clasped behind his back, his full silvery beard unfurling in the wind. Reminiscences of long-forgotten episodes from the Year of Hsin Hai half a century ago came floating back to him again, until his grandson Hsiao-hsien came and tugged at his sleeve. With his hand on the boy's shoulder, the two of them, grandfather and grandson, went in to dinner together.

Love's Lone Flower

Peach Blossom and I always used to go home together every night after we knocked off work at the Mayflower. Sometimes on summer nights we'd hail a pedicab and take a slow ride back to our little apartment on Kinhwa Street. It's different now. Now I often go back by myself first, fix a midnight snack, and wait up for Peach Blossom. Sometimes I wait till dawn.

I spent my life's savings to buy this little Kinhwa Street apartment. Back in the Shanghai days, when I was with the Myriad Springs Pavilion, I managed to save a few dollars. I'd been in this line of work much longer than Baby Five and the rest of them—in fact, I was the one who took care of Baby Five, showed her the ropes and taught her to fend for herself. But by the time I fled to Taiwan I had lost 'most everything except for a pair of emerald jade bracelets I'd been wearing all the time. That pair of bracelets was left to me by Baby Five; no matter what hardships and dangers I went through, I could never bear to part with them.

I didn't really want to go with the Mayflower. When I first got to Taiwan, I used to hang out with racketeers like Yu the Hunk and run hot goods for the black market. We didn't figure on being raided, not just once but many times on the Keelung dockside—the upshot was that not only did the Hunk lose his own stash, but my jewelry went, too. Finally the Hunk had the nerve to try to rip those bracelets off my arms! I grabbed a pair of long scissors, pointed them at him and shouted, "Just you try and lay a finger on these bracelets!" He spat right in my face and yelled, "You cheap whore!" I've been in this business all my life but that's one word I can't stand, especially out of a man's mouth. It stinks.

It's not an easy life in one of these Taipei winehouses, let me

tell you. The boss at the Mayflower was impressed with me. I had
plenty of experience, I knew how to handle people, and I knew a little
Peking opera, too. So he'd send me specially to take care of honorable
gents from the mainland and sing a few arias to keep them happy.
Occasionally I'd run into some of my old Shanghai clients and they'd
still call me by my old professional name, "Fragrant Cloud Number
Six." Once I happened to meet Ninth Master Lu, name of Lu Ken-
jung. The minute he saw me, he stamped his foot as if to say what a
pity.

"Number Six, how the devil did you land back in a hole like
this?"

I smiled at him. "Well, Ninth Master, I guess that's just my
fate!"

You really should give me credit, a mainlander like me, thrown
in with those little Taiwanese chicks at the Mayflower and still able
to lay away some dough over the years. Quite an accomplishment, I'd
say. After a while I sweet-talked the boss into making me one of the
managers who look after the girls. Flora Hu and I are the only women
managers at the Mayflower; the rest of them are just a bunch of
hoods. It doesn't bother me really. I've been clawing my way up
among men all my life and doing just fine, thank you. The guests have
given me the title "Commander-in-Chief," they say I've got all the
top brass under my command—Princess Beauty, Heart o' Plum, and
whatnot—just like I was riding herd on the Army, the Navy, and the
Air Force. As a manager all I get is my salary—and I couldn't bear to
squeeze too much of that flesh-peddling money from those little
chicks—so I got to be a lot harder up than before. In the end I had to
call in all the money I'd loaned out. I counted it over and over and
tried figuring it every way I could, but I still had to sell those two
emerald jade bracelets to raise enough money to buy the little apartment on Kinhwa Street. I did it all for Peach Blossom's sake.

Peach Blossom used to be one of Mousie's girls. She was new
at the Mayflower; I'd run into her several times before, all right, but
I'd never paid much attention to her. To tell the truth, when those
Mayflower girls are all dolled up with powder and rouge you can't tell
one from another. Then, one winter night, over a year ago, I went up
to Room 313 on the third floor on my rounds. When I pushed the door
open I saw Peach Blossom standing there, singing a Taiwanese ballad.

Half the table was Japanese wolves; they were really whooping it up with Princess Beauty and Heart o' Plum and the other hot numbers, some grabbing them around the waist and some feeling up their boobs. The whole room stank of cigarette smoke, wine, and men; no one was really listening to Peach Blossom sing. She was over in the corner; she had on a black satin cheongsam with a small white cape and was wearing her long hair down—it brushed over her shoulders— her waist was pulled in so tight you could span it with one hand. Grouped behind her were three musicians, Third-Son Lin in the lead. Blinking his ulcerated, nearly blind eyes, he accompanied Peach Blossom on his old beat-up accordion with its plaintive, wheezing tone. She was singing something called "Love's Lone Flower." Her head to one side, her face tilted upward, eyes closed, eyebrows knit together, her long hair falling over one shoulder, she sang in a thin, quavering voice, not really knowing for whom she sang:

> The moon is sinking in the west,
>   the moon is sinking.
> With all my heart of you I'm thinking—
>   and you not knowing!
> A tender bush; who cares to tend it?
> From my fallen leaves
>   the pains of love are growing . . .

This ballad was by Third-Son Lin himself. During the time of the Japanese rule he was a fairly famous musician, and he wrote his own songs. They say he fell in love with a winehouse girl by the name of White Jade, who worked at the Fairyland. She was an epileptic, and in one of her seizures she fell into the Tamsui River and drowned. It was in memory of her that he wrote "Love's Lone Flower." Embracing that accordion of his with its greasy yellow keys and blinking those ulcerous eyes, he kept playing that same song day in and day out. I've heard it sung by God knows how many girls in the Mayflower, but not one of them sang with as much bitter sorrow as Peach Blossom, note by note as if she was pleading all the wrongs she'd suffered. I don't know why, but for just a moment the way she looked reminded me of Baby Five. Peach Blossom and Baby Five didn't really look that much like each other; Baby Five had finer features, yet when Baby Five sang opera she had that same sorrowful look. In those days, when we were called out to banquet performances, we used to like to sing something from the opera "Lovers Reincarnate" together; I was the heroine, the beauteous Lady Meng, and Baby Five played the maid Su. Baby Five also had this way of knitting her brows; there was one passage in the tragic *Erh-huang* mode where she seemed to pour out her grievances straight from the heart. Both girls had pinched, triangular faces, pointed chins, high cheek-bones, sunken eyes; and both of them had that look of a castaway drifting to a no-good end.

The instant Peach Blossom finished singing, a bald, stubby Japanese snared her by the waist and sat her down on his lap. He forced a cup of wine down her throat first thing; when she finished he poured her another and pushed her on to the next guest for a drinking bout. Peach Blossom didn't put up any fight. She lifted her cup and gulped the wine down in one long breath. Then she wiped away the drops in the corner of her mouth with the back of her hand, looked at the guest, and gave him a smile. I saw that shadow of a smile float across her small, pale, triangular face—sadder than weeping it was. I'd never seen a winehouse girl allow herself to be pushed around so easily. Now my girls Princess Beauty and Heart o' Plum, for instance, it would take a helluva lot of doing before a man could force anything down *their* throats. But Peach Blossom just let those Japanese push her around and pour wine down her throat. She didn't resist, she didn't even protest; after each cup she'd smack her lips and smile helplessly. When her round drew to a close she'd already downed seven or eight cups of Shaohsing, and her face had turned greenish. Before she left, she stood up and excused herself, nodding to the guests who'd ganged up on her. That sad, stiff smile floated across her face again.

That evening, after I'd taken care of business and was ready to leave, I went to the bathroom on the third floor. When I opened the door I was stunned. There on the floor, flat on her back, was Peach Blossom, dead drunk, her face ashen, her black satin cheongsam spattered all over with vomit. The faucet hadn't been turned off and water was spilling over onto the floor; Peach Blossom's hair was drenched, dripping wet. I rushed over to prop her up, took my coat off, and wrapped it around her. That night I took Peach Blossom back to my apartment; at the time I was still living by myself on Ningpo West Street.

I washed Peach Blossom up, changed her clothes, and put her to bed in my bed; she was out the whole time, still shivering as though she had a chill. I got out a heavy quilt, covered her up, and tucked the quilt in under her chin. Suddenly I realized how many years it was since I'd done that. Back when Baby Five and I slept together in the same room, I often used to get up in the middle of the night and put her covers back on. She could only handle two cups of wine; when she was called out to drink with gents, she'd come home totally pie-eyed. In her sleep, whenever the aftereffects of the wine got to her and made her hot and restless, she'd kick off all her covers. I'd always get a blanket out and wrap her up real snug. Sometimes she got beat up and hurt by that old reptile of a pimp, Hua the Third, and she couldn't sleep well and I had to get up several times during the night. Whenever I tried to give her some advice, she'd thrust her arm out from under the covers up at my face and say with a scornful laugh:

"This is my lot, Sister."

Stamped on her snow-white arm was a row of coin-size blisters from marks Hua the Third had branded on her with his opium pipe. When I saw she was in severe pain, I would lie beside her and give her a massage and keep her company until daybreak. I felt Peach Blossom's forehead; it was icy from cold sweat. She'd drunk herself sick for sure. She tossed and turned the whole night.

The next day, Peach Blossom woke at dawn. Her face looked ghastly pale, and her eyes were opened wide and glassy; she said she had a splitting headache. I got up to boil a bowl of ginger soup with brown sugar to feed her in bed. She sat up and I wrapped a quilted jacket around her shoulders. She only drank half of the soup and said she didn't want any more. Head lowered, she rubbed her temples vigorously, her long hair falling forward, hiding her face. After a while, without looking up she suddenly said, "I saw my mother in a dream again." Her voice sounded very strange, faraway, hollow, each word fading off.

"Where is she now?" I sat down next to her.

"I don't know." She looked up, shaking her long hair. "Maybe she's still in our Su-ao countryside—she's a madwoman."

"Ohh—" I stretched out my hand to wipe away the beads of cold sweat breaking out on her forehead. I noticed Peach Blossom's eyes also looked very strange; they were dark and deep; even when she stared blankly her eyes were still full of fear, the pupils like two black tadpoles darting about.

"My father put an iron chain around her neck and locked her in the pigsty. When I was little I didn't know she was my mamma. My father never told me. And he wouldn't let me go near her. When I went to feed the pigs, I often saw the neighbors' kids pick up rocks and throw them at her; when she got hit she'd raise her hands like claws and gnash her teeth and howl. The kids laughed, and I laughed with them—" Peach Blossom laughed nervously, her small pale, triangular face slightly distorted. "One day, look—"

She pulled her collar open and pointed down at her throat; there lay a red scar, as thick as your finger, like a shiny earthworm.

"One day my aunt came. She took me to the pigsty and told me through her sobs, 'That's her, that's your mother!' That evening I got together a bowl of food on the quiet, crawled into the pigsty, and handed it to my ma. She took ahold of it, stared at me for a while, and grinned. I moved up and stroked her face with my hand, but the minute I touched her she let out a bloodcurdling wail. Dashing the bowl to the ground, she reached out her claws and in one swoop grabbed me, and before I could make a sound her teeth were already sinking into my throat—"

Peach Blossom laughed nervously again, her two tadpole pupils jumping. I hugged her and caressed that scar on her throat; all of a sudden I felt that red earthwormlike scar turn slippery, as if it were beginning to squirm.

Once Baby Five and I made a wish: in days to come, when we saved up enough money, we'd buy a house, live together, and make it our home. We even said we were going to redeem a little virgin sing-song girl and bring her up as our own. Baby Five had been kidnapped from the Yangchow countryside by a white slaver. When she was sold to the Myriad Springs Pavilion, she was only fourteen; she was dressed in a flower-print cotton jacket and pants wrapped tight at the ankles; her hair was cut in a pageboy, fastened with a copper butterfly pin.

"Where's your mother, Baby Five?" I'd asked her.

"I haven't got a mother." She smiled.

"Stupid-head," I scolded her. "You haven't got a mother? Who gave birth to you?"

"Oh, I don't remember." She waved her short hair around and tittered. I caught her to my bosom, held her cheeks, and gave her a couple of kisses. From then on I grew to feel a maternal pity and tenderness for her.

"Peach Blossom, this *is* our home now."

That's what I told her, my arm around her shoulders, when we moved into our little apartment on Kinhwa Street. Baby Five died early, so that wish of ours never came true. I spent half my life knocking around until I met Peach Blossom; only then did the idea of building a home come back to me. I just let things slide, never got used to doing the laundry and cooking and all that housekeeping business, but I thought Peach Blossom was too frail for the heavy work, so I wouldn't let her do too much around the house. Every day she slept way into the afternoon, yet I couldn't bear to wake her up. Especially when she came back from turning a trick, she looked so worn-out my heart went out to her. Don't I know it! When men get into bed there isn't one dirty trick they won't pull. One old motherfucker damn near strangled me with his hands around my neck, and he got sore, that bastard! kept asking me, "Why aren't you panting? Why aren't you panting?" The night of Baby Five's initiation, the dude who copped her cherry was an army man, strong as an ox. The morning after, Baby Five crawled into my bed, rolled against my bosom, and cried till her eyes were bloodshot; her tiny little breasts were black and blue, covered all over with toothmarks.

"Who was the one who deflowered you, Peach Blossom?" Once when Peach Blossom got up very late after a call, I asked her while I was combing her hair.

"My father."

I stood behind her and just kept on combing her hair, without a sound.

"Whenever my father got drunk, he'd come straight into my room . . ." She talked with a cigarette in her mouth, an exhausted look on her face. "I was just fifteen then. The first night, I was scared and I bit him. He grabbed me and began knocking my head so hard against the headboard my head swam and I blacked out. From then on, every time he'd bring me back some rouge and lipstick from I-lan and coax me into doing it with him—" Peach Blossom laughed drily, the cigarette in her mouth bobbing up and down.

"When I got knocked up, my father would drag me to the door every day, point his finger right in my face in front of all the neighbors and cuss me out. 'You slut! Been sleeping around, huh!' Then I felt my swollen belly and I got frightened and started to cry. My father got hold of a handful of bitter herbs and crammed it down my throat. That night I dropped a clot of blood—" As she said it, she giggled nervously again; her face was so twisted up you couldn't tell her eyes from her eyebrows. Gently I caressed her bony back; I felt as though I was stroking a sick kitten that someone had thrown out on a pile of garbage and left to die.

When Peach Blossom got through dressing, we'd leave for work at the Mayflower. On the street I watched her long hair blow about in the evening wind, her tiny waist swaying this way and that as if it would snap at any moment. At the mouth of the street we ran up against a huge setting sun that looked as if it had just rolled out of a dyeing-vat, making Peach Blossom's pale triangular face look like it was splashed with blood. From the cast of her face, I had a secret feeling a dark fate awaited her. How many unatoned-for sins from former lives, I wondered, weighed upon this swaying, fragile body?

It's only recently that Peach Blossom's begun staying out all night. One hot, humid night in June I was lying in bed; I hadn't slept a wink all night waiting for her; I watched it grow light little by little outside the window, my back soaking wet. Peach Blossom didn't come home till seven or eight in the morning, reeling from side to side like she was still drunk, her face white with fatigue; her mascara had run and spread into two big black circles—it made her eyes and eyebrows look like they were rotting. She walked into the room and kicked off her high heels; without a word she struggled out of her cheongsam, fell back onto the bed with her eyes closed, and lay there, totally inert. I sat down next to her and took off her bra; her nipples had been bitten through and were swollen up like two overripe oxblood plums; something sticky was oozing from them. On her neck there was a ring of blue toothmarks that made her earthwormlike red scar stand out even more. I lifted her arm. To my horror I saw a row of four or five black needlemarks in the vein.

"Peach Blossom!" I called to her.

"Yama K'o Lao-hsiung—" Peach Blossom muttered, her eyes closed. She turned her head away and passed out.

As I kept watch by her side, everything that had happened at the Mayflower the night before last flashed across my mind. That night when K'o Lao-hsiung, nicknamed Yama, the King of Hell, came to the Mayflower I had sent Princess Beauty and Heart o' Plum over; he didn't want either of them; he told them to "fuck off"; for some reason he had his eye on Peach Blossom. Three years ago he was a regular at the Mayflower, a smuggler, a gambler, and a dope addict into the bargain; there was nothing he wouldn't do. A known underworld chief all right. He was a big spender in those days, and had gone through quite a number of winehouse girls. There was one called Graceful Phoenix who had shacked up with him less than a month and then suddenly she was dead. There was a lot of talk around the Mayflower that he was the cause of her death, so he stayed out of sight for a couple of years. Now here he was, twice as nasty and more ferocious than ever. By the time Peach Blossom was there on her rounds, he was already eighty percent loaded, in with a gang of cardsharps who were talking all kinds of filth. Yama took off his shirt, baring his massive dark red arms, showing the two big clumps of dark hair in his armpits; his belt was loosened, the zipper on his fly halfway down. He was a skinhead; the back of his enormous head was shaved and shiny, but a tuft of hair stiff as pig bristles stood up on his crown. He had a big, mean jaw that stuck out like a carp's gills and a pair of pig eyes, bloodshot, with swollen lids; between his bulging thick black lips flashed a mouthful of gold teeth. His head was sweaty, his body was sweaty; even before I got near him I caught a whiff of his odor, like fish.

As Peach Blossom approached, he rolled his pig eyes and looked her over from head to toe. Without warning he stretched out a beefy red arm, seized her by the hand, and pulled her toward him. He grinned, his gold teeth flashing. Peach Blossom lost her balance and fell right into his lap. His bare arm clutching her tiny waist, he tried to pour a cup of wine down her throat; before she'd finished it, he snatched the cup out of her hand; smacking his lips, he drained the rest. He thrust his nose out and sniffed around Peach Blossom's neck, one hand pawing her breasts; then abruptly he pulled Peach Blossom's arm up, stuck out his tongue, and gave her armpit a quick lick. Peach Blossom couldn't help but let out a piercing laugh, her feet kicking violently.

Yama wouldn't relax his grip; he caught her hand and pulled it down below his belly.

"Afraid?" he leered.

The gang around the table cackled. Peach Blossom struggled wildly; in Yama's arm her slender waist twisted as if it had been broken in two. I could see those tadpole eyes of hers in her pale face all but leaping out in panic.

I don't understand what it is in Peach Blossom's fate that's brought about such retribution, that's attracted such demons. Ever since she got mixed up with Yama, it's as if her soul was snatched away. Whenever he came to the Mayflower to pick her up she'd go along meekly; every time she came back she was all bruises, her arms full of needlemarks. I did everything I could to stop her; I told her just how dangerous these underworld thugs are. Peach Blossom just looked at me vacantly, as if she were under a spell.

"Don't you understand? Peach Blossom!" Sometimes I'd get so worked up, I'd grab her by the shoulders and shake her, hard. Then she would shake her head and smile sadly.

"I can't help it, Commander—"

Without a stitch on except her bra, she'd go sit on the window-sill; she hunched over, one leg drawn up, picked up a bottle of Cutex, and began painting her toenails while she plaintively hummed snatches of "Yearning for You," "Three Forlorn Sighs," those weepy ballads, her voice hollow, like a widow wailing. Every few lines she'd blow her nose with a wad of Kleenex. She's become a heroin addict.

Yama took Peach Blossom to a hotel once and she got picked up by the police as a hooker. I had to spend quite a bit of money before I could bail her out. From then on I wanted Peach Blossom to bring Yama home; at least he wouldn't dare go too far with her at my place. I'm always afraid one day Peach Blossom will lose her life to that King of Hell. A couple of times I've taken her horoscope to be read; they've all said she's got an extraordinarily violent destiny.

Every time they come home I excuse myself and go into the kitchen; I can't stand the sight of those gold teeth. They remind me me of that pimp Hua the Third. When he beat Baby Five up, he'd bare all his gold teeth and curse; I'll beat you to death, you stinking whore! While I'm in the kitchen stewing the lovage-tonic chicken for Peach Blossom's late-night snack I keep my ears open all the time; I hear Yama's lewd laugh, his bark, Peach Blossom's agonized whimpering like a sick kitten; not until Yama leaves do I draw Peach Blossom's bath and go into the room to see her. One time I went in to find her sitting mother-naked on the bed, holding a wad of crisp hundred-dollar bills, counting this way and that, over and over, like a little child playing with bubble-gum cards. I went up close and saw a dark-red spot of blood, as big as a fingernail, on her small face by the corner of her mouth.

On the fifteenth day of the seventh lunar month, the Ghost Festival, it finally happened.

That evening Yama had taken Peach Blossom off to the town of Sanchung for the wild jamboree there. I came home earlier than usual, bought silverfoil ingots and candles, prepared four sacrificial dishes, and took them to the terrace behind the kitchen as offerings to Baby Five. The night was so hot it made you feel dizzy; the whole sky looked as if it had been scorched; even the huge moon had turned red. By the time I'd finished burning the ingots, I was dripping with sweat; my cheeks were feverish. I don't usually think about it, but when I counted I realized it's already been fifteen years since Baby Five died. Whenever I think about her, it's as if everything is right before my eyes: the way she lay on Hua the Third's opium couch, dead, her mouth stuffed with opium scum, her eyes wide open; I can still see it. Over and over Baby Five had sworn: I'll turn into a ghost and hunt him down!

It was almost midnight before Yama came in dragging Peach Blossom along, both of them reeling, Yama's face flushed purple. "Damn your mother's soul!" The minute he walked in he spat and cursed. He literally yanked Peach Blossom off the ground and took her into the other room. As I sat in the kitchen I felt a burning in my heart; I simply couldn't calm down no matter how hard I tried. This time Yama's howls turned savage, and now and again there were sounds of a scuffle. The scene right before Baby Five's suicide suddenly reappeared—Baby Five sits down hard on the floor in Hua the Third's room; Hua grabs her by the hair and keeps twisting her head around as if he's turning a handmill; the copper opium pipe in his hand slashing down at her, sending out a shower a gold sparks. I see her two hands in the air swinging and grasping like mad, and then comes her scream for dear life, SISTER!—I summon up all my strength and smash the window with my fists. The broken glass cuts my hands; blood comes—an ear-piercing shriek made me start up in fright. I snatched up the cleaver and rushed into the other room. As I burst through the door, there was Peach Blossom, stark naked, astride Yama's body. He lay flat on the floor; he was naked, too. She raised a black flatiron in her two hands and hammered it down on Yama's skull. Thump, thump, thump, one blow after another—her long hair flying, her mouth wide open, shrieking like a wildcat gone mad. Yama's skull split open, his grayish brains, like beancurd dregs, splashed all over the floor; that tuft of pig's bristle hair on his crown still intact, stuck there; those huge red arms of his were thrust up in the air, quivering. Peach Blossom's bluish white breasts jounced up and down, spotted with blood. Riding on Yama's dark red corpse, her thin white body all of a sudden grew larger and larger. A wave of dizziness washed over me; the cleaver in my hand dropped to the floor.

Peach Blossom's case never went to court: she had gone completely insane. They've locked her up in an asylum by the sea, in Hsinchu. It was more than two months after I filed my application before they gave me permission to see her. Third-Son Lin came along to keep me company. When Peach Blossom was at the Mayflower, Lin was very fond of her and taught her many Taiwanese ballads. That song he wrote, "Love's Lone Flower," Lin had taught her himself.

We got to see Peach Blossom at the Hsinchu asylum. They had handcuffs on her; they said she bit people. They had her hair cut short, to ear length, curling up around the ends; it made her look like a fifteen- or sixteen-year-old girl. She was wearing a gray cotton robe with a low neck; that earthworm scar on her throat showed. She didn't know us any more; only after I called her name several times did she smile a little. That triangular little face of hers looked even paler and thinner. But, oddly enough, her smile no longer had that touch of sadness; instead she had taken on a dash of mad, childlike innocence. We stayed for a while, but we didn't have much to say. I left her a basket of apples I'd bought; Third-Son Lin had brought her two boxes of Water Pavilion cookies. Two male nurses ushered her inside; I knew they would never let her out again, ever.

When Third-Son Lin and I left the asylum it was already dusk; the sea breeze had blown sand up onto the road; when the setting sun shone on it it looked like a cloud of yellow dust. It was quite a walk to the bus station, and since Third-Son Lin was almost completely blind, he could only walk very slowly. He wore dark glasses and guided himself with a cane. I held onto his arm and the two of us trudged along step by step down the endless dirt road. There was no one in sight; on both sides of the road paddy-fields stretched one after another. The autumn harvest was already over; all that was left standing in the parched fields were clusters of withered stalks. After we'd been walking for some time, I suddenly began to feel lonely.

"Third-Son, sing your song, 'Love's Lone Flower,' for me."

"All right, Commander."

Third-Son Lin cleared his throat. In a falsetto, imitating those winehouse girls, softly he began to hum:

> A tender bush; who cares to tend it?
> From my fallen leaves
>   the pains of love are growing . .

Glory's by Blossom Bridge

Talk about our Glory's by Blossom Bridge—now *there* was a shop with a name to conjure with. Of course I'm talking about the rice-noodle shop Grandpa owned at the head of Blossom Bridge just outside River East Gate back in Kweilin. I tell you, there was nobody in all of Kweilin City who didn't know about Grandpa Huang T'ien-jung* and his noodles. Grandpa made his start in life selling horse-meat and rice-noodles. He sold them at two coppers a dish, and he was always sure to sell a hundred or more orders a day. If you got there a little late you wouldn't get to eat any, because they'd be all sold out. I can still remember Grandma with her red woollen strings threading those little copper coins, string after string, laughing so she could hardly keep her mouth closed. She used to point at me and say, "Sissy, when the time comes, you sure won't have to worry about your dowry." Even when they had parties in the grandest homes in the city, they'd sent out for our noodles. I used to go with Grandma to make the deliveries. When those swell ladies in the fancy homes saw how cute I was and how I always said the right things, they'd stuff handfuls of tips in my pockets and call me "Rice-noodle maid."

But this place called Glory's by Blossom Bridge that I run now hasn't got the old glamour. I never would have dreamed I'd end up opening a restaurant after fleeing to Taipei. My husband wasn't a businessman in the first place; he was in the service back on the main-land. As a matter of fact, I was even a battalion commander's missus for a few years back then. Who would have expected that in the battle of Northern Kiangsu my husband would be missing in action, swept

---

* The name literally means "Heaven-Glory."

This story was translated by William A. Lyell and is published here for the first time.

off to God knows where. In the panic that followed, we military dependents were evacuated to Taiwan. The first few years, I asked around for news of my husband wherever I went. But later on when he appeared time after time in my dreams, and always covered with blood, I knew he must have gone. Here I was, a lone woman stranded in Taipei. Had to find *some* way to make a living. I scraped together a few dollars here and there and finally had enough to open this little restaurant here on Changchun Road. Before I knew it I'd already been a "Boss-Lady" for over ten years. Why, I can tell you the name of every last person who lives along this section of the road, even with my eyes closed.

Mostly, the people who eat at my place are government workers living from hand to mouth—you know, city clerks, elementary-school teachers, district staff workers, what have you—every one of them with their pockets as flat as dried-out bedbugs. They order a little bit of this and a little bit of that—never anything fancy, just plain run-of-the-mill fare. You have to work harder than an old ox turning a millstone to squeeze any extra fat out of a bunch like that. But I have to say it's been these poor old customers of mine who've supported me all these years; without them, my restaurant would have folded a long time ago.

Quite a few of my customers are from Kwangsi, my home province; it's the taste of real down-home cooking keeps them coming back to my place year after year. I've got a group of them on monthly meal tickets, and every last one of that crew is a good old Kwangsi boy. Whenever we got to chewing the fat, seems like it always turns out we're kinfolk, one way or another. These old live-alones, some of them have taken their meals at my place three to five years at a stretch; a few made it for as long as seven or eight years and swallowed their last mouthful right here. Like old man Li. He was big in the lumber business way back when in Liuchou. Everybody called him "Half-the-Town Li"; talk was he owned half the houses in town. His son runs a general store down in Taichung; he just took and dumped the old fellow in Taipei, leaving him all by himself and sending him a check every six months. He ate at my place for eight long years—must have broken two dozen of my rice bowls. Had the palsy, and his hands would shake every time he picked up a bowl. The old bird loved to sing the opera *Retribution by Thunder-*

bolt. The minute he started singing, his nose began to run and two streams of tears flowed down his face. And then one night he ordered himself a whole big spread, cleaned it all up, said it was a grand occasion, his seventieth birthday. Who would have guessed he'd hang himself the next day! We all ran over to see. There he was, the old fellow, hanging from a big old withered tree, his grayed cotton shoes fallen to the ground and his black felt hat rolled away off to one side. As for the food money he still owed me, I tried asking his son for it, but all I got out of that gallows-bird was a big helping of mean back-talk.

We people in the restaurant business can't afford to carry a bunch of free-loaders. After all, we're in it to make a living, not run a poorhouse. It's just my luck that I should have let Crazy Chin eat at my place for over half a year without paying a single cent. He'd been doing fine at his job with the city, and then he had to go and try to get fresh with a female employee and got himself sacked. That's when he went crazy—*woman*-crazy if you ask me. He said he used to be a magistrate in Junghsien back in Kwangsi; even had two concubines! One day he was a little too free with his hands with a lady customer in my restaurant, and I had to show him the door. Well, then he marched along the street, head cocked to one side and eyes all askew, waving his arms wildly in the air, foaming at the mouth and yelling, "Clear the road! Clear the road! His Honor the Magistrate is coming!" Another time he went to the market and felt up a vegetable hawker's neenies. She grabbed her basket pole and hit him one right on the head, cracked it open just like a melon. Last August when we had that big typhoon, this area around Changchun Road was completely flooded. Even the tables and chairs in my place floated away. When the water finally went down, heaps of dead chickens and cats came popping out of the ditch along the street, some so cruddy they were covered with maggots, and with the sun beating down on them the whole street stank to high heaven. When the Board of Health came by to decontaminate the area, they drained the ditch and fished up Crazy Chin. He was covered from head to toe in a coat of mud and stiff as a board. Looked like a big tortoise on its back with all four legs in the air. Nobody knew when he had fallen in.

To tell the truth—and I'm not just sticking up for us folks

from Kweilin—in a place like our Kweilin, with its heavenly scenery, you'd expect the people to be a bit extraordinary, too. You look at people from little holes like Junghsien and Wuning, those bucktoothed clods with their jawbreaking native jabber—if you ask me, they've all got a wild Miao tribesman in their family tree somewhere, how could the likes of them compare with us Kweilin folk? You take any of us, man or woman, some of the natural beauty of our mountains and waters is sure to have rubbed off on us. I used to tell that crew of bachelors that came in here: Don't you sell your fairy godmother short. In my day back in Kweilin I was the belle of River East Gate, I'll have you know! When I worked for Grandpa, the soldiers from Headquarters would gather round the door of our noodle shop like flies after blood, you couldn't shoo them away. That was how my husband and me got together. And it was no wonder. Back home there were green hills everywhere—your eyes'll grow brighter just looking at them—and blue waters—you wash in them and your complexion turns smooth and fair. Those days I never dreamed I'd ever live in a dump like Taipei—a typhoon one year, an earthquake the next. It doesn't matter what kind of beauty you are, this weather is enough to ruin *anybody's* looks.

Of all my customers, Mr. Lu was the only one from my home town, Kweilin. You didn't even have to ask; you knew it the minute you saw him. He was polite, thoughtful, an educated gentleman; taught Chinese at the Changchun Elementary School for years. As I remember, he must have been thirty-five or so when he first started eating at my place. He had such refined manners, always quiet and unassuming. Every time he came in for a meal he'd just sit down, bend over his bowl, and mind his own business. When I'd go over to his table to serve him another helping of rice or something, he'd always get up a bit from his seat and say to me with a gentle smile, "Thank you very much, Boss-Lady."

Mr. Lu was a thin fellow, kind of tall, and a little stooped. Had a pale face and a nose straight as a scallion. He looked old for his age, and a bit run-down. His hair had turned gray early, and whenever he smiled you could spot a whole bunch of crow's feet at the corners of his eyes, but underneath it all you could still see the outlines of what must have been a handsome face at one time. I often bumped into him on the street. He'd always have a long string of school kids hopping and skipping along after him. Every time they crossed the street, he'd stand in the middle of the intersection and spread out his arms to stop the traffic, shouting "Careful, now! Careful!" until the little ones were all safely on the other side. I don't know why, but whenever I saw the patient way he had with his pupils, it always made me think of a gentle rooster I used to have. Why, that rooster would actually mother those chicks. Many a time I saw him spread his wings way out and shelter a whole flock of them underneath.

It was only after I started chewing the fat with him that I discovered his grandfather was none other than Old Mr. Lu, the well-known philanthropist in Kweilin, Lu Hsing-chang. Old Mr. Lu had been a high official in Hunan Province, an Inspector General. He was the one who set up the Foster Virtue Middle School just outside River East Gate. Old Mrs. Lu used to be very fond of Glory's rice-noodles in thick soup, and I had even been to the Lu residence with Grandma to deliver his orders.

'Mr. Lu," I said to him, "I used to go over to your home in the old days. That was some grand mansion you had there!"

He smiled a bit; after a while he answered, "When we retreated from the mainland our own troops put the torch to it. Burned it down to the ground."

"What a shame!" I sighed. I could still remember that garden of theirs, all red and white with peonies.

Now I ask you, can anybody blame me for playing favorites with a gentleman like Mr. Lu? Think what a good family he came from, and fallen on evil times, too, just like all of us here. You could tell he was a man of real culture, the way he went about his own business and never said anything that would cause the least trouble. He wasn't at all like some of those Miao types from Kwangsi who came in here smashing bowls and breaking chopsticks, yelling and hollering, always bitching about something or other like sand in their rice or flies in their food. I couldn't help getting mad at them. In times like these we're lucky to be alive. But instead of making the best of things they had to be picky about the food. I didn't care what they thought or how envious they were, I always put something extra in Mr. Lu's order—beef, I'd give him the shank cut; pork, all lean meat. At least once a week I'd go into the kitchen and make him a piping-hot bowl of noodles with my own hands: braised beef liver and hundred-leaf tripe, sprinkled with parsley and sesame oil, and topped off with a handful of deep-fried peanuts. I'd serve it to him steaming hot. I'll bet you couldn't find another restaurant in all of Taipei where you could get a meal like that—and don't talk to me about your extra-fine Yunnan noodles either! Well, I gave Mr. Lu that dish as a special treat. To tell the truth, the reason I was trying so hard to get in good with him was on account of Hsiu-hua.

Hsiu-hua was my husband's niece. She was married to a soldier, too, a platoon leader. He was lost in the fighting on the mainland, the way my husband was, but in all this time she hadn't given up hope. She waited and waited; got herself a job in a plant here, weaving hemp sacks. She worked so hard her hands were all calluses, but still she was one of our Kweilin girls, neat, fresh-faced, very decent-looking. Well, I finally got hold of her and tried to make her see the light.

"Hsiu-hua, dear child," I said, "you and Ah Wei loved each other very much. I can understand your wanting to wait for him for the rest of your life; that's a beautiful thing. But take me, your aunt, for an example. Don't you think your uncle and I felt the same way about each other? Yes, I waited, too. Waited till I am what you see today. I'm not complaining, but if I'd known I was going to end up like this, I'd have done things a good deal differently ten or more years ago. Let's suppose your Ah Wei *is* alive. You still can't be sure you'll ever see him again. And what if he's already gone? Then, my dear, I'm afraid all your suffering will have been for nothing."

In the end my words must have found some echo in Hsiu-hua's heart; she covered her face and broke down and cried. If it were anyone else, I'd have thought about it a bit before butting in. But Hsiu-hua and Mr. Lu were both from Kweilin. If I could get them together, it would be a wonderful match. As for Mr. Lu, I even found out how he was situated in a financial way. You see, Mrs. Ku, his landlady, was a mah-jong crony of mine. That old Hupei bag had a tongue as sharp as a knife; when *she* started jawing about anyone he'd be lucky to escape with his skin! Still, she always stuck up for Mr. Lu, said she'd never in all her born days seen such a well-behaved man. He didn't eat much, didn't spend much, and, except for playing his *Hu-ch'in* and singing a little opera, he didn't have any vices at all. You could always find half a dozen or so school kids at his place at night. He raised chickens with the money he earned from this extra tutoring.

"And those chickens! Why, they're like Mr. Lu's great-grandpa and great-grandma, that's how well he takes care of them!" says Mrs. Ku, laughing. "You've never seen anything like it—the way he tends those chickens! Such patience!"

Every New Year's Mr. Lu would bring two big basketfuls of his black-and-whites to sell in the market. Every last one of the birds had a bright red comb and shiny white feathers. They must have weighed a good seven or eight pounds each. One time, I bought a couple of them myself; cut a big bowl of chicken fat just off the rumps alone. The way Mrs. Ku had it totaled up, counting all the compound interest on his small loans and betting-pool money over the years, Mr. Lu had at least forty or fifty thousand Taiwan dollars stashed away; he could easily afford to take himself a wife.

And so, one New Year's Eve I invited Mr. Lu and Hsiu-hua to come over. I cooked a whole tableful of Kweilin dishes and heated up a steaming pot of Shaohsing wine. I tried my darndest, with a little tug here and a little push there, to get the two of them together. Hsiu-hua did seem interested and kept smiling coyly, but Mr. Lu, big grown man that he was, started acting shy. When I egged him on to drink a toast with Hsiu-hua, he actually blushed.

I collared him on the street the next day and asked, "Well, Mr. Lu, what do you think of our Hsiu-hua?" He was so flustered he couldn't say a thing. I gave him the eye and smiled.

"Our Hsiu-hua's been saying such nice things about you."

"Please don't kid me—" he stammered.

"Who's kidding?" I cut him short. "You'd better give me a treat right away, and I'll be your go-between. Why, I can taste the wine at your wedding feast already!"

"Boss-Lady." All of a sudden Mr. Lu pulled a long face and said to me seriously, "No more of this joking, please. I was engaged back on the mainland a long time ago."

He gave me the back of his head and walked off. That made me so mad I shook all over and couldn't say a word for hours. Well! Find me another miserable man like that under the sun! So he thought he was going to eat my hot noodle soup, did he! So who else wasn't paying me three hundred and fifty a month for meals? From now on, just like everybody else—it's fat pork for you, Mister Lu! After that, several times, he tried to strike up a conversation with me, but I gave him the cold shoulder. Not until Hsiu-hua was married, and to a solid businessman at that, did I let some of my anger at Mr. Lu blow away. After all, he was still one of us Kweilin folks. If he'd been from any other place . . . !

One mid-September day, when the heat of early autumn came in fierce as a tiger I was at the restaurant all day and dripping with sweat. By five or six in the afternoon I simply couldn't take it any longer, I turned things over to my cook, grabbed my rushleaf fan and went down to that little park at the end of the street to get some fresh air. There were some stone benches under the big elm tree where you could sit and cool off. I caught sight of Mr. Lu in a T-shirt and a pair of wooden clogs, sitting there by himself. His head was bowed; he was completely wrapped up in his *Hu-ch'in.* I listened to it. Why! He was playing one of our Kweilin operas! It made me tingle all over. Back in the old days in Kweilin I used to be a great opera fan; when stars like Little Gold Phoenix and Seven-Year-Old Prodigy sang, I'd go to the theater every day.

I went right up to him and said, "My, Mister Lu, so you know Kweilin opera!"

He stood up in a hurry and greeted me. "Oh, not really, I just play and sing to myself for the fun of it."

"Wouldn't it be wonderful if I could hear Little Gold Phoenix sing again someday."

"She used to be my most favorite opera singer, too," said Mr. Lu.

"Oh yes! When she sang 'Homecoming to the Cave' it was enough to wring your heart!"

I had to coax him quite a while before I got him to tune up his instrument and sing a passage from "Hsueh Ping-kuei's Homecoming to the Cave." I had never dreamed Mr. Lu could sing a female role, but his voice was pleasant and clear. In fact, his style rather reminded me of Little Gold Phoenix. *"Eighteen long years have taken their toll on Lady Precious Bracelet"*—my heart gave a little twinge when I heard those words.

Mr. Lu stopped playing. "You see?" I said to him with a sigh. "That young wife Precious Bracelet waited eighteen long years, she waited for Hsueh Ping-kuei and got him back after all—" He just smiled and didn't say anything.

"Mr. Lu," I asked him, "What family is your fiancée from?"

"She's one of the Los. Lo Chin-shan is her father."

"Oh, she's one of the Lo girls." I told Mr. Lu about how I often used to go to the Lo store, the Woven Jade Pavilion, to buy silks and satins. Back then in Kweilin their family was making money hand over fist. He listened to me in silence. Afer a long time he started to talk, thoughtfully and in a low voice.

"She and I grew up together, from the time we were little. We were schoolmates at Foster Virtue." He smiled and clusters of wrinkles appeared at the corners of his eyes. As he spoke, he lowered his head, picked up his bow and absentmindedly played snatches of whatever came to mind. The sun began to set and darkened to a dull red. A breeze blew up. It was warm against the body and blew hard enough to ruffle Mr. Lu's gray hair. I leaned back against the stone bench and closed my eyes, listening to the plaintive note of his bow as it went gently back and forth across the strings. My eyes grew heavy and I dozed off. One moment I saw Little Gold Phoenix and Seven-Year-Old Prodigy on stage in "Homecoming"; the next moment Hsueh Ping-kuei turned into my husband and came galloping toward me on his horse.

"Boss-Lady—" I opened my eyes and saw that Mr. Lu had put away his violin and was getting ready to leave. The sky was already filled with stars.

There came a time when Mr. Lu suddenly seemed on top of the world, a rosy glow spread all over his sallow face. Mrs. Ku told me he was actually fixing up his room; he'd even bought a brand new quilt with a red silk cover.

One day in my place I noticed him sitting alone grinning to himself. "Happy news, Mr. Lu?" I asked. He blushed right away. Then he groped around in his pockets until he finally fished out an envelope of coarse paper, yellowed, but carefully folded.

"It's a letter from her . . ." he said softly, swallowing hard. He was so choked up he could hardly get the words out. He told me a cousin of his in Hong Kong had finally managed to get in touch with his fiancée. She'd already made it to Canton.

"It will take ten gold bars. Comes to exactly fifty-five thousand Taiwan dollars. If this had happened a little while back, I'd never have been able to scrape together that much, but . . ." He blurted out his good news in gasps, pausing for breath in between, and it wasn't until he'd gone on for some time that I figured out he was paying some big operator in Hong Kong to smuggle his fiancée out of the mainland. The going rate was ten gold bars a head. The way he clutched that letter in both hands while he was talking, you'd think it was his very own life he was holding on to.

Mr. Lu waited for a month. The waiting made him so fidgety that just by looking at him I could tell that though his body was still here his soul had flown off someplace else. One day he came in for his meal as usual, took a mouthful, got up again, and walked right out. His face was ashen and his eyes were bloodshot. I ran out and stopped him on the street.

"Is there anything wrong, Mr. Lu?"

His mouth kept opening as though he was about to say something, but he couldn't get it out. And then all of a sudden he shouted with a sob in his voice:

"He's not even human!" He went on talking, and the more he spoke the faster he went, pointing and waving his arms, and out came a whole heap of words. What he said was so garbled you'd have thought he was talking with a mouthful of marbles, but I did manage to make out that he'd sent the money to a cousin of his in Hong Kong; the guy simply pocketed the cash, and when Mr. Lu got someone to look him up the cousin pretended he didn't know a thing about it.

After he'd caught his breath, he mumbled with a bitter laugh, "I'd been saving that money for *fifteen years*—" He nodded his head up and down, up and down, his gray hair sticking out every which way. Somehow or other I was reminded of those black-and-whites he used to raise. Every year at New Year's time he'd be standing in the market holding a rooster with a bright red comb and black and white speckled feathers. How fat he used to get every single one of those birds he fed.

For half a year or so he lost all interest in food and drink. He was a quiet man to begin with, but now you couldn't get a word out of him. When I saw how thin and drawn his face had gotten—it was no bigger than the palm of my hand—I went back to my old habit of feeding him my best piping-hot noodles. I never imagined he'd ever lose his appetite for those noodles of mine, but he did; time after time he'd leave half his bowl untouched. Once he didn't show up for two weeks in a row, and I thought he'd taken sick. I'd just about made up my mind to go pay him a visit when I ran into his landlady Mrs. Ku in the market. As soon as that old Hupei bag set eyes on me she grabbed me by the shoulder, walking beside me, cackling as she went, swearing and spitting.

"These men!" she said.

"My dear Mrs. Ku, what news have you got this time?" My shoulder still hurt where she'd grabbed it. The old snoop, if any married woman in the neighborhood slept with another man, she'd talk about it as though she was keeping watch under her bed.

"What can I say?" She spat hard again. "To think even a man like Mr. Lu would be messing around like that. You'll never guess who he's shacked up with—Spring Maid! The washerwoman."

"Mercy!" I couldn't help letting out a yell.

That female had a pair of boobs on her would be bouncing off your face before she was close enough for you to make out who it was behind them. She wasn't much over twenty and already that rump of hers was puffed out like a drum. When she was scrubbing clothes, there wasn't a single part of her body that didn't jiggle; those big melons of hers would be going up and down like a pair of mallet-heads. Whenever she laid eyes on a man, she'd give him the old come-on smile and bedroom eyes. The thing I remember most about her was that day in the market when a young vegetable hawker did something or other to cross her. Before you knew it, those giant knockers of hers were already rammed into that poor man, all he could do was stumble backwards several steps while she sprayed a volley of spit over him and exploded "Fuck your mother's————!" What a spitfire! What a tramp!

"Whenever Spring Maid delivered Mr. Lu his laundry in no time flat she'd be worming her way into his room," Mrs. Ku continued. "I knew right off that Taiwanese trollop was up to no good. And then one afternoon when I was passing by Mr. Lu's window I heard all kinds of groaning and moaning. I thought he'd had some kind of accident, so I stood on tiptoe and peeked inside between his curtains. Pew!" Mrs. Ku spat on the ground as hard as she could. "There they were, the pair of them, stark naked in broad daylight! That damn piece was riding on top of Mr. Lu, her hair flying all over the place, she looked just like a lioness. To run into a thing like this, now you tell me, Boss-Lady, isn't that just my luck!"

"Well! No wonder you've been hitting Thirteen Odds at mah-jong all the time these days. You sure stumbled onto a rarity!" I couldn't help laughing; that old nine-headed Hupei bird,* all she did was pry into other people's secrets.

"Aw, you're full of bull!"

"Well," I sighed, "I guess Mr. Lu's got a good thing going there. From now on at least he won't have to worry about finding somebody to do his laundry."

"But that's just the funny part about it!" Mrs. Ku clapped her hands. "Her wait on him? Not on your life! It's Mr. Lu who serves her and treats her like a living treasure. Miss High-and-mighty doesn't even wash clothes any more. Just sits around all day long, her finger-nails painted bright red, and listens to Taiwanese opera on the radio. And you'd think Mr. Lu was some old horse or ox, the way he works himself. He's bought a stove so he can cook for her. But the thing that really ticks me off is that now Mr. Lu even washes his own sheets. You can imagine how clean he gets them! When I see them drying out there in the courtyard with all the dirty spots on them, it's enough to make me throw up."

The next day I ran into Mr. Lu and Spring Maid on the street. They were coming right at me, with the woman in the lead. She had her head stuck way up in the air and that big bust of hers sticking out. She was wearing real flashy clothes, had a big splash of bright red rouge on each cheek—even her toenails were painted. She went strutting down the street in full sail, her wooden clogs pounding clip-pety-clop. Mr. Lu followed along behind her, carrying a shopping

---

* A deprecatory saying about natives of Hupei Province goes, "In the sky the nine-headed geese, on earth the Hupei-ese." Hence, Hupei people are sometimes nicknamed *chiu-t'ou niao* (nine-headed birds).

basket. When he got close to me I did a double-take. At first I thought
he was wearing a black hat, but now I saw he'd dyed his hair jet
black. Hadn't done a good job, either; it was coarse and stuck out
from his head like wires. His face was so chalky white he must have
had cold cream on; his eyes were sunken, the sockets so dark his face
was nothing but two black caves in a spooky ground of white. I don't
know why, but suddenly I thought of an old actor named White Jade
from the days when I used to go to the opera in Kweilin, a man well
over fifty who kept on singing young romantic leads. Once I saw him
in a piece from *The Dream of the Red Chamber* called "Pao Yu Wails
by Black Jade's Coffin." I was sitting in the front row. He'd absolutely
caked himself in white powder for the role, but when he came to the
wailing part every wrinkle on his aged face showed through; when he
opened his mouth to sing, all you saw was a mouthful of black
tobacco-stained teeth. Just to look at him made me feel sick at heart;
imagine that part of the young and handsome Pao Yu being played
like that! Mr. Lu brushed past me; he turned his head the other way,
pretending not to know me, and just walked away behind that Taiwanese wench.

All up and down Changchun Road everybody knew about the
incident between Mr. Lu and Spring Maid. I'm talking about the time
Mr. Lu got beaten up by Spring Maid and badly hurt. What happened
was, she was balling a man in Mr. Lu's room—that young stud from
down the street, you know, Little Horse, the shoeshine boy. Mr. Lu
ran home so's to catch them in the act. Little Horse flattened Mr. Lu
with one kick and took off. Mr. Lu struggled to his feet and slapped
Spring Maid's face a couple of times.

"And that's how he brought the whole disaster down on himself!" Mrs. Ku told me the same day. "Could you imagine a more
cruel and vicious female in this world? Did you ever see such a thing
in your life! She lit into Mr. Lu like a hurricane, climbed all over him,
tearing and clawing. And then, with one bite she bit half his ear off!
If it hadn't been for me running out into the street and screaming for
help, that bitch would have finished Mr. Lu off right then and there!"

Mrs. Ku went on complaining about what bad luck it was to
have such an ugly thing happen in her house. She said if she'd had
her way she'd have thrown Mr. Lu out that very day. But he'd taken
such a beating he just lay there on his bed and couldn't move. When

his wound healed, he started boarding at my restaurant again. There was nothing left of him but skin and bones. He still had some bruises on his neck, and his left earlobe was gone; there was a piece of white adhesive on the wound. He'd stopped dyeing his hair, but he hadn't washed out all the old dye; the new hair growing out at his temples was white as could be, but the hair on top of his head was still black, like a pot-cover; you wouldn't believe how funny it looked. As soon as he came in, all those old Kwangsi duffers who boarded at my place winked at each other and smiled.

One day when I was standing at the bus stop by the Changchun Elementary School, I happened to see Mr. Lu. He was leading a group of kids just out of school; they were all jabbering and horsing around when Mr. Lu suddenly turned and shouted at them.

"Stop fooling around!"

You could tell he was mad as hell; his face turned absolutely purple, his neck was all red, and the veins in his forehead seemed about ready to burst. The kids got really scared and settled down right away, all except one little girl who broke out giggling. Mr. Lu bounded over, stuck a finger in her face, and barked, "How dare you laugh? How dare you laugh at me?"

That made the little moppet shake her pigtails back and forth and laugh even harder. Mr. Lu slapped her face so hard she lost her footing and ended up sitting on the ground. "Wa—" She opened her mouth as wide as she could and started bawling. Mr. Lu hopped up and down screeching at the top of his voice. He pointed down at her.

"You little devil, you've got the gall to push me around, too? I'll beat you, I'll beat you, I'll beat the living daylights out of you, so help me!" and he reached out to grab her by the pigtails.

The other kids were so scared they started crying and yelling for help. People on the street began to crowd around, some of them trying to comfort the kids; then two male teachers from Changchun Elementary grabbed him and hauled him off. His arms waving wildly as he went, Mr. Lu was foaming at the mouth and screeching, "I'll kill her! I'll kill her!"

That was the last time I saw him. He died the next day. When Mrs. Ku went into his room, she found him slumped over his desk. At first she thought he'd fallen asleep; his head was resting on the desk; his fingers were still gripping his writing brush; a stack of composition books was piled up next to his head. Mrs. Ku said the coroner had examined his body for hours without being able to find anything wrong. Finally he filled in the blank under *Cause of Death:* "Heart failure."

Mrs. Ku warned me never to let on to anyone who might come around looking for a room that Mr. Lu had died at her place. She paid some Buddhist and Taoist monks to come over and chant the scriptures so's to help Mr. Lu's soul along on its journey to the next world. I bought some candles and paper money myself and burned them outside the front door of my restaurant. After all, Mr. Lu must have taken his meals at my place for five or six years all told. For that matter, when old man Li and Crazy Chin died, I'd burned quite a bit of spirit money for them to use in the next world, too.

I got out Mr. Lu's bill and totaled it up; he still owed me two hundred and fifty dollars. First I went to the police station and obtained a permit, then I came over to Mrs. Ku's to try to get some of Mr. Lu's belongings so I could sell them and get my money back. A woman like myself in a small business just doesn't have any spare cash—I can't afford bad debts. Mrs. Ku greeted me with a broad smile, probably thought I'd come to ask her to a mah-jong game. When she found out what I was there for, she sneered:

"Think there's anything left for you? Where'd you expect I'd go to recover my back rent?"

She shoved his room key into my hand and stomped back to her kitchen. I went to his room; sure enough, it was empty. There were a few old books stacked on his desk, and a raggedy old writing-brush still stood in its holder. That old Hupei bag must have taken everything that was worth anything and stashed it away somewhere. I opened the closet and found a couple of white shirts with frayed collars hanging inside; in one corner of the closet were a few pairs of yellowed panties. When I gave the room another once-over, I noticed that *Hu-ch'in* of his hanging on the wall, all covered with dust. There were a few photographs hanging next to it. What was this? Wasn't that bridge in the large framed photograph in the middle Blossom Bridge? Our own Blossom Bridge, just outside River East Gate, back in Kweilin? I grabbed a chair and climbed up in a hurry and took the picture down. I carried it over to the window and wiped off the glass with the corner of my jacket, held it to the light, squinted my eyes and took a good look. Oh, yes, there it was, our Blossom Bridge, with the River Li flowing underneath, and there were the two stone pillars with carved dragons on them at the head of the bridge. Two youngsters were standing next to the pillars, a boy and a girl. The boy was Mr. Lu, and the girl must be the Miss Lo he was engaged to. Mr. Lu was in student uniform and duck-billed cap, looking very handsome and clean-cut. I took another look at that girl and couldn't help a silent "Bravo!" Now *there* was a Kweilin girl for you! Her whole body had the grace of the flowing waters of the river, and her eyes, bright and innocent, had the classic upward tilt. Just to look at her was enough to melt your heart. The two of them were standing close together, shoulders touching, leaning against each other, smiling happily. They couldn't have been more than eighteen or so at the time.

No matter how hard I tried I couldn't scare up a thing worth any money in Mr. Lu's room, so I took the photograph. I planned to hang it in my restaurant. Someday if anybody from Kwangsi comes along I'll point to it and tell them that's the Glory Noodle Shop by Blossom Bridge my Grandpa used to run back in Kweilin—right there at the crossroads by the head of the bridge, on the bank of the River Li.

Autumn Reveries

"Now, Miss Lin, tell me the truth. Between Ambassador Wan's lady and me, which of us wears her years better?" Madame Hua was reclining on a red velvet chaise longue in her boudoir when she put this question to the young beautician. Miss Lin, seated on a low pouf at her feet, was giving her a manicure; on her lap was a box of small scissors of all sorts, eight pairs of them.

"How could Madame ask such a question!" Miss Lin protested, raising her head. "How can there be any comparison between you and Madame Wan?" she added with a snigger. "Why, she's even been to our Soothing Fragrance Salon for surgery."

"Really?" Madame Hua sat up; she had just finished her facial and already her powder and rouge were smoothly applied, her eyebrows plucked to a fine line and pencilled to her temples. "When did that happen?"

"Please don't tell anyone I said anything, Madame," Miss Lin lowered her voice. "It was last spring. Dr. Chou it was gave her a face-lift. I'm not sure if something went wrong with the operation or if her skin was just no good to begin with, but her forehead's begun to sag again recently. Every time I go give her a facial, she takes it out on me—Madame Wan is so hard to please!" Miss Lin shook her head and sighed, laughing. Madame Hua began to laugh, too. She leaned back on the chaise longue, her head back, her eyes closed, and breathed a little sigh.

"I'm not just saying this in front of Madame." Miss Lin laid down her scissors and lifted Madame Hua's right hand, her face filled with envy and admiration. "Of all the ladies I've seen in Taipei Madame's complexion has got to be the finest! I've never seen anything like it, a skin with such beautiful, natural color!"

Madame Hua extended her left hand and studied it with satisfaction, eyes narrowed. The hand had already been manicured; her fingers, white as a handful of spring scallions, tapering and pearl-sheened, were gracefully raised; and on her ring finger was a jade ring of sea green deep as the color of an emerald. "What's so beautiful about it now . . ." she sighed, smiling.

"Madame certainly knows how to take care of herself! Your skin has stayed so delicate and soft." Gingerly Miss Lin drew Madame Hua's right hand back to her knee.

"I haven't paid that much attention to it, really; there, look." She pursed her lips in the direction of the French-style dressing-table, trimmed in white and gold, arrayed from one end to the other with glass bottles and jars of all shapes and hues. "Those things there are just for show—all sent me from abroad by my daughter; that girl never stops trying to make me over in the latest fashion."

"Madame is really fortunate to have such a devoted daughter."

"Devoted indeed! It's just her little-girl nonsense!" Madame Hua laughed. "The other day, in front of everybody, Madame Wan tried to make fun of me, calling me 'the chic Grandma.' Why, she's the chic one, if anyone is! Painting on her eyeshadow blue and green like that—"

"Isn't she, though!" Miss Lin echoed. "I've had to massage her under the eyes over a hundred times every sitting, and she still wasn't pleased. She's got a bad case of the bags, you know; they'll show if she dosen't wear heavy make-up." She and Madame Hua broke out laughing again. Miss Lin held Madame Hua's daintily manicured hand in hers, turning it this way and that as if she were appreciating a work of art. From the vanity box she pulled out a rack of nail enamels in twelve different shades.

"What color dress will Madame wear today?"

"That one, there." Madame Hua pointed. On the bed lay a *ch'i-p'ao* of Indian silk, black wavy designs on a royal blue ground.

"Burgundy to go with the royal blue, what does Madame think?" Miss Lin drew out a burgundy shade.

"I'm wearing jade today; I wonder, will it stand out?" Madame Hua took the bottle of enamel and held it against the large jade ring on her finger.

"This shade of red isn't flashy at all; it's just perfect with jade."

"This will do, then." Madame Hua held out her right hand and leaned back on the chaise longue again, her eyes closed, in repose.

"Madame," her maid Lotus came in. "Ambassador Wan's lady is just telephoning again to ask you to please hurry. Madame Ch'in and Madame Hsüeh are already there. Madame Wan says will Madame please come to the Wan residence right away."

"I've never seen the like of it. What's the rush? She'll be the death of me yet!" Madame Hua laughed, her eyes still closed. "Go tell Madame Wan I'll be there in half an hour. Er, Lotus—"

Lotus stopped at the door and turned around. Madame Hua sat up and thought for a moment.

"If Madame Wan asks, just tell her I'm changing. Don't say Miss Lin is here."

"Very good, Ma'am," Lotus replied with a smile, and went out.

Madame Hua and Miss Lin exchanged a look and grinned. Miss Lin replaced all eight pairs of scissors in the box.

"Those mah-jong fiends!" Madame Hua shook her head with a sigh and rose gracefully. "Every day they come to snatch me away. Really, the way they pester me, it's driving me crazy."

Miss Lin hurried over to pick up the royal blue *ch'i-p'ao* from the bed; holding it up carefully in both hands she brought it to Madame Hua and helped her into it.

"Take a look at this, Miss Lin. I'm not really pleased with it." Madame Hua sat down at the dressing table. She looked in the mirror, her head turning this way and that, and frowned. "I've just been to the Cent Joies Belles today. That Number Thirteen of mine got sick again; it's a new hairdresser who did my hair. He practically combed it to death!"

"Let me tease it a little, and see if Madame likes it better."

Miss Lin selected a styling comb from the dressing table and began to comb Madame Hua's Imperial Favorite chignon. Madame Hua opened a jewel case on the table; inside was arranged a parure of emerald green jade: a pair of pearl-size ear pendants, a link bracelet, and a phoenix-rampant brooch the size of a begonia leaf. Madme Hua picked up the brooch; fingering the cool, smooth jade, she pinned it on the front of her gown. In the mirror her hand was snow white against the royal blue silk, the green phoenix glimmered in her slender fingers, her fingertips were as red as drops of blood.

"Oh—are there some again?" Madame Hua asked, her eyes raised, a faint quiver in her voice. In the mirror she saw Miss Lin's head bent over hers, eyes squinting as her fingers ran through the hair on the upper part of her right temple.

"Only one or two strands," Miss Lin answered, her voice hushed. "I'll try and smooth it out for you; then it won't be noticeable."

With utmost care Miss Lin gave Madame Hua's hair several light brushstrokes. "Does that look all right now, Madame?"

Madame Hua leaned closer to the mirror; turning her head to one side, she took a good long look at herself; then, gently, she caressed the hair at her right temple.

"Well," she said at last, wistfully, "let's leave it at that. Thank you, Miss Lin."

Madame Hua stepped out into the garden; a breath of chill wind swept over her, blowing her long autumn coat open. She quickly fastened it and slipped on her pearl-gray silk gloves. A fall of evening sun poured down on the lawn. Already the tips of the zoysia were tinted brown; on the stone path leading to the main gate, a few fallen leaves whirled about, rustling in the wind. As Madame Hua walked along the path, a wave of cool fragrance suddenly assailed her. She looked back, and her eyes were greeted by a sweep of blossoming "Handful-of-Snows" that leaped and tumbled in the east corner of the wall. She halted in spite of herself and hesitated a moment, as if she'd just thought of something; finally she turned and went over to the flowers. She stooped and inhaled deeply. The dozens of waist-high plants poured forth chrysanthemums, great balls of them, cluster upon cluster, crystal puffs as big as your fist, of a feathery white like new-fallen snow. She bent to an especially large and gorgeous mum and smelled it. Everybody says this is *the* superior white chrysanthemum in Taiwan; it has even won a special award at the Flower Show in New Park; it's a little too delicate, though. They were planted last year and at first almost all of them withered and died, so she told the gardener to mulch them with chicken-feather ashes all spring long, and then they came back to life again. You'd never have thought they'd flourish so magnificently, all at once! No wonder that the last time Pearl Wan was here, when these "Handful-of-Snows" had just begun to bud, she had complained: "Madame Hua, are those chrysanthemums of yours really that superior? Can't you bear to part with one or two for me to use in my flower arrangements?" So. Madame Wan is taking Japanese lessons. Madame Wan is learning the tea ceremony. And now Madame Wan is practicing flower arranging! And with a Kyoko-san, mind you. Pearl Wan—that woman, what could she possibly understand about the tea ceremony and flower arranging? Why, she's got herself a houseful of pots, jars, jugs, and cups—all bought in Japan, she said, Japanese goods are *so* well made, nowadays! Tokyo has become unbelievably prosperous since the war! How odd, the Japanese these days—why, even their looks have changed for the better! As if she's terrified people won't know Ambassador Wan has just been assigned to Japan. Even when she walks, even when she pours tea, she has to bend over and hunch her shoulders, bowing and scraping, looking every inch the Nipponese wench. Don't tell me I have to surrender these really superior "Handful-of-Snows" to her to be ravaged? Madame Hua plucked a double-calyx chrysanthemum, the twin blossoms quivering in the wind. But how well she knows Pearl Wan, that vain woman with a tongue sharp enough to kill; if you give her a flower the least bit too small you can be sure she'll torment you for it. "Chic Grandma" indeed! As if she hasn't become a full-fledged grandmother herself. Madame Hua stepped into the flower grove and looked around; in the center she noticed one or two especially abundant stalks; she walked forward, brushing stalks and leaves aside with her hand; under all those luxurious blossoms she was startled to find there lay many flowers that had already rotted and died. Some were withered and blackened; white mold had grown on them, and one by one they hung on the stems like rotten dumplings; some had only just begun to droop—their petals had turned a rusty yellow. A few of the rotted blossoms, spotted and streaked, were covered with crawling "chrysanthemum tigers" chewing at the flowers' hearts, from which a murky amber juice kept dripping. A gust of wind whipped by; mingled with the cool perfume of the perfect flowers Madame Hua could smell the rank, pungent odor of rotting plants. Pain jolted her heart; she vaguely remembered those few days;

his room, too, was filled with a strange odor like this one; she watched over him at his bedside and saw the doctor stick a rubber tube into that cancerous tumor on his throat, swollen and shiny, all black, drawing pus from it day and night. On his bedside table, in that white porcelain gall-bladder vase, there were three white chrysanthemums, each the size of a ricebowl; she had picked them in the garden herself and placed them there. The hundred or more chrysanthemum plants in their garden were all the famous variety "Handful-of-Snows," which had been transplanted from Ch'i-hsia-shan—the Mountain of Evening Glow. That autumn after the Japanese devils had been chased out, people all said that the crabs in Yangch'eng Lake suddenly fattened and the chrysanthemums in Nanking City blossomed more luxuriantly than ever. The day he led his army into the city of Nanking, old men and women wept and laughed in the streets, cheering and wiping away their tears; the noise of firecrackers exploding all over the city was enough to deafen you. She bowed, laughing too, and said to him, "Welcome home, General! Welcome to you and your triumphant legions—" He put his arm through hers; his military cape flared high in the wind; the sword by his side shone and clanged; his riding boots with their white brass spurs clicked exultantly. Holding her, he walked her into the garden; he raised a cup of fiery wine and toasted her lips, his face all smiling, calling to her in a low and gentle voice: *Yun-hsiang*— At that instant, the hundred or more full-blooming "Handful-of-Snows" that filled the garden waved behind him like roaring, galloping white breakers in a sea of snow. That autumn, people all said even the chrysanthemums were blossoming more luxuriantly than ever—

"Madame, the car has already been brought around."

Madame Hua raised her head and saw the old gardener Huang Yu-hsin standing there on the stone path. His eyebrows were white, he was white at the temples, his back was bent; he stood there shivering, holding a bamboo broom for sweeping the fallen leaves. Madame Hua hesitated a moment and abstractedly picked another chrysanthemum; she stepped out of the flower grove and walked toward the main gate, the large bunch of white chrysanthemums glowing at her bosom.

"Huang Yu-hsin—" Madame Hua walked a few steps, then stopped.

"Yes, Madame," Huang Yu-hsin replied, staying his broom.

"Go and trim those chrysanthemums a little; quite a few have already wilted."

A Sky Full of Bright,

Twinkling Stars

It's always been like this. Always, he would wait until all the bright, twinkling stars in the sky slowly darkened and faded one by one before he would lean back against the stone balustrade around the lotus pond in New Park and begin to recite to us those ancient tales of his.

Maybe it's one of those stifling hot days in July or August; the ramblers in the park linger on and on, unwilling to leave, then we start to circle hurriedly around and around on the terrace surrounding the pond, treading on each other's shadows. In the thick, torrid darkness a tuft of white hair floats here, there a ravaged bald head sways, a stooped silhouette, anxiously on the prowl, beetles to and fro, until the last pair of eyes filled with desire vanishes into the murky grove; then, only then, do we start our gathering. By that time our legs are so exhausted we can hardly raise them.

We all call him "the Guru." Ah Hsiung the Primitive says that among his people, the aborigines, at the season when the first spring rain comes all the youths run naked into the rain and perform the Spring Sacrifice Dance and there will always be a white-haired, white-bearded elder presiding at the altar as the Chief Priest. Once we threw a dance party at Dark-and-Handsome's house in Wan Hua and Ah Hsiung the Primitive got drunk. He tore off all his clothes and started his tribal dance for the Spring Sacrifice. The Primitive is a strapping lad, dark and wild, with muscles bulging all over his body. He leaped around and flew through the air with abandon, his large aborigine eyes rolling like two balls of dark fire—our acting coach, Old Man Mo, says Ah Hsiung is a born martial-arts star for the movies—and the rest of us watched him, mesmerized. Then, yowling and roaring, we all ripped off our clothes and joined in the Spring Sacrifice Dance with him. We danced and danced, and suddenly Dark-and-Handsome sprang onto the table, his sinuous body undulating like crazy. In a voice piercing as a young cockerel's he declared, "We all belong to the Cult of the Spring Sacrifice!"

When you stop to think about it, who but the Guru could be our Guru? Sure, he belongs to our grandfathers' generation, yet there are plenty among those night sprites that roam the Park who outrank him in seniority. But they're a cheap lot; they haven't got the kind of style our Guru has that somehow inspires awe in people. After all, his is a unique past; in the thirties he was the biggest star under contract with the Galaxy Motion Picture Corporation in Shanghai—we have that from Dark-and-Handsome, who likes to worm his way into some of the old movie directors' homes and call their wives his godmothers. According to Dark-and-Handsome, the Guru was a star of the first magnitude in the silent movie days; he once saw a still of the Guru in the role of T'ang Po-hu in the film classic "Three Smiles."

"You just wouldn't believe it . . . !" Dark-and-Handsome gasped, with his mouth popped open and his eyes rolled upwards.

But the Guru had been at the peak only a short time; once the talkies came in, he was eclipsed. He was a Southerner and couldn't speak Mandarin. At that time, Old Man Mo had told Dark-and-Handsome, everybody at the Galaxy Motion Picture Corporation poked fun at the Guru; they called him "Chu Yen, the Cardboard Lover." That night at the stone balustrade around the pond in the Park, we followed the Guru and started calling him by his professional name, Chu Yen–Crimson Flame. He turned abruptly, raised a forbidding finger and waved it at us vehemently.

"Chu Yen? Did you say Chu Yen?—He died a long time ago!"

We all began to laugh; we thought he was drunk, and indeed, the Guru had downed more than he could hold that night. His hoary mane stood out wildly, quivering in the wind; his eyebrows drew close together and made the three lines in his forehead deeper than ever. Have you ever seen furrows so deep on a person's face? It's as though they had been etched with a sharp-pointed knife, the three straight lines, right across his broad forehead, so deep that they appeared dark. He was tall and broad-shouldered; once he must have had a very impressive carriage, but now his back is bowed; he was always wrapped in an old topcoat of gray herringbone tweed; as he walked, his coat flapping in the wind gave you a sense of infinite desolation. But those strange eyes of his—what did they resemble, after all? In the dark, they were two orbs of burning emerald, they sent forth a flame that refused to die, like the eternal lamps in an ancient tomb.

"What are you laughing at?" he shouted at us. "Do you think you're going to live forever?" He walked over and jabbed a finger at Ah Hsiung the Primitive's chest. "*You* think you've got a strong body, huh?" He chucked Dark-and-Handsome under the chin. "*You* think you've got a pretty face, do you? Think you'll all live till you're forty? Fifty? Some people live long, see, like him—" He pointed at an ancient fortune-teller, a graphologist, who was dozing off at his table by the Park fence. "He can live until his beard drags along the ground, until there's nothing left of his face but a few dark holes—he'll still be alive! But Chu Yen died early—1930, 31, 32"—he laughed coldly, counting on his fingers—"Three years, he only lived three years! 'T'ang Po-hu?' All those people at the studio rushed up to call him by that name, but the moment the cameras stopped grinding on 'Loyang Bridge' they announced, 'Chu Yen is finished!' They wanted the *Shun Pao** to sign his death warrant: 'An actor whose artistry is dead and gone.' They not only pushed him down a well, they dumped stones in after him. Buried him alive! Didn't even give him a chance at one last breath—"

As he was saying these words, his hands suddenly closed around his own throat, his eyes bulged, he uttered stifled sounds, his face turning purple; he looked frightful, as if he was actually being strangled. We all broke out laughing, we thought he was acting. The Guru had a terrific talent all right; no matter what he played or mimicked, he made it seem real.. Dark-and-Handsome said the Guru could have become a famous director, but he took to drinking; and being headstrong and full of pride, he offended all the big stars. So a first-rate film never came his way.

"Like this! It was just like this!" The Guru let go of himself. "Little brothers, you don't know what it's like to be buried alive, it's as if someone had you by the throat and you couldn't utter a sound, but you could see their faces, you could hear their voices, you could see them shooting straight at you with the camera under the klieg

---

* A leading newspaper in Shanghai in those days; its movie reviews could make or break a reputation.

lights; and you? Your pulse beat slower and slower, and one by one your nerves deadened, with your own eyes you saw your limbs rot away piece by piece—And that was why I gritted my teeth and told my Prince Charming, 'Son, you must show them, for my sake!' Chiang Ch'ing was a good boy; he really didn't let me down. The day *our* 'Loyang Bridge' premiered at the Grand Theater in Shanghai, the crowd was so big it stopped the traffic on Bubbling Well Road. The minute he came galloping onto the screen in his robe of sea-green silk astride his white horse I heard myself cry out in my heart, 'Chu Yen lives again! Chu Yen lives again!' To remake 'Loyang Bridge' I staked everything I owned. Once, when I was directing him in a scene, I slapped him across the face and left five bloodred marks. But no one can ever know how much I cherished him. 'Chu Yen's Prince Charming' they all called him. He was born to be a great star; there was a spiritual quality about him—little brothers, don't think you're such charmers: not one of you has it!''

He went round the circle pointing at each of us; when he came to Dark-and-Handsome, the boy made a face and sneered; we all roared. Dark-and-Handsome thought he was some hotshot. Some day for sure he was going to make it to Hollywood, he said. We advised him to order a pair of those Italian high-heeled boots; he was only five foot five and where was he going to find a foreign dame short enough to play opposite him?

"But why? Why?" Without warning, the Guru caught Ah Hsiung the Primitive by the arm. Ah Hsiung started; laughing, he struggled to free himself, but the Guru held him fast; he thrust his head with its mane of unruly white hair up close to Ah Hsiung's face. "Why didn't he listen to me? 'Son,' I said, 'you're a genius; whatever you do, don't ruin yourself.' The first time I laid eyes on her I knew Dandelion Chen was bad luck! Imagine, the little witch was thrown clear, not a hair on her head was injured; and later on she even became a top star at the Supreme Studios. And him? He was burned to a lump of charcoal sitting in that sports car I gave him. They wanted me to claim the body. I refused. I refused to acknowledge it. That heap of charred flesh was not my Prince Charming—" It was as if a piece of bone were stuck in the Guru's throat; he became unintelligible. "Burnt to death—we both got burnt to death—" he muttered; his burning emeralds of eyes flashed so that sparks seemed to leap from them. Ah Hsiung freed himself; panting, he ran back to us. The Guru leaned back against the stone balustrade, his head slightly bowed; a big lock of his white hair slipped forward and hung there. Behind him the enormous yellow moon was languidly sinking through the row of coconut trees on the west shore of the pond. The lotuses flowering in the pond breathed out waves of fragrance with increasing intensity. Dark-and-Handsome stood on tiptoe, stretched and yawned; we all began to feel drowsy.

There was a time several months long when you couldn't find a trace of the Guru in the Park. Within our circle there were all kinds of rumors; they all said the Guru had gotten himself arrested and put in prison by the police from the Fourth Precinct; and not only that, he had been booked on a morals charge—all this was spread around by one of those fancy boys from Sanshui Street. The way that little fancy boy told it, one night, after he left the Park as he passed through West Gate Square he saw the Guru in the China Plaza arcade. The old cuss was running after a student and trying to buttonhole him. "That schoolboy was some gorgeous bastard!" the little fairy recalled, smacking his lips. The Guru looked absolutely soused; he could hardly walk. He was swaying from side to side, trying to catch up with that student and asking him if he wanted to be a movie star. At first the student just tried to get out of his way and kept turning around and laughing; at the corner, the Guru caught up with him; he threw his arms around him and hugged him mumbling "Loyang Bridge! My Prince Charming!" and all that. The student cried out in panic, a big crowd gathered, and then the police came.

Finally one night we saw the Guru reappear in the Park. It was a most unusual summer night: for two months there hadn't been a single drop of rain in Taipei. The wind was hot; the stone balustrade in the Park was hot; the outlines of those lush tropical trees wavered in a sultry, smoky haze; the lotus flowers in the pond smelled so sweet the air tasted sticky. In the dark, thickening sky the moon—have you ever seen its like? Have you ever seen such a lewd, demonic moon before? Like an immense ball of flesh, bloodshot, floating up there, flesh-red. In the Park human shadows flickered, circling around wildly like the images on a revolving lantern. Dark-and-Handsome was sitting on the stone balustrade, decked out in a tight-fitting scarlet

T-shirt, black Bermuda shorts, and sandals. Head in the air, legs swinging, he was showing off like a little peacock spreading its tail for the first time. He'd just landed a small part in "Dawn of Spring," directed by Old Man Mo. In front of the cameras for the first time in his life, he was so satisfied with himself he damn near forgot who he was. But Ah Hsiung the Primitive seemed determined to steal the scene. He showed up sporting a snug bright purple Thai silk shirt that turned the upper part of his body into an inverted triangle and white denim pants so tight they looked painted onto his bulging, sinewy legs; his steel belt-buckle was as big as a goose egg, flashing like silver. His whole body was bursting with saturated maleness, tinged with the primitive wildness of the aborigines.

When he sat next to Dark-and-Handsome, for sure they were the most eye-catching pair in the Park; but that gang of fancy boys from Sanshui Street refused to be upstaged. In groups of threes and fives, their arms around each other's shoulders, their wooden clogs clicking, they marched to and fro on the terrace as if they were demonstrating, humming amorous melodies. When a fat, bald-headed foreigner in a loud Hawaiian shirt made his way over, furtively exploring, the fancy boys brazenly hailed him with a chorus of "Hel-lo!"

Just when the excitement in the Park was at its height, the Guru arrived out of nowhere; his appearance was so sudden everybody was astounded, awestruck. At once they all fell silent and quietly watched the Guru's huge shadowy shape move up to the terrace. He wore a brand new sharkskin suit, pale blue and shiny. He was unusually well-groomed, which made his shock of white hair all the more striking, but he was walking with difficulty, as if he were wounded somewhere.

He'd probably gone through a lot in prison, you know; the police could be very cruel sometimes, especially to people in on morals charges. Once a little Sanshui Street fairy hooked a wrong customer and got arrested; the police really fixed him good. By the time he got out he'd been so scared he'd lost his voice; when he saw people he could only open his mouth and go *ah, ah*. People said he'd been beat up with a rubber hose. The Guru dragged his feet along heavily, with great dignity, step by step; eventually he made the stone balustrade at the end of the terrace. He stood there by himself against the balustrade, his white, unruly head lifted up high, his tall, gaunt silhouette jagged and erect, ignoring the whispers and snickers buzzing around him. In a moment excitement returned to the terrace. The night was deepening; steps grew more urgent, one by one the shadows went searching, exploring, yearning. The Guru stood there alone. Not until that flesh-ball of a red moon had languidly gone all the way down did he leave the Park. When he left he took a Sanshui Street boy along with him. The boy was called Little Jade; he was a pretty-faced little thing, but he was a cripple, so not many people paid him attention. The Guru put his arm around the boy's shoulder, and the two of them, one tall, one small, supporting each other with their incompleteness, limped together into the dark grove of Green Corals.

Wandering in the Garden, Waking from a Dream

The K'un-ch'ü, or K'unshan opera, named after its place of origin, K'unshan in Kiangsu Province, is the oldest form of opera still performed in China. Dating back to the Ming Dynasty (1368–1644), K'un-ch'ü dominated the Chinese stage for over two hundred years. The famous Ming dramatist and musician Wei Liang-fu developed K'un opera. Later it was popularized in the capital, Peking, and from there spread throughout the country. It became a favorite entertainment for the literati, many of whom wrote plays for this theater, refined it, and brought it to a peak of artistic perfection. K'unshan opera is an elegant art form, combining music, dance, and poetry. It demands the highest standards of its singers. Unlike the later form of Peking opera, the primary accompaniment to K'un-ch'ü consists of flutes and reeds.

In time, the K'unshan opera became an exclusive art for aristocratic connoisseurs. By the end of the Ch'ing Dynasty (1644–1912), it had been supplanted in the popular theater by the P'i-huang, the dominant strain in what was to become the Peking opera. However, many features of the K'un-ch'ü have been absorbed into the Peking opera, and some of its major works are still performed, in somewhat modified form. The best known of these is "Wandering in the Garden, Waking from a Dream."

A perennial favorite in the traditional Chinese theater, "Wandering in the Garden" is based on the classic Ming drama The Peony Pavilion by T'ang Hsien-tsu (1550–1616). This is a poetic romance that celebrates the triumph of love over death. The heroine Tu Li-niang, Tu the Beauteous Maid, the young daughter of a government official, leads a secluded life in her parents' home. One beautiful spring day, she wanders out into the garden with her maid. Seized with the restlessness of spring and her first longings for love, she laments the waste of her youth. Returning from the garden, she falls asleep and in her dream meets a handsome young man, Liu Meng-mei. In this dream, one of the most passionate and lyrical scenes in all Chinese drama, the lovers have an amorous tryst in the garden. Upon waking *from the dream, Tu the Beauteous Maid pines away, longing for her dream lover. She dies and is buried by her parents in the garden. But the dream lover exists in real life: a young scholar, also named Liu Meng-mei. After many adventures, Liu reaches Tu Li-niang's garden and discovers her portrait. Her spirit appears to him. Moved by her great love, the Judge of the Underworld restores her to life. The lovers marry, and after a number of further trials, the dream ends happily.*

The K'unshan opera "Wandering in the Garden, Waking from a Dream" is adapted from Scene Ten of The Peony Pavilion. *In the twentieth century, the celebrated actor of women's roles, Mei Lan-fang, is regarded as the greatest performer of the role of Tu the Beauteous Maid. Some of Tu Li-niang's brilliant arias figure prominently in our story.*

When Madame Ch'ien arrived at the Tou villa in the elegant Taipei suburb of Tien Mu, the road near the house was already packed on both sides with parked cars, most of them black official sedans. As her taxicab drove up to the gate, Madame Ch'ien ordered the driver to stop. The villa's iron gates were wide open, the lamps burning high above. A guard stood on either side of the gate; a man in the uniform of an aide-de-camp was busy attending to the guests' chauffeurs. As soon as Madame Ch'ien got out of the cab, the aide hurried over. A man graying at the temples, he was outfitted in a Sun Yat-sen tunic of dark blue serge. Madame Ch'ien took a calling card from her purse and handed it to him. He bowed deeply as he took it, his face all smiles, and greeted her in his northern Kiangsu accent.

"Madame Ch'ien, I'm Liu *Fukuan*. Madame probably doesn't remember me any more."

"Is that you, Liu *Fukuan*?" Madame Ch'ien glanced at him, a little startled. "Of course. I must have seen you then, at your General's residence in Nanking. How are you, Liu *Fukuan*?"

"I'm fine, thanks to Madame's blessings." Again, he bowed, and, hurrying ahead, led the way with a flashlight along a concrete driveway around the garden towards the main building.

"Madame has been well, I presume?" He turned to her and smiled.

"Quite well, thank you. And how are your General and his lady? It's been many years since I saw them."

"Madame is well; the General has been rather preoccupied lately with official business."

The garden of the Tou villa was deep and wide. Madame Ch'ien looked around her; everywhere swaying shadows of the trees and flowers and plants moved back and forth across each other. The garden walls were thickly lined with rows of coconut palms. A clear late-autumn moon had already risen above their lofty tops. Madame Ch'ien followed Liu the aide-de-camp around a little grove of coir palms—suddenly the two-story Tou mansion loomed up before her. The entire house, upstairs and down, was ablaze with lights, as if on fire. A wide flight of stone steps led up to a huge curved terrace. Along the stone balustrade stood big pots of cassia in a neatly spaced row—there were more than ten of them, all grown chest-high. As Madame Ch'ien stepped onto the terrace, a wave of strong fragrance enveloped her. The main doors were wide open, and inside, servants could be seen shuttling to and fro. Liu stopped at the door, bowing slightly, and extended his hand in a respectful gesture.

"This way, please, Madame."

As Madame Ch'ien entered the antechamber, Liu summoned one of the maids. "Go, quickly, and report to Madame. General Ch'ien's lady has arrived."

The only furnishings in the antechamber were exquisite redwood chairs and side tables. On the low table to the right stood a group of cloisonné vases; one, shaped like a fish-basket, held a few sprays of evergreen. Set in the wall over the table, was a large oval pier glass. Madame Ch'ien went up to the mirror, removing her black autumn evening coat; a maid hurried forward to take it from her. Madame Ch'ien stole a glance in the mirror and quickly smoothed a stray lock of hair at her right temple. At six o'clock that very evening she had gone to the Red Rose on West Gate Square to have her hair dressed, only to have the wind ruffle it as she had walked through the garden. Madame Ch'ien took a step closer to the mirror; she even felt that the color of her emerald green Hangchow silk *ch'i-p'ao* was not quite right. She remembered that this kind of silk shimmered like sea-green jade when the light shone on it. Perhaps the antechamber was not well-lit; the material looked rather dull in the mirror. Could it really have faded? She had brought this silk with her all the way

from Nanking. All these years she hadn't been able to bring herself
to wear it; she had dug it out of the bottom of her trunk and had it
cut just for this party. If she had known, she would have bought herself a new length of silk at the Swan. But somehow she always
thought Taiwan materials coarse and flashy; they hurt your eyes, especially the silks. How could they compare with mainland goods—
so fine, so soft?

"Fifth Sister, you've come after all." There was a sound of
footsteps, and Madame Tou appeared. She took Madame Ch'ien's
hand in hers, smiling.

"Third Sister," exclaimed Madame Ch'ien, smiling graciously
also, "I'm late. I must have kept you waiting."

"Not at all. You're right on time. Dinner's just about to start."

As she spoke, she walked Madame Ch'ien arm in arm toward
the main drawing room. In the corridor Madame Ch'ien cast a few
glances at Madame Tou out of the corner of her eye. She couldn't
help observing to herself: So, Fragrant Cassia really hasn't aged after
all. The year they were to leave Nanking, she'd thrown a party at her
own villa in Plum Garden, hadn't she, in honor of Fragrant Cassia's
thirtieth birthday. Practically all her sworn sisters from the Terrace
of the Captured Moon had come, including Fragrant Cassia's real
sister, Heavenly Pepper, Number Thirteen, who was later to become
concubine to Governor Jen—Jen Tzu-chiu, that is, and her own
sister, Number Seventeen, Red-red Rose. The whole group had
chipped in, Western-style, and ordered a big two-layer birthday cake,
measuring thirty inches across and decorated with no fewer than
thirty red candles. She must be well past forty by now, surely? Madame Ch'ien stole another glance at her old friend. Madame Tou was
wearing a *ch'i-p'ao* of silver gray chiffon dusted with vermilion span-
gles and matching silver high-heels. The ring finger of her right hand
bore a diamond as big as a lotus seed, and a platinum bracelet studded
with tiny diamonds twisted around her left wrist. A crescent-shaped
coral pin held her hair; a pair of inch-long purple jade earrings hung
below, setting off her full, pale face and making it look all the more
aristocratic and dignified. In those Nanking days, she recalled, Fragrant Cassia had never had this special air about her. Then she was
still a concubine, her husband, Tou Jui-sheng, a mere Deputy Minister. He's big in the government now, of course, and Fragrant Cassia

has risen to be the official Madame Tou. You had to give her credit: she had sweated out all those years; now, at last, she could hold her head high.

"Jui-sheng's gone to the south to attend a meeting. When he heard you were coming tonight, Fifth Sister, he asked me specially to give you his warmest regards." Madame Tou turned to Madame Ch'ien with a smile.

"Ah," said Madame Ch'ien, "that's so thoughtful of Brother Tou." As they neared the drawing room, a swell of laughter and chatter flowed toward them from the inside. Madame Tou stopped at the entrance, again taking Madame Ch'ien's hands in hers.

"Fifth Sister, you should have moved to Taipei long ago," she said. "It's been on my mind all this time. It must be very quiet for you now, living alone in a place like that down south. You simply had to come to my party tonight—Thirteen's come, too."

"She's here, too?"

"Well, you know, as soon as Jen Tzu-chiu died, she moved out of his house." She leaned close to Madame Ch'ien's ear. "He was quite well off, and Thirteen's all by herself—you could say she's living comfortably. She was the one who clamored for tonight's party; it's the first time since we came to Taiwan. She's invited a few of her friends over from the Tien Hsiang Opera Club—gongs, drums, pipes, flutes, the whole works. And they all expect you to get up there and show your stuff."

"Come on, now, really, I can't do that sort of thing any more!" Madame Ch'ien hurriedly freed herself from Madame Tou, laughing and waving her hands in a gesture of deprecation.

"Don't be so modest, Fifth Sister," Madame Tou laughed. "If the famous 'Bluefield Jade' can't sing,* who else would dare utter a note?" Giving Madame Ch'ien no chance to argue, she led her into the drawing room.

The main drawing room was already filled; groups of guests in dazzling evening dress were scattered here and there like clusters of flowers embroidered on silk. It was an enormous room with an alcove, furnished in a blend of Chinese and Western styles. On the left-hand side were grouped armchairs and sofas with soft cushions; on

*Bluefield Mountain in Shensi Province is famous for its rare jade. In China, jade symbolizes spiritual essence.

the right, tables and chairs of red sandalwood; in between, the floor was covered with a thick carpet depicting two dragons vying for a pearl. The two large sofas and four armchairs, all covered in black velvet with a design of wine-red begonia leaves, faced each other in a circle. Inside the circle on a low rectangular table stood a tall gall-bladder vase of fine blue porcelain; from the vase sprang forth a bunch of Dragon-beard chysanthemums, their red petals veined in gold. To the right, surrounded by eight sandalwood chairs, was an Eight-Immortals table with a marble top, laden with all sorts of bonbonnières and tea things. In the alcove stood a towering ebony screen with an inlaid-mica design of bats and drifting clouds. The screen was flanked by six redwood chairs in a semi-circle, three on each side. Madame Ch'ien noticed the cymbals and stringed instruments arranged on the chairs. In front of them were two stands: one held a small drum and the other was hung with flutes and pipes all in a row. The room was resplendent. Two floor lamps were trained on a large gong, making it glitter with a golden radiance.

Madame Tou ushered Madame Ch'ien to the left side of the drawing-room, where a woman, fiftyish, wearing a pearl-gray *ch'i-p'ao* and covered with jade ornaments, was seated on a sofa.

"Madame Lai, this is Madame Ch'ien. You must have met before."

Madame Ch'ien recognized her. Lai Hsiang-yun's wife. They'd met several times in Nanking, on social occasions. At that time, Lai Hsiang-yun was an Army Commander, probably. Since coming to Taiwan, she seemed to see his name quite often in the newspapers.

"This must be His Excellency General Ch'ien's lady." Madame Lai was in the middle of a conversation with a gentleman; now she turned, looked Madame Ch'ien up and down for a moment and rose gracefully with a smile. She shook hands with her; touching a finger to her forehead, she added: "But your face does look familiar!"

She turned to the guest beside her, a stout bald-headed man with a swarthy face, attired in a long gown of royal blue silk.

"I've been chatting with the President's Staff Advisor, General Yu—I just can't remember which opera Mei Lan-fang starred in the third time he came down to Shanghai to appear at the Cinnamon Theater No. 1. See what a memory I have!"

General Yu was already on his feet. Smiling broadly, he bowed to Madame Ch'ien.

"It's been a long time since I've had the pleasure of seeing you, Madame. That year in Nanking, at the gala performance sponsored by the Officers' Moral Endeavor Association, I had the great good fortune to be in your audience. As I recall, Madame sang in 'Wandering in the Garden, Waking from a Dream.' "

"Oh, yes!" Madame Lai put in. "I've heard so much about Madame Ch'ien's great reputation. Tonight, at last, I'll have a chance to enjoy your artistry."

Madame Ch'ien hastened to reply modestly to General Yu's compliments. She remembered he had been once to her villa in Nanking, but she also seemed to recall that he'd gotten involved in some major political scandal, been relieved of his post, and retired. Presently Madame Tou took her around and introduced her to the guests one by one. She didn't know any of the other ladies. They all looked rather young; most likely they'd arrived socially only after they came to Taiwan.

"Let's go to the other side; Thirteen and her Opera Club friends are all there."

So saying, Madame Tou showed Madame Ch'ien to the right side of the drawing room. A lady in red came mincing quickly up to greet them. She slipped her arm through Madame Ch'ien's, shaking with laughter.

"Fifth Sister," she declared, "Third Sister told me a little while ago that you were coming. I was so thrilled I yelled, 'Wonderful! Tonight we've really got the Star to come out.' "

When Madame Ch'ien first learned from Madame Tou that Chiang Pi-yueh was to be present, she had wondered whether, after being married so many years, the fiery Heavenly Pepper would have mellowed a bit. In Nanking, when the whole group was performing in the Confucius Temple District at the Terrace of the Captured Moon, Heavenly Pepper would always thrust herself into the limelight, coaxing their Master into allowing her to sing all the crowd-pleasing numbers. When she was on stage, she would look straight at the patrons, defying all the rules of their profession, her eyes reaching out like a pair of hooks all the way into the audience. The two sisters were born of the same mother, yet how different their characters were! In her worldly wisdom and generosity, Fragrant Cassia was second to none. Heavenly Pepper made the most she could for herself out of her sister's every opportunity. Jen Tzu-chiu had already presented Cassia with the betrothal gifts when Heavenly Pepper had the nerve to snatch him right from under her eyes. Surprising that Cassia could have such forbearance. She had had to wait ever so many years until finally, not without a certain sense of grievance, she had reluctantly agreed to become Tou Jui-sheng's second concubine. No wonder that every now and then Cassia would sigh: It's always your own younger sister, your flesh and blood, who'll do you in! Again Madame Ch'ien looked at Heavenly Pepper, Chiang Pi-yueh. She was all aflame in a red satin *ch'i-p'ao*. On her wrists she wore no fewer than eight gold bracelets, jingling and jangling with her every move. Her makeup was in the height of fashion: her eyelids painted with eyeshadow, the corners of her eyes heavily pencilled, her hair pouffed in a beehive, and at her temples tiny little seductive curls, like crescent hooks. After Jen Tzu-chiu died, this Heavenly Pepper, contrary to expectation, had become more vivacious than ever, even more flamboyant. On this woman you could find no trace of the war and turmoil that had been our lot these many years.

"Say! You people really have a treat in store for you. Madame Ch'ien here is the real female Mei Lan-fang!" Chiang Pi-yueh steered Madame Ch'ien toward her friends, the men and women of the Opera Club, and made the introductions. The men stood up hurriedly, bowing to Madame Ch'ien.

"Pi-yueh, don't talk nonsense. You'll make a laughingstock of me before these connoisseurs." Returning their bows, Madame Ch'ien mildly reproached her.

"Pi-yueh is right, actually," Madame Tou interposed. "Your K'unshan opera is of the true Mei School."

"Now, Third Sister, . . ." Madame Ch'ien murmured in protest. But when it came to K'unshan opera, even her husband, Ch'ien P'eng-chih, had said to her, "Fifth, my dear, I've heard the finest singers north and south, and I must say your voice ranks right up there with theirs."

Ch'ien P'eng-chih had told her that when he went back to Shanghai from Nanking after having heard her in "Wandering in the

Garden, Waking from a Dream," he thought about her day and night and simply couldn't get her out of his mind. Eventually he returned and married her. He had told her all along that if only he could have her by his side to amuse him with singing a few bars from his favorite K'unshan opera, he would be content for the remaining years of his life. She had just risen to stardom then at the Terrace of the Captured Moon. One phrase from a popular K'unshan aria in that inimitable voice of hers and she would bring down the house. The Master of the Moon Terrace had said, "Of all the singers in the Confucius Temple District, Bluefield Jade is the one who must be regarded as the most classic."

"That's just what I say, Fifth Sister. Come along and meet another friend. —Mrs. Hsu here is a Queen of K'unshan opera, too." Chiang Pi-yueh led Madame Ch'ien to a quietly refined young lady in a black *ch'i-p'ao*; then, turning to Madame Tou, "Third Sister," she said, "in a little while we'll have Mrs. Hsu sing 'Wandering in the Garden' and Fifth Sister here sing 'Waking from a Dream.' Do let's stage a grand revival of this hallowed masterpiece of K'unshan opera. Let these two great stars shine on the same stage and give our ears a big treat."

Mrs. Hsu rose at once, saying she wouldn't dare be so presumptuous. Madame Ch'ien quickly made some polite remark as well, but in her heart she was annoyed at Heavenly Pepper's lack of tact. Among all these people here tonight there probably wasn't one who didn't know opera; very likely this Mrs. Hsu beside her was a first-rate singer; later, if they actually got her to perform, she'd better not take things for granted. When it came to the techniques and skills of operatic singing, she had nothing to fear from these people; but she'd been in the south so long, and in all this time she hadn't really been in training; she wasn't at all sure of her voice. Besides, her dressmaker had been right after all: In Taipei, the long *ch'i-p'ao* has gone out of fashion. Everyone sitting here, including that old Madame Lai, her face so wrinkled it looked like chicken skin, had the hem of her gown almost to her knees, exposing a good half of her legs. In the Nanking days, a lady's gown was so long it almost touched her feet. She was sorry she hadn't listened to her tailor; she wondered whether she wouldn't look ridiculous in front of all these people if she stood up later in this long gown. When one goes onstage it's essential to create a presence instantly. In those Nanking days, when she herself gave opera dinners at Plum Garden, every time she got up to sing, her presence would hush the audience and hold it spellbound even before she uttered a note.

Smiling, Madame Tou escorted Madame Ch'ien to an officer who looked to be in his thirties. "Colonel Ch'eng, I'm turning Madame Ch'ien over to you now. If you don't take the very best care of her, I'll penalize you—you'll have to treat us all tomorrow." She turned and whispered to Madame Ch'ien. "Fifth Sister, you sit here and chat a while with the Colonel. He's a true opera buff. I must go look after the banquet."

"Madame Ch'ien, this is a great honor."

Colonel Ch'eng stood facing Madame Ch'ien and bowed smartly, military fashion. He was in dress uniform, beige gabardine, his Lieutenant-Colonel's insignia, a pair of shiny gold plum blossoms, on each lapel, his jump boots together, raven-glossy, water-smooth. Madame Ch'ien noted that his smile showed his even white teeth. He boasted a fine-chiselled face, a smooth-shaven gleaming blue chin, long slender eyes slanting upwards, with a pair of loftily raised eyebrows thrusting up into his temples. His inkblack hair was carefully brushed; his nose was straight and slender as a scallion, the tip slightly hooked. He was tall and slim, in uniform he looked extraordinarily dashing, yet Madame Ch'ien felt a touch of gentleness in the way he greeted her, without any trace of military coarseness.

"Please sit down, Madame."

Colonel Ch'eng gave her his chair, straightening the soft cushions. He went quickly to the Eight-Immortals table and returned with a cup of jasmine tea and a bonbonnière with four kinds of candied fruit and melon seeds. When Madame Ch'ien reached for the pomegranate-red porcelain cup, Colonel Ch'eng said in a gentle voice, "Be careful not to scald your hand, Madame."

He opened the gold-trimmed black lacquer bonbonnière; bending, he presented it with both hands to Madame Ch'ien, beaming, watching her intently, waiting for her to choose one. Madame Ch'ien took a few pine nuts, but Colonel Ch'eng hastened to dissuade her.

"Madame, those are bad for the voice. May I suggest you try one of the honeyed dates; they're good for your throat."

He fixed a honeyed date on a toothpick and handed it to Madame Ch'ien. She thanked him, popped the date into her mouth and tasted a penetrating honey-sweetness, a delightful scent. Colonel Ch'eng brought another chair and sat on her right.

"Have you been to the opera lately, Madame?" When he spoke, he leaned towards her a trifle, as if with total concentration. Again Madame Ch'ien noticed his white teeth, shining like crystals in the light.

"I haven't been for quite a while," she answered. She lowered her head and took a dainty sip of jasmine tea. "I live in the south; one rarely gets to see good opera there."

"Chang Ai-yun is playing the 'Nymph of the River Lo' at the National Theater right now, Madame."

"Really?" Madame Ch'ien's head was still lowered. She sipped her tea, sunk in thought for a moment, before resuming, "When I was in Shanghai, I saw her perform the "Nymph" at the Heavenly Toad Theater. . . . That was a long time ago."

"She's still got her acting. No wonder they called her 'Peerless in the *ch'ing-i* roles.'* She portrayed the love affair of Lady Mi and the poet Tsao Tzu-chien with great subtlety—a marvelous piece of acting."

Madame Ch'ien raised her head and met Colonel Ch'eng's eyes; immediately she averted her face. Those slender eyes of the young officer covered you like a net.

"Whose acting is so subtle and marvelous?" Chiang Pi-yueh, the Heavenly Pepper, chimed in with a laugh. Colonel Ch'eng stood up quickly and yielded his seat. Chiang Pi-yueh snatched up a handful of sunflower seeds for herself and sat down, crossing her legs and cracking the seeds open while she carried on. "Colonel, everybody says you are knowledgeable about the theater, but Madame Ch'ien is the All-Knowing First Lady of opera. If I were you, I'd stop sounding off in front of a real pro."

"Madame Ch'ien and I have just been discussing Chang Ai-yun's 'Nymph of the River Lo.' I was asking Madame Ch'ien's expert opinion," Colonel Ch'eng replied, glancing sideways at Madame Ch'ien.

"Oh, were you talking about Chang Ai-yun?" Chiang Pi-yueh

* *Ch'ing-i*, literally "dark dress," roles are those of virtuous wives, maidens in distress, faithful lovers, and the like.

chuckled. "It's all right for her to do a little opera teaching around Taiwan, but to appear as the 'Nymph of the River Lo'! Why, she couldn't pass for Lady Mi even in full costume and makeup! Last Saturday I finally made it to the National—got a seat in the back row —and all I saw were her lips moving. I couldn't hear a thing. Barely halfway through the opera her voice failed. —Well, here comes Third Sister now to invite us in to the banquet."

Sliding doors of mahogany with carved openwork swastikas led to the banquet hall. A servant opened them and Madame Tou emerged from the magnificent room. It was pale silver, luminous as a snow cave. The two banquet tables were spread with fine scarlet linen; the plates, bowls, spoons, and chopsticks, all of silver, glowed against the scarlet. There was much standing on ceremony after the guests filed in; no one ventured to take the place of honor at the head of the table.

"I'd better take the lead. If we go on waiting for each other like this, we'll never sit down to dinner. In which case, we'd be abusing our hostess's hospitality!" That was Madame Lai, who thereupon went to the head of the first table and sat down. She beckoned to General Yu. "General, come sit next to me, why don't you. We haven't reached any conclusions about Mei Lan-fang's operas yet."

"At your command, Ma'am!" Grinning broadly, General Yu folded his hands in an elaborate operatic salute. The guests burst out laughing and one after another took their seats. When they reached the second table, again everybody started deferring to each other. Laughing, Madame Lai called from the first table, "Madame Ch'ien, I think you'd better follow my example."

Madame Tou came over and escorted Madame Ch'ien to the head of the second table. "Fifth Sister, please do sit down," she whispered. "If you don't take the lead, the others will have trouble getting seated."

Madame Ch'ien looked around. The guests were all standing there watching her and smiling. She made a vague attempt to decline the honor, but at last she sat down; for a moment her heart fluttered, her face even flushed a little. It certainly wasn't as if she'd never been through this sort of high-society ceremonial, but she'd not entertained or been entertained for so long she'd become rather unused to it. When her husband was alive, nine times out of ten she would be

first to take the seat of honor at banquets. Naturally Madame Ch'ien
P'eng-chih would be at the head of the table; she'd never had to yield
pride of place to anyone. Of all the ladies in government circles in
Nanking not many could be numbered among her superiors. Of course
those officials' concubines couldn't compare with her. She was Ch'ien
P'eng-chih's legitimate wife; he, a widower, had taken her in marriage
with all due ceremony. Poor Fragrant Cassia hadn't even been allowed
to act as hostess in her own right; hadn't *she* been the one who'd
given the party for Cassia's birthday? Only since her arrival in Taiwan has Cassia dared to come out and stage such a grand spectacle,
and yet she herself, when she was a singing-girl barely turned twenty,
was transformed overnight into a general's lady. A singsong girl mar-
rying into an ordinary family is enough of an event to cause comment;
imagine the talk when she married one of the high and mighty! Even
her own sister, Number Seventeen, Red-red Rose, had let fall a cutting
remark or two.

"Sister, it's about time you cut off your braid, or when you go
out for a walk with General Ch'ien people could mistake you for his
granddaughter!" The year Ch'ien P'eng-chih married her he was almost sixty. She didn't care what anybody said, she was his true and
honorable second wife. She understood her position, and she guarded
it jealously. In the dozen or so years she was Ch'ien P'eng-chih's help-
meet, she always handled banquets and such as if she were walking
on eggs, smoothly, perfectly, no matter how great the occasion. Whenever she appeared in public, she carried herself with such elegance
and grace that nobody would dare whisper she was the "Bluefield
Jade" who had sung at the Moon Terrace by the Chin Huai River.

"It must have been hard on you, Fifth," Ch'ien P'eng-chih often said to her, caressing her cheek. Whenever she heard that, she felt
a twinge in her heart. There was no way she could make him see what
was troubling her deep down. After all, how could she possibly lay
the blame on him? She had entered the thing with her eyes open.
When he married her he'd been frank with her, told her clearly that
only after he'd heard her in "Wandering in the Garden, Waking from
a Dream" had it occurred to him to take her as the companion of his
old age. Well, wasn't it just the way her sister Red-red Rose had put
it? Ch'ien P'eng-chih might as well be her granddaddy! What else
could she have expected? It had been fulfilled after all, that ironclad

prophecy made by their *shih-niang*,* the blind woman who was their Master's wife at the Terrace of the Captured Moon. Fifth, my girl, she told her, the best thing your sort of people can hope for is to get married to an older man who'll love you like a daughter. As for the young fellows, can you trust them? As if that weren't enough, *shih-niang*, blind as she was, had to go and take hold of her wrist and feel the bone, blinking her sightless eyes and adding with a sigh: worldly glory, wealth, and position—you shall enjoy them all, Bluefield Jade. Only it's a pity you've got one bone in you that's not quite right. It's just your retribution from a previous life! What else was it, if not retribution? Except for the moon, which he could not pluck from the sky, Ch'ien P'eng-chih had tried bringing her in both hands all the gold and silver and treasures of the world that would make her happy. She appreciated his thoughtfulness: he was afraid her humble origins would weigh on her mind and she'd be diffident, intimidated by the high-ranking officials and the wellborn ladies; he tried in every way to encourage her to show off her wealth, to live it up. Certainly the high style of Madame Ch'ien's parties at Plum Garden was the talk of Nanking; it was practically a sin, the number of silver dollars she tossed around at the Ch'ien residence on banquets alone. Take that birthday party she gave for Fragrant Cassia! No fewer than ten tables were laid out; for entertainment she engaged the top flutist, Wu Sheng-hao of the Rainbow Club; to preside over her kitchen she spent ten silver dollars just to transport the chef from the famed Willow Lodge at Peachleaf Ferry.

"Madame Tou, where did you find your chef?" asked Madame Lai. "It's the first time I've had such superb shark's fin since I came to Taiwan."

"He used to be Chief Cook at Minister Huang's home in Shanghai," Madame Tou replied. "Huang Ching-chih, you know. He came to us only after we got to Taiwan."

"No wonder!" General Yu put in. "His Excellency the Minister is a well-known gourmet."

"If I could borrow your chef someday to make shark's fin, it would add so much prestige to my dinner-table," said Madame Lai.

"What could be simpler?" rejoined Madame Tou. "I'd be more

---

* *Shih-niang*, literally "teacher-mother." See note on p. 18.

than happy to go out for a free meal!" This brought a laugh from all the other guests.

"Madame Ch'ien, won't you have a bowl of shark's fin?" Colonel Ch'eng ladled a bowl of the red-cooked shark's fin, adding a spoonful of Chenchiang vinegar, and set it before her. He murmured, "This is our cook's most famous dish."

Madame Ch'ien had hardly tasted her shark's fin when Madame Tou came over from the other table and proposed a toast to the guests. She made a point of telling the young colonel to refill her cup, and moving to Madame Ch'ien's side, she put her hand on her shoulder and said warmly, "Fifth Sister, it's been so long since the two of us drank to each other."

She clinked her cup with Madame Ch'ien's and downed the wine in one gulp; daintily Madame Ch'ien drank hers. As Madame Tou was leaving, she turned to Colonel Ch'eng. "Colonel, be sure you drink another round with everyone for me. Your General's not here; you'd better do the honors at this table."

Colonel Ch'eng rose to his feet. Holding a silver decanter, he bent down, all smiles, and started to pour wine into Madame Ch'ien's cup. She hastily stayed his hand.

"Colonel, why don't you serve the others. My capacity is quite limited."

Colonel Ch'eng didn't move but looked at Madame Ch'ien with a smile and replied, "Madame, this *hua-tiao* is not at all like other wines; it fades away easily. I know you'll be singing in a while, but this wine's been heated; it won't hurt your voice to drink a little."

"Madame Ch'ien's capacity is unlimited. Don't let her off!" Chiang Pi-yueh, who was seated opposite Madame Ch'ien, came around; without waiting to be served she poured herself a full cup and raised it to Madame Ch'ien. "Fifth Sister," she said, her voice ringing with laughter, "I, too, haven't had a chance to drink a cup with you for a long time."

"Pi-yueh, if we keep drinking this way, we'll get drunk." Coughing slightly, Madame Ch'ien fended off Chiang Pi-yueh's hand.

"So you won't do your little sister the honor. All right! I'll drink double. If I get drunk later, I'll just let them pick me up and carry me home."

Chiang Pi-yueh threw back her head and drained the cup.

Colonel Ch'eng promptly presented her with another; she took that, swallowed it and turned the silver winecup upside down, brandishing it before Madame Ch'ien's face.

The guests applauded. "Good show, Miss Chiang!"

Madame Ch'ien had no choice but to raise her cup; she finished her *hua-tiao* unhurriedly. The wine certainly was well-heated; once down your throat it coursed like a warm current through your whole body. Still and all, Taiwan *hua-tiao* was not nearly as good as what you used to get on the mainland, not that smooth and mellow— it felt a little scratchy on your throat. Though they say *hua-tiao* fades away easily, does it ever trip you up if you drink it down too fast! She'd never dreamed the aged *hua-tiao* she'd ordered brought directly from Shaohsing could have packed such a wallop. That night finally she fell into their trap. *The whole gang insists: How could you possibly lose your voice with a few cups of* hua-tiao? *It's such a rare occasion; it's Fragrant Cassia's special day. . . . We sisters don't know when if ever we'll get together like this again. . . . If you, our hostess, won't drink up, how can your guests let themselves go? Even Red-red Rose, her own little sister Seventeen, sides with them and chimes in: Sister, let's you and me drink bottoms up and be real pals for a while. Red-red Rose is arrayed in a flashing red and gold satin ch'i-p'ao, gorgeous as a parrot, her liquid eyes flashing this way and that. Sister, you won't do me the honor, she says. So you'll make your little sister lose face, she says. She's practically stolen the whole show, made off with all the prizes, and here she's handing me the sweet talk. No wonder Fragrant Cassia sighed: It's always your own younger sister, your flesh and blood, who'll do you in! Red-red Rose—well, granted she was young and didn't know better, but he, Tseng Yen-ching he should have known better than to join in that charade. But he, too, comes holding out a brimming cup to her, his white teeth flashing, Madame, may I also drink to you, he says. His cheeks glowing red with the wine, his eyes smoldering like two balls of dark fire, his spurred riding boots clicking smartly together, he bends down and whispers to her tenderly: Madame . . .*

"It's my turn now, Madame." Colonel Ch'eng rose, holding his cup high in both hands, grinning.

"Really, Colonel Ch'eng, I can't any more," Madame Ch'ien murmured, her head lowered somewhat.

"I'll drink three cups first as a token of my respect; please drink as much as you like, Madame."

Colonel Ch'eng drank the three cups one after the other; a mild glow from the wine spread over his face. His forehead began to glisten, beads of sweat appeared on the tip of his nose. Madame Ch'ien took up her winecup and barely touched it to her lips. Colonel Ch'eng served Madame Ch'ien a wing from the Chicken Imperial Favorite and helped himself to a chickenhead as a relish with the wine.

"My, my!" Chiang Pi-yueh trilled from across the table, "What ever are you toasting me with?" She stood up and leaned over to take a sniff of General Yu's wine. He was holding a rare gold "bird-bath" cup in his hands.

"Young lady, this here is the wine called 'Nocturnal Carousing.'" General Yu laughed roguishly; already his swarthy red face had turned liver color.

> " 'Fie, fie, be off!
> Who is here will carouse the night with you?"

With a grand wave of her hand Chiang Pi-yueh declaimed operatically from "The Imperial Favorite Drunk with Wine."*

"Miss Chiang," Madame Lai called from the other table, "the banquet at the Hundred-Flower Pavilion isn't laid yet, and here you're already 'Drunk with Wine.'" The guests burst into a roar of laughter.

Madame Tou stood up. "We'd better get ready for the show," she announced. "Will everyone move to the drawing room, please."

The guests rose, Madame Lai taking the lead. They filed into the drawing room and seated themselves here and there. The men from the Opera Club took their places on the redwood chairs in front of the screen and began tuning their instruments. There were six of them, counting the *Hu-ch'in*—one played the *erh-hu*, one played moon

---

* A historical drama about the romance of the T'ang Emperor Hsuan Tsung and his favorite Imperial Concubine, Yang Kuei-fei. Yang and Mei-fei, the Plum Concubine, are rivals for the Emperor's favor. Yang Kuei-fei has prepared a banquet for the Emperor at the Hundred-Flower Pavilion, but His Majesty goes to visit Mei-fei instead; whereupon Yang Kuei-fei drinks herself tipsy out of jealousy and chagrin.

guitar,* and one kept time with the small drum and wooden clappers. The other two performed standing, one holding a pair of cymbals, one a large brass gong.

"Madame, that Mr. Yang is superb on the *Hu-ch'in*." Sitting beside her on a leather hassock, Colonel Ch'eng pointed out the man who played the Tartar violin, whispering in Madame Ch'ien's ear. "He's also a fantastic flutist; you won't find another like him in Taiwan. You'll know the moment you hear him play."

Half reclining in the soft armchair, savoring the fresh cup of jasmine tea that Colonel Ch'eng had offered her, Madame Ch'ien followed the direction of his hand and watched Mr. Yang. He was a man of about fifty, clad in a soft silk gown the color of ancient bronze with round designs faintly woven into the fabric. His features were lean and strikingly refined; he had long, slender hands with fingers like ten panpipes of white jade.

He pulled his *Hu-ch'in* from its cotton bag, laid a pad of blue cloth over his knee and placed the instrument on top of it, adjusted the bow, and casually warmed up a little, his head inclining a bit forward and his arm extended, and suddenly the sound of the strings leaped into the air like an outflung rope. His playing of the intermezzo "Deepening Night" was clear, crisp, plangent. The moment he finished, General Yu was first to spring to his feet, applauding, "Wonderful *Hu-ch'in!*" The other guests all clapped. Immediately the gong and drum struck up the overture "The General's Command." Madame Tou went around the drawing room inviting each guest to perform. While the guests were still politely urging each other forward, General Yu, his arm around her, had already walked Chiang Pi-yueh over to the master *Hu-ch'in*.

"May it please Your Ladyship," he announced in the shrill tones of an opera clown, "this here is the Hundred-Flower Pavilion."

Clapping both her hands to her mouth, Chiang Pi-yueh bent over with laughter, causing her gold bracelets to jingle without stop. The guests followed with a burst of applause, and the *Hu-ch'in* launched into the *Ssu-p'ing* Air from "The Imperial Favorite Drunk with Wine." Not even turning sideways, but boldly facing the audi-

* The *Hu-ch'in*, Tartar violin, is the main instrument that accompanies Peking opera singing. The *erh-hu* is the deeper-toned "second violin," and the moon guitar is a stringed instrument with a round, flat body, played like a guitar.

ence, Chiang Pi-yueh began to sing. When she came to an interlude, General Yu ran off and re-entered holding aloft the gold bird-bath cup on a vermilion tray. With one hand he lifted the hem of his robe, pantomiming the role of Kao the Eunuch in a half-kneeling posture before her. "May it please Your Ladyship!" he piped, "Your slave offers wine."

Chiang Pi-yueh, on cue, assumed a drunken air, swaying from side to side and striking one operatic attitude after another. Then with a twist of her body she lunged into a "Reposing Fish" pose and lifted the cup with her teeth. Tossing it to the floor with a clang, she warbled the initial lines of the famous aria:

> Like to a vernal dream
> is our life in this world;
> So will I for mine own ease drink
> my measure full!

By now the guests were rolling with laughter. Madame Tou laughed till she was gasping for breath, calling out hoarsely to Madame Lai, "I think our Pi-yueh is high as a kite tonight!"

"Miss Chiang!" Madame Lai called loudly, laughing so hard she kept wiping away her tears with her handkerchief, "There's nothing wrong with being high, just be careful you don't follow the example of the Imperial Favorite and drink your fill of vinegar."*

Though the guests cheered Chiang Pi-yueh on, she swaggered off and, hustling Mrs. Hsu to center stage, declared, "The Queen of K'unshan opera will now sing 'Wandering in the Garden' for us; then we'll ask Madame Ch'ien, the Goddess of K'unshan opera, to follow with 'Waking from a Dream.' "

Madame Ch'ien looked up. She laid her cup down on the teapoy to her left and saw that Mrs. Hsu had already taken her place before the screen, her body half turned away from the audience, one hand resting on the ebony woodwind stand. She wore a black velvet *ch'i-p'ao*, and her long hair was loosely knotted at the nape of her neck. She faced outward a little, a jade-green pendant in a white earlobe showing through her hair. The trumpet-shaped floor lights shone

---

* To "drink vinegar" is a Chinese idiom meaning to be jealous of someone who has alienated your lover's affections.

on the drawing room like spotlights, casting her slender shadow gracefully onto the mica screen.

"Fifth Sister," Chiang Pi-yueh came over and plunked herself down next to Colonel Ch'eng. "Listen carefully and see if Mrs. Hsu's 'Wandering in the Garden' can top yours," she whispered, leaning over, one hand tapping Madame Ch'ien's shoulder.

"Madame," Colonel Ch'eng also turned around and spoke smilingly. "Tonight it will be my great good fortune to have the opportunity of hearing you sing."

Madame Ch'ien looked intently at the bright gold bracelets darting and flashing on Chiang Pi-yueh's wrists; suddenly she felt dizzy, a wave of tipsiness rose to her head, and it seemed that the few cups of *hua-tiao* she'd swallowed earlier were taking their effect— her eyes felt feverish and her vision was growing hazy. Chiang Pi-yueh's red *ch'i-p'ao* flared up like a globe of flame, catching Colonel Ch'eng's body in a flash, and the golden plum blossoms on his lapels started to leap forward like sparks. Chiang Pi-yueh's eyes were dancing like two balls of dark quicksilver on her glowing face, Colonel Ch'eng's long, slender eyes narrowed, shooting out threatening rays, the two faces confronting her at once, showing their even white teeth, smiling towards her, the two faces so red they shone slowly closing in on each other, merging, showing their white teeth, smiling towards her. The high and low flutes began to sound in unison, the high flute's notes like flowing water, lifting the low flute's trailing fall and carrying it into the aria set to "Black Silk Robe" from "Wandering in the Garden":

> The glorious purples
> > the enchanting reds
> > > once everywhere in bloom
> Alas that these must yield
> > to broken wells
> > > and crumbling walls
> This joyous time
> > this fairest scene
> > > yet Heaven grants me not
> Then in whose gardens do hearts
> > by happiness delighted
> > > still rejoice—

You could say these lines, sung by Tu the Beauteous Maid, are the most challenging in the entire K'unshan operatic repertoire. Even the great flutist Wu Sheng-hao had said, "Madame Ch'ien, your singing of 'Black Silk Robe,' why, Mei Lan-fang himself couldn't do better." *But why does Wu Sheng-hao play the music so high-pitched? (Master Wu, the girls have made me drink too much tonight; I'm not sure of my voice any more—a bit lower, please.) Wu Sheng-hao has said: The first thing a singer should stay away from is wine, and yet Red-red Rose, Seventeen, comes over with that cup of* hua-tiao *in her hands, saying, Sister, let's you and me drink bottoms up. She's arrayed in flashing red and gold, still there she is, saying, Sister you won't do me the honor. Don't talk like that, Sis, it's not that Sister won't do you the honor, it's that really he's the retribution in your Sister's fate. Hadn't the blind woman, our* shih-niang, *said, Worldly glory, wealth, position—Bluefield Jade, only it's a pity you've got one bone that's not quite right. Oh, my retribution. Isn't he the retribution in your Sister's fate? Understand? Sis, it's retribution. And yet he, too, comes over with a winecup in his hands and salutes: Madame. A Sam Browne belt, bright gold insignia pinned on his lapels, his waist belted tight, stance erect, his high riding boots, raven-glossy, water-smooth, with white copper spurs clicking together, his eyelids peach-pink with wine, he salutes: Madame. Is there anyone who doesn't know Madame Ch'ien of Plum Garden in Nanking? Ah yes, His Excellency General Ch'ien's lady. Ch'ien P'eng-chih's lady. Ch'ien P'eng-chih's aide-de-camp. General Ch'ien's lady. General Ch'ien's aide. General Ch'ien. It must have been hard on you, Fifth, Ch'ien P'eng-chih said. Poor thing, you're still so young. As for the young fellows, how could they have kind hearts? The blind woman, our* shih-niang, *said, Ah, your sort of people only the old ones can love and cherish. Worldly glory, wealth, position—only it's a pity, one bone is not quite right. Understand? Sis, he is the retribution in your Sister's fate. General Ch'ien's lady. General Ch'ien's aide-de-camp. General's lady. Aide-de-camp. Retribution, I say. Retribution, I say. (Master Wu, a bit lower, please, my voice is failing. Oh dear, this passage set to 'Sheep on the Mountain Slope')—*

> Spring fever
> that did me by stealth surprise

I cannot send away
Unspoken discontent
  too suddenly
    wells all within my heart
All for that I was born
  a fair maid
    and have been so ever
To be conjoin'd with one worthy our house
  match'd to perfection
    the celestial pair
Then why sweet Fortune
  must my verdant spring be tossed
    so far
and who is here
  to see
    my sleep's affection—

Fiercely the ball of red flame shot up again, burned till those loftily raised eyebrows glistened dark green with sweat. The two wine-red faces were once more closing in on each other, showing their white teeth, smiling. Those fingers like jade panpipes flew up and down the flute. That slender shadow shimmered among the lights on the snow-green mica screen. The flutes sank even lower, grew more and more plaintive, as if they voiced all the Beauteous Maid's wistful longing. The Beauteous Maid was about to enter into her dream, and it was time her dream lover, Liu Meng-mei, appeared onstage. *But Wu Sheng-hao has said that the secret tryst in "Waking from a Dream" is the most suggestive passage. (Master Wu, a bit lower, please, I've drunk too much tonight.) And yet he has to come over with a winecup in his hands, saluting: Madame. His riding boots, raven-glossy, water-smooth, click together, the white copper spurs sting your eyes. His eyelids peachpink with wine, still he salutes: Madame. Allow me to help you mount, Madame, he said; in his tight fitting breeches his long slender legs looked muscular, trim, like a pair of fire-tongs clasping the horse. His horse was white, the road was white, the tree trunks were white, and his white horse shone in the blazing sun. They say that all along the wayside the road to the Sun Yat-sen Mausoleum is full of white birch trees. His white horse galloped through the birch groves like a hare darting about among stalks of wheat. The sun beat down on the horses' backs sending up steam-*

ing white smoke. *One* white. *One* black. *The two horses were sweat-
ing. His body was stained with the odor of horse sweat pungent to
the nostrils. His eyebrows turned dark green, his eyes smoldered like
two balls of dark fire, beads of sweat came running down his forehead to his flushed cheeks. The sun,* I cried, *the sun glares;* I can't
open my eyes. *Those tree trunks, so white and pure, so smooth, shed-
ding their skin, layer after layer, unveiled their tender naked flesh.
They say that all along the wayside the road is full of white birch
trees. The sun,* I cried, *the sun has pierced my eyes. And then he
whispered in a gentle voice:* Madame. General Ch'ien's lady. General
Ch'ien's aide-de-camp. General Ch'ien's—*Fifth,* Ch'ien P'eng-chih
called, his voice choked. Fifth, my dear, *he called, his voice dying,
you'll have to take care of yourself. His hair tangled like a patch of
withered white straw, his eyes sunk into two dark holes, he stretched
out his black, bony hand from under the white sheet:* Take care of
yourself, Fifth. *His hands·shaking, he opened that gold-inlaid jewel
case.* These are emeralds; *he pulled out the first drawer.* These are
cat's eyes. These, jade leaves. You'll have to take care, Fifth my dear,
his blackened lips quivering, Poor thing, you're still so young. Worldly glory, wealth, position—*only it's a pity, you've got one bone that's
not quite right.* Retribution, Sis, *he is the retribution in your Sister's
fate.* Do listen to me, Sis, it's my retribution. Worldly glory, wealth,
position—*but I only lived once.* Understand? Sis, *he is my retribution.
Worldly glory, wealth, position—there was only that once. Worldly
glory, wealth, position—I only lived once.* Understand? Sis, listen to
me, Sis. *But Red-red Rose comes over with that cup of wine in her
hands and says,* Sister won't do me the honor, *her liquid eyes flashing.
So you won't give your little sister the face, she's all red and gold,
flashing like a ball of fire she sits down right beside him.* (Master Wu,
I've drunk too much hua-tiao)—

> Languishing
>   where may I tell
>   my unquiet heart
> Seething
>   how shall I redress this life
>   so ill-fulfilled
>   except I sue to Heaven—

Right at that moment, this life so ill-fulfilled—she sits down beside him right at that moment, all red and gold, at that moment, the two wine-red faces slowly closing in on each other, right at that moment, I see their eyes: her eyes, his eyes. It's over, I know, right at that moment, except I sue to Heaven—(Master Wu, my voice.) It's over, my throat, feel my throat, is it quivering? It's over, is it quivering? Heaven—(Master Wu, I can't sing any more.) Heaven—it's over, worldly glory, wealth, position—but I only lived once—Retribution, Retribution, Retribution,—Heaven—(Master Wu, my voice.)—right at that moment, right at that moment, it's gone—Heaven—oh, Heaven—

"Fifth Sister, it's time for your 'Waking from a Dream.' " Chiang Pi-yueh rose and advanced on Madame Ch'ien, beaming, stretching out her gold-bangled arms.

"Madame—" Colonel Ch'eng called softly. He rose, too, and stood before Madame Ch'ien, bowing slightly.

"Fifth Sister, please, it's your turn now." Madame Tou came over, extending her hand in an inviting gesture.

All the instruments struck up in unison—the gong, the drum, the *sheng*,* and the flute—playing the codetta "Ten-Thousand-Year Jubilation." The guests sprang up from their seats. Madame Ch'ien saw a roomful of waving and clapping hands encircling Mrs. Hsu. The winds blew with mounting intensity; raised high in the air the brass gong was struck, radiating gold in all directions.

"I can't sing now," Madame Ch'ien muttered, gazing at Chiang Pi-yueh, slowly shaking her head.

"That just won't do!" Swiftly Chiang Pi-yueh caught Madame Ch'ien's hands. "Fifth Sister, you are the star. We can't let you off tonight, no matter what!"

"My voice is gone," Madame Ch'ien sputtered. Suddenly she tore herself away from Chiang Pi-yueh's grasp; she felt all the blood in her body rush to her head, her cheeks burned, her throat smarted as if it had been slashed by a razor. She could hear Madame Tou intervene:

"Fifth Sister doesn't want to sing; let her be. —General Yu,

---

* The *sheng* is a small pipe-organ made of bamboo, held in the hands and blown into.

I think we'd better have you, the 'Thunder Warrior,'* for the finale tonight."

"Hurrah! Hurrah!" Madame Lai chorused from the other side. "It's been a long time since I've had the pleasure of hearing General Yu sing 'Eight Great Blows.'"

Madame Lai propelled General Yu toward the gong and drums. Once onstage, General Yu clasped his hands in a salute. "My Humble Performance!" he announced. This brought forth a burst of laughter from the audience. He began to sing to the tune of "Touching Up Red Lips" for the Tartar General Wu Chu's entrance; as he sang he swept up the hem of his robe, mimed mounting a horse, and started circling the middle of the room "at a trot." His broad, fleshy face purple-red with drink, his eyes round and staring, his bushy eyebrows standing straight up, he drowned out the *Hu-ch'in* with his battle cries. Madame Lai, bent double with laughter, ran up and followed General Yu around, clapping her hands in appreciation. Chiang Pi-yueh immediately fell in behind them and kept shrilling, "Bravo, Thunder Warrior! Bravo!" Several other ladies joined in, circling around and cheering, the laughter rose higher in the drawing room, wave on wave. As soon as General Yu finished singing, maids in white jackets and black trousers appeared, bearing bowls of dragon's-eye soup cooked with red dates to soothe the guests' throats.

Madame Tou accompanied the guests outside to the terrace. The night air was dewy and chill. The guests had put on their overcoats; Madame Tou had tossed a large white silk shawl around her shoulders and walked down the terrace steps. Standing by the stone balustrade, Madame Ch'ien looked up; she saw that the autumn moon had just reached the center of the sky; it coated the trees, the garden paths, the steps with a layer of white frost. The potted cassia on the terrace sent forth a wave of fragrance even more powerful than before; it broke over her face like wet fog.

"Madame Lai's car has arrived." Liu the aide stood at the foot of the stairs announcing the guests' cars. First to draw up was Madame Lai's brand new black Lincoln; a uniformed chauffeur jumped

---

* The Thunder Warrior, literally, *hei-t'ou*, "black head," is a character actor on the operatic stage with a black-painted face, usually in the role of a heroic general or an upright judge.

out of the car, opened the door with a respectful bow, and waited. Madame Lai came down the steps with General Yu and took her leave of Madame Tou. After she got into the car, she stuck her head out.

"Madame Tou," she laughed, "your opera program tonight was simply marvelous—even better than Mei Lan-fang and Chin Shao-shan in the old days."

"Why, yes!" Madame Tou replied, half in jest. "General Yu's Thunder Warrior certainly had it all over Chin 'The Tyrant.' "*

The guests on the terrace laughed and waved goodbye to Madame Lai. The second car to drive up was Madame Tou's own sedan; it carried off the group from the Opera Club. Then Colonel Ch'eng pulled up in his jeep, and Chiang Pi-yueh strutted right down; scooping up her long *ch'i-p'ao*, she tried to climb on. Colonel Ch'eng hurried round to help her in next to the driver's seat. Leaning out, she giggled, "Why, this jeep hasn't even got a door! I could get tossed out on the road any minute."

"You'd better drive carefully, Colonel Ch'eng," said Madame Tou. She waved him over and said something in his ear. He smiled and nodded.

"Don't worry, Madame."

He turned to Madame Ch'ien, clicked his heels and bowed deeply; he looked up at her with a smile. "Madame Ch'ien, allow me to take my leave." He leaped nimbly into the jeep and started the engine.

"Goodbye, Third Sister! Goodbye, Fifth Sister!" Chiang Pi-yueh thrust out her hand, waving. Madame Ch'ien saw the bracelets on her arms making gold circles in the night.

"Madame Ch'ien's car?" Almost all the guests were gone; at the foot of the staircase Madame Tou spoke to Liu the aide.

"Madame," Liu stood to attention, "General Ch'ien's lady came in a taxi."

"Third Sister, . . ." Madame Ch'ien called from the terrace; earlier she had wanted to ask Madame Tou to get her a taxi, but there

---

* Chin Shao-shan: famous *hei-t'ou* actor in Peking opera. He was known to opera fans as "Chin the Tyrant" for his great performance in the role of the Tyrant of Ch'u in the play "The Tyrant's Farewell to his Lady-Love," in which Mei Lan-fang played the heroine.

were too many guests around and she had been reluctant to speak up.

"Then as soon as my car comes back, call it in for Madame Ch'ien," Madame Tou said without hesitation.

"Yes, Madame." Liu retired.

Madame Tou turned and walked up to the terrace; in the moonlight her white shawl looked like a cluster of clouds hovering over her shoulders. A breeze brushed past, rustling the coconut palms all around and billowing Madame Tou's large shawl gently. Madame Ch'ien hurriedly pulled her coat tight; her cheeks, burning a moment ago, tingled, stung by the wind. She gave a little shiver.

"Let's go inside, Fifth Sister." Madame Tou, her arm around Madame Ch'ien's shoulder, walked with her to the house. "I'll have them make a pot of tea. Now the two of us can have a good talk together. —It's been so long since you've been here. Do you find Taipei at all changed?"

Madame Ch'ien hesitated for a moment, then she turned her head: "Oh, it has changed a great deal," she said. As they walked to the gate, she added softly, "It's changed so I hardly know it any more. . . . They've put up so many tall buildings."

Winter Night

Winter nights in Taipei, it usually rains cold rain. This evening, a bleak wind suddenly rose up and the rain began to fall pitterpatter again. In no time the water had risen an inch in the alleys around Wen-chou Street. Professor Yü Ch'in-lei, a pair of wooden clogs on his feet, walked to the mouth of the alley and peered in all directions. He was holding up an oilpaper umbrella; the paper had torn and raindrops fell through the large hole onto his bald head. They sent a chill through him that made him hunch his shoulders and shiver. He was wrapped in his old padded gown, thick and heavy enough, but still it couldn't ward off the damp, bone-chilling cold of a Taipei winter night.

The alley was veiled in hazy gray mist. Not even the shadow of a human being could be seen anywhere. A soft, thick silence reigned, broken only by the murmur of the rain falling like a gentle sifting of sand on the tiled roofs of the low houses far and near. Professor Yü stood in the cold rain under the torn umbrella; after a while, he turned and trudged back to his house in the alley. His right leg was lame, and as he limped along awkwardly in his clogs, his body lurched to one side at every step.

The house that sheltered Professor Yü looked exactly like the other University faculty quarters in the alley: they were all old structures left over from the period of Japanese occupation. Long years of neglect had left the doors and windows broken and decayed. The living-room floor was still covered with tatami; from years of dampness the mats gave off a musty odor of rotten straw. The living room's furnishings were modest and sparse: a desk, a tea-table, a pair of tattered armchairs, so worn with age that their cotton insides were showing through. On the chairs, on the tables, on the tatami, everywhere, strewn every which way, were books that had once had hard covers, but now the bindings had come off some, others were frayed and moldy, and many were so battered that they looked like so many dismembered corpses lying there. Mingled throughout were rental-library knight-errant romances covered in brown paper. Ever since the time Professor Yü had flown into a tantrum at his wife, no one dared touch any of the mountainous pile of books in his living room. She had put his books out to sun and lost a sheaf of notes left between the pages of the Oxford edition of Byron's Collected Poems—notes that contained his own inspired reflections on the English poet, written more than twenty years before when he was teaching at Peking University.

Professor Yü came into the living room and sank into one of the tattered armchairs, panting slightly. He massaged his right knee vigorously a few times; whenever it turned damp and cold, his injured leg would start acting up. That afternoon, just before his wife went over to Professor Hsiao's next door for a game of mah-jong, she had instructed him:

"Don't forget, now! Stick on that plaster from the Yü Shan Drug Emporium."

"Would you mind coming home a bit earlier tonight?" he had tried to persuade his wife. "Wu Chu-kuo is coming."

"What's so special about Wu Chu-kuo? Won't you be enough company for him?" His wife wrapped up a wad of bills in her handkerchief and walked out the front door. He'd just happened to have a copy of the *Central Daily News* in his hand, and he'd wanted to stop her to show her Wu Chu-kuo's picture in it, with a caption reading:

Professor Wu Chu-kuo, our world-renowned authority on history, presently residing in the United States, yesterday gave a lecture at the Academia Sinica. Over one hundred scholars and dignitaries attended.

But his wife had already raced off next door. She never missed a single one of Mrs. Hsiao's Tuesday, Thursday, and Saturday mah-jong games. Whenever he tried to protest, she would shush him. "Don't spoil my fun, old boy! I'm going to win a hundred dollars and stew a chicken for you." He couldn't impose economic sanctions on her either, for she always won at the game and she had her own nest egg to draw from. He'd suggested they invite Wu Chu-kuo over for a family dinner, but he had no sooner raised the subject than his proposal was vetoed. As he watched her broad, corpulent back disappear, he was suddenly overwhelmed by a feeling of helpless resignation. If Ya-hsing were still alive, she would surely have gone into the kitchen and cooked a tableful of Wu Chu-kuo's favorite dishes to welcome him back. That time in Peiping when they gave Wu Chu-kuo a farewell banquet, Wu Chu-kuo ate and drank until he was quite expansive and aglow with delight. "Ya-hsing," he had said, "Next year when I come back from abroad I'll have more of your Peking duck." Who could have known that Peiping would fall that next year? Wu Chu-kuo's one trip abroad had lasted twenty years. When Professor Yü saw him the other day at Sung-shan Airport, Wu Chu-kuo was engulfed in such a flood of people—government officials, newspaper reporters, curious onlookers—that not another person could squeeze through. He himself was elbowed to the edge of the crowd and didn't even get a chance to greet him. Wu Chu-kuo had on a black woolen overcoat; he was wearing a pair of silver-rimmed glasses. His hair had all turned snow-white, till it shone. Pipe in hand, he looked completely poised as he answered the reporters. His scholarly and awe-inspiring bearing seemed to have grown mellower with the years. In the end, it was Wu Chu-kuo who had spotted him in the crowd; Wu Chu-kuo had made his way through to him and gripped his hand.

"Why don't I come see you in a couple of days," he whispered in Yü Ch'in-lei's ear.

"Ch'in-lei—"

Professor Yü started up; he limped over to greet his visitor. Wu Chu-kuo was already walking into the vestibule.

"I went to the head of the alley a while ago to wait for you. I was afraid you might not find the way." Professor Yü crouched down, fumbled around in the low wall-cabinet, and fished out a pair of straw slippers for Wu Chu-kuo to change into; one of them was so worn out it had popped open at the toe.

"These Taipei alleys are a regular labyrinth," Wu Chu-kuo smiled. "Even more confusing than the Peiping *hutungs*."*

---

* Residential alleys in old Peking.

His hair was wet from the rain, and his glasses were spotted with water. He took off his overcoat, shook it a couple of times, and handed it over to Professor Yü. Underneath, he had on a Chinese jacket of padded silk. As he sat down, he pulled out his handkerchief and gave his head and face a brisk rub; his silvery white hair got all fluffed up and ruffled.

"I've been wanting to ask you over for days." Professor Yü took out the thermos glass he reserved for his own use, brewed some Dragon Well tea in it, and set it before Wu Chu-kuo; he still remembered that Wu Chu-kuo had never liked black tea. "I can see how busy you must have been the last few days. I felt I had better not join the crowd and add to your burden."

"Yes, we Chinese still love to entertain, don't we!" Wu Chu-kuo shook his head with a smile. "I've been invited to banquets every day for the past few days, course after course, well over a dozen each time—"

"At this rate, if you stay longer, I'm afraid you'll eat your way back to your old stomach trouble," said Professor Yü, smiling in turn. He sat down opposite Wu Chu-kuo.

"You're absolutely right! I can't take it any more, as it is. Shao Tzu-ch'i gave a dinner tonight, and I hardly touched a thing. —He told me it's been a good many years since he saw you last. You two . . ." He looked at Professor Yü intently.

Professor Yü passed his hand over his bald head and heaved a gentle sigh. "He's a government official now, and a very busy man, you know." He smiled. "Even if we were to meet, we wouldn't have much to talk about. Besides, I'm not all that good at idle chat, least of all with him. It's probably just as well we don't run into each other. You remember, don't you, the year we all joined the Moral Endeavor Society? What was the first oath we took?"

Wu Chu-kuo let out a chuckle. " 'Not to become a government official for twenty years!' "

"And to think Shao Tzu-ch'i was the one who led the oath-taking that day! Of course, of course, the twenty-year time-limit has long since expired—" Professor Yü and Wu Chu-kuo both broke out laughing. Wu Chu-kuo put his hands around the glass of Dragon Well tea; he lifted it, blew aside the tea leaves floating on the surface, and had a sip. The hot steam from the tea fogged his spectacles. He took them off and wiped them, at the same time letting out a sigh as though deep in thought.

"Yes, now I've come back, and most of our old friends from the Society have passed away . . ."

"Chia I-sheng died last month," Professor Yü responded. "It was tragic the way he died."

"I read about it in the papers abroad; they didn't report it in detail, though."

"Very tragic . . ." Professor Yü murmured. "I saw him on the campus the day before he died. His neck was paralyzed, and his mouth was twisted to one side—six months ago he had fallen and ruptured a blood vessel—when I saw how ill he looked, I urged him to go home and rest. All he did was force a smile. I understood he was in serious financial trouble, and besides, his wife was in the hospital. That very evening he had to teach someplace else—moonlighting, you know. At the school entrance, he tripped and fell in the gutter—and he was gone." Professor Yü turned his hands palms up and gave a dry laugh. "So ended Chia I-sheng, just like that."

"So that's how . . ." Wu Chu-kuo mumbled.

"I heard somewhere that Lu Ch'ung had died, too. Living abroad, you're probably better informed about it."

"I could see how Lu Ch'ung would end up long ago," Wu Chu-kuo sighed. "During the Communists' 'Hundred Flowers' backlash, the students at Peita purged him. They accused him through his own *History of Chinese Philosophy* of being a lackey of the Confucian cult and forced him to write a confession. How could a man of Lu Ch'ung's character take that? He jumped off the building. Right in front of everybody in Peita."*

"Good! Good for him!" Suddenly Professor Yü got excited and slapped his knee twice. "What a man! I bow to him. He deserves to be called a true Confucian scholar with his unbending spirit!"

"Still, wasn't that one of life's great ironies," Wu Chu-kuo remarked sadly. "Time was when he was one of those who rallied to the call to tear down the 'Confucian Shop.' "†

---

* Abbreviation for *Peiching Tahsüeh*: Peking University.
† From one of the slogans of the May Fourth Movement for intellectual reforms: "Down with the Confucian Shop!"

"Wasn't it, though?" Professor Yü agreed with a resigned smile. "Just look at us—Shao Tzu-ch'i, Chia I-sheng, you, me, and that big traitor, Ch'en Hsiung, who collaborated with the Japanese and was executed—when we were all at Peita, what plans didn't we make together?"

Wu Chu-kuo got his pipe out and lit it. He took a deep draw and blew the smoke out slowly. He remained silent for a while, lost in thought. All of a sudden he began to shake his head, chuckling to himself. He leaned over. "You know, Ch'in-lei," he said, "Most of the courses I give at universities abroad only cover our history up to the T'ang or the Sung. I've never taught a course on the Republican era. Last quarter at Berkeley, I gave a course on the T'ang political system. The students are rioting all over America these days, and the UC students are the worst! They've burned down buildings on campus, chased the Chancellor out, and beaten up professors. The way they carry on—it really galls me! One afternoon, I was lecturing on the civil examination system in Early T'ang. Outside the students were scuffling with the police; they were spraying tear gas all over the campus; it was absolutely insane! Just imagine—there I was in the middle of all that, lecturing on the civil examination system in seventh-century China. How could that possibly interest those shaggy-haired, barefoot American kids, hell-bent on action? They were sitting there staring out the window. So I put down my book.

" 'You call this a riot?' " I said to them. 'Over forty years ago, Chinese students in Peking started a riot ten times, a hundred times more ferocious than yours!' That shook them up all right; they all looked at me in disbelief: *Chinese* students? Rioting?" Wu Chu-kuo and Professor Yü chortled.

"Well, then I told them all about it: 'On May Fourth, 1919, with the Peking University students in the vanguard, a mob of student rioters out in protest against Japan fought their way into the house of a traitorous government official. They set it on fire, dragged out the envoy to Japan, who happened to be in hiding there, and gave him the beating of his life.' All at once those American students sat up and listened to me with awe. They talk and talk against the war in Vietnam, but after all they don't dare burn down the Pentagon. I continued: 'Later, all those students were arrested and imprisoned in the Law School at Peking University, over a thousand of them.' When I saw I had their complete attention, I announced gravely, 'The leader of those Chinese students who beat up the envoy to Japan is standing right here in front of you.' The whole classroom roared at this, some stamping their feet and others clapping, forgetting all about the police gunfire outside—"

Professor Yü shook with laughter, his bald head bobbing up and down.

"They were falling all over themselves asking how we stormed Chao's Pavilion.* I told them we formed a human pyramid and climbed into Ts'ao Ju-lin's house. The first student to jump over the wall had his shoes knocked off; he ran barefoot all around the courtyard setting everything on fire.

" 'Where is that student now?' they asked with one voice.

" 'He's at a university in Taiwan,' I said, 'teaching Byron.' The American kids were overjoyed to hear this, and they rocked with laughter . . ."

Professor Yü blushed at this, his wrinkled face breaking into a boyish smile. He grinned sheepishly and looked down at his feet. He didn't have his slippers on, just a pair of heavy woolen socks with large black patches on the heels. Unconsciously, he put his feet together and rubbed them against each other a couple of times.

"I told them: 'While we were imprisoned in school, a lot of girl students came to cheer us up. The belle of the Women's Normal College and the barefoot arsonist eventually got married; they were China's Romeo and Juliet of the day—' "

"Aw, Chu-kuo, you really know how to make a joke!" Professor Yü ran his hand over his bald head; a nostalgic smile appeared on his face. Seeing that Wu Chu-kuo's tea was cold, he got up and hobbled over for the thermos bottle. As he refilled Wu Chu-kuo's glass with boiling water, he retorted, "Why didn't you tell your students about the student leader who carried the flag in the demonstration that day and got his glasses knocked off in the fight with the police?"

It was Wu Chu-kuo's turn to laugh a little self-consciously. "Well, as a matter of fact, I did tell them how Chia I-sheng slit his

---

* "Chao's Pavilion" (Chao Chia Lou) is the historical name for the residence of Ts'ao Ju-lin, a pro-Japanese cabinet minister in the warlord government, as were Lu Tsung-yü and Chang Tsung-hsiang, mentioned later in this story.

finger and wrote GIVE US BACK TSINGTAO* on the wall in characters of blood and how Ch'en Hsiung paraded through the streets, dressed in mourning and carrying a funeral banner that proclaimed TS'AO, LU, AND CHANG WILL LIVE TEN THOUSAND YEARS IN INFAMY—"

"Yes, Chia I-sheng . . . You know, all his life he wanted to do something grand for his country . . ." Professor Yü sat down with a doleful sigh.

"I wonder, did he ever finish that book of his, *The History of Chinese Thought?*" Wu Chu-kuo asked with a look of concern.

"I've just been editing his manuscript, actually. He'd only gotten as far as the Neo-Confucianism of the Sung and the Ming, and besides—" Professor Yü knitted his brows. "The last few chapters seemed a bit slapdash. His reasoning wasn't at all as keen and original as it used to be. I haven't been able to find a publisher for the book yet. Even his funeral . . . the few of us, his old friends, had to put up the money to pay for it."

"Oh?" Wu Chu-kuo was taken by surprise. "Was he really that . . ."

Professor Yü and Wu Chu-kuo sat facing each other, and they fell silent. Wu Chu-kuo slid his hands into his sleeves, while Professor Yü kept patting his stiff, aching leg.

"Chu-kuo—" After a long while, Professor Yü raised his head and looked at Wu Chu-kuo. "I must say, you're the most successful of us all."

"Me? Most successful?" Wu Chu-kuo looked up, startled.

"Yes, really, Chu-kuo!" Professor Yü's voice grew agitated. "All these years I've accomplished nothing. Every time I'd read in the papers about how your name has become known all over the world, I couldn't help feeling heavy-hearted, and at the same time I felt comforted. At least we have you to vindicate us in the scholarly world—" As he spoke, he stretched out his hand impulsively and took Wu Chu-kuo's arm.

"Ch-in-lei—" Wu Chu-kuo cried; abruptly he tried to free himself. Professor Yü heard the anguish in his voice. "If you keep

---

* The Chinese port of Tsingtao, which had been under German control from 1898 to 1914, fell under Japanese control as a result of the First World War. The Paris Peace Conference backed Japan against China's claim to reassert its sovereignty over the territory.

saying things like this, I won't know where to hide myself!"

"Chu-kuo?" Professor Yü murmured, drawing back his hand.

"Ch'in-lei, let me tell you something. Then you'll understand how I have felt, being away from the country all these years." Wu Chu-kuo put his pipe down on the table, took off his silver-rimmed glasses and pinched the bridge of his nose, knitting his brows together. "I've spent all this time giving lectures here, attending conferences there, all over the world. It all seemed very exciting, all right. Last year the Oriental History Association held a convention in San Francisco. At the session I attended, there was an American student, a graduate fresh from Harvard, who read a paper entitled 'A Re-evaluation of the May Fourth Movement.' Right from the start that young fellow tore the Movement to pieces. He concluded with quite a burst of eloquence. In an iconoclastic outbreak against tradition, he said, these overzealous young Chinese intellectuals completely overturned the Confucian system that had prevailed in China for over two thousand years. These young Chinese, ignorant of the current conditions in China, blindly worshipped Western culture and had a superstitious belief in Western democracy and science. This gave rise to unprecedented confusion in the Chinese intellectual world. But this generation, which had grown up in a patriarchal society and which had neither a system of independent thought nor persistence of willpower, suddenly found itself bereft of its spiritual sustenance once the Confucian tradition crumbled; then, like a tribe of parricidal sons, they began to waver in panic; they became lost—they had overthrown Confucius, their spiritual father—carrying the heavy burden of their guilt, they set out on their spiritual self-exile. Some hurled themselves into the arms of totalitarianism; some turned back and embraced the remnants of their long-since-shattered tradition; some fled abroad and became wise hermits taking refuge in their isolation. Their movement disintegrated, deteriorated. He ended by saying: 'Some Chinese scholars have called the May Fourth Movement a Chinese Renaissance, but I consider it at best an aborted Renaissance.' As soon as he finished, there was great agitation in the audience, especially among the several Chinese professors and students, all of whom turned to look at me, thinking I would certainly stand up to speak. But I didn't say a word and quietly left the conference room."

"Oh, Chu-kuo—"

"Actually, some of that youngster's theses wouldn't be too hard to refute, but Ch'in-lei—" Wu Chu-kuo's voice choked; he gave a nervous laugh. "Just think, I've been a deserter abroad for so many years—several decades! On such an occasion how could my own pride permit me to stand up and speak for the May Fourth Movement? That's why in all my years abroad I've never wanted to talk about the history of the Republic. That time at Berkeley, I only mentioned May Fourth because I saw how excited the students were by the riots and it put me in the mood to talk about it—I just wanted to have some fun with them; it was nothing more than a joke. It's so much easier to talk about China's past glories. I don't have to feel ashamed at all when I tell my students: In its time, the T'ang Dynasty built the most powerful and culturally the most splendid empire in the world—just like that, I've been thundering forth these pronouncements all these years abroad. Sometimes I can't help laughing to myself and feeling, when I talk to these foreigners, like one of Emperor Hsuan-tsung's white-haired court ladies who never ceased boasting about the glories of the T'ien-pao Reign—"

"But Chu-kuo, you've published so many books!" Professor Yü interrupted, almost in protest.

"Oh, sure, I've written quite a few books: *The Powers and the Office of the T'ang Prime Ministers*, *The System of Garrison Commands in the Latter T'ang*. I've even written a monograph, *The Pear Garden Actors of T'ang Ming Huang*. Altogether several hundred thousand words—empty talk, all of it!" cried Wu Chu-kuo, waving his hand. "Those books," he sneered. "They're stashed away in the library, and probably only some American student working on his Ph.D. would want to flip through them."

"Chu-kuo, your tea is cold, I'll go get you a fresh cup." As Professor Yü got up, Wu Chu-kuo suddenly seized his hand.

"Ch'in-lei, let me tell you the truth." He looked up at Professor Yü. "I wrote those books only in order to satisfy the requirements of the American universities. If you don't publish, they won't hire you or you won't get promoted, so every couple of years, I grind out a book. If I didn't have to publish, I wouldn't have written a single one of them."

"I'll just go make you another cup of hot tea," Professor

Yü faltered. He saw a slight spasm pass over Wu Chu-kuo's elegant face. He dragged himself over to the tea-stand in one corner of the living room, emptied the cold tea into the spittoon, and brewed a fresh cup of Dragon Well tea. Holding the thermos glass with both hands, he limped painfully back to his seat. His right leg was feeling stiffer and stiffer from sitting for so long, and a numbing pain seemed to seep out in waves from his knee joint. After he sat down he couldn't help giving it a hard squeeze.

"Your leg seems to have been pretty badly hurt." As he accepted the hot tea, Wu Chu-kuo looked at Professor Yü with concern.

"It's that injury from the time I got run into; I've never fully recovered from it. It's pure luck I haven't turned into a cripple by now," Professor Yü said with an air of self-mockery.

"Have you tried everything possible to treat it?"

"Oh, don't talk about treatment." Professor Yü waved his hand. "I stayed in Taiwan University Hospital for five months. They operated on me, they gave me electrotherapy, they did this, and they did that, the more they did the worse I got. Damned if I didn't get thoroughly paralyzed. Then, over my strenuous objections, my wife got some acupuncturist from God knows where. A few jabs and what d'you know! there I was, feet on the ground and running around again." Professor Yü threw up his hands, laughing helplessly. "I guess we Chinese are pretty weird when it comes to illness; sometimes Western treatments just won't work, and we have to turn to some secret native cure of our own—acupuncture, for example. A random jab of the needle and just maybe you hit the magic spot—"

Wu Chu-kuo shook his head, echoing Professor Yü's helpless laughter. He reached out and patted Professor Yü's injured leg gently. "You have no idea, Ch'in-lei. While I was abroad, whenever I thought of you and Chia I-sheng, I couldn't help feeling ashamed of myself. Life here has been so austere for the two of you, and yet you stick to your posts, educating our own young people—" Wu Chu-kuo's voice started to shake; he gave Professor Yü another gentle pat. "Ch'in-lei, it really hasn't been easy for you—"

Professor Yü gazed at Wu Chu-kuo without saying a word.

Then he scratched his bald head. "All my students are girls now; last semester, there wasn't a single boy left."

"Well, you are teaching the Romantic period, after all; naturally girls take to it," Wu Chu-kuo tried to explain.

"There was one girl student who asked me, 'Was Byron really that handsome?'"

"'Byron was a cripple,' I told her, 'Probably a worse one than I am.'"

"She looked so stricken I had to comfort her. 'But he did have a devilishly handsome face—'" Professor Yü and Wu Chu-kuo broke out laughing. "On my final exam last semester, I asked them to write an essay on the Romantic spirit in Byron. One girl wrote down an impressive list of Byron's mistresses; she even included his half-sister Augusta."

Wu Chu-kuo doubled over with mirth. "Oh yes, teaching girls is fun, too! How's your translation of Byron's *Collected Poems* doing? It must be in great demand here, surely?"

"Byron's *Collected Poems* . . . I never finished translating it."

"Oh . . ."

"Actually, I only have the last few Cantos of *Don Juan* to go. But I haven't translated one word these past seven or eight years, and even if I had translated the whole of Byron, I'm afraid there wouldn't be many people who'd want to read it now . . ." Professor Yü uttered a forlorn sigh and looked Wu Chu-kuo straight in the eye. "Chu-kuo, I haven't been at all as you've imagined me all these years; I never really made any effort to 'stick to' my post; in fact, all along I've been trying to figure out a way to go abroad.
. . ."

"Ch'in-lei—you—"

"I haven't just *wanted* to go abroad, either; I've jumped at every chance, at every scheme that might get me there. Every year, the minute I learned about any foreign grants to our humanities faculty, I'd be the first to apply. Five years ago, after a great deal of trouble, I finally won a two-year Ford Foundation grant from Harvard, almost $10,000 U.S. a year. All the formalities and my travel arrangements had been taken care of. The day I went to the

American Consulate to get my visa, the Consul himself shook my hand and congratulated me. Would you believe, the moment I walked outside the Consulate gate a Taita* student drove his motorcycle straight into me; the next thing I knew, I had a broken leg."

"Ah, Ch'in-lei!" Wu Chu-kuo moaned.

"When I was hospitalized I should have announced I was surrendering the fellowship immediately. But I didn't. I wrote Harvard to say that my leg had suffered only a minor injury and that I would leave for the United States as soon as I had recovered. I wound up staying in the hospital for five months, and by then Harvard had withdrawn the fellowship. If I had given it up early, Chia I-sheng would probably have gotten it."

"Chia I-sheng?" Wu Chu-kuo exclaimed.

"He had applied for it, too, Chia I-sheng. That's why I felt so miserable when he died; I felt I had done him a great wrong. If he had gotten the fellowship and gone to America, he probably wouldn't have died like that. When he passed away, I ran around everywhere to raise money for the funeral expenses and his family. You know, his wife was very sick in the hospital, too. I wrote to Shao Tzu-ch'i, and all he did was send somebody over with a NT $1,000 contribution—"†

"Good grief," Wu Chu-kuo sighed.

"But Chu-kuo," Professor Yü looked at Wu Chu-kuo in chagrin, "The fact is, I badly needed that fellowship myself. When Ya-hsing passed away, my two sons were still small. Just before she died, she made me promise to bring them up properly and give them the best possible education. When my older son went abroad to study engineering, he didn't have a scholarship; I had to borrow the money—a considerable amount, as it turned out. I've been paying it back for a number of years, but I'm still in the red. So I thought at the time if I got the fellowship and used it sparingly, I'd be able to pay off all my debts. Who could have known . . . " Professor Yü shrugged, with a mirthless laugh.

Wu Chu-kuo raised his hand as if he were about to say something, but he only moved his lips a little and fell silent. After

* Abbreviation for National Taiwan University.
† On the average, NT$40 equal US$1. NT$1,000 is about $25 in American money.

a while, he forced himself to smile. "Ya-hsing . . . she was the kind of woman you always remember."

Outside the window, the rain came soughing down more and more heavily. The cold chill kept creeping in through cracks along the windows and doors. The front door opened and banged shut, and a tall, slender young man in a navy blue plastic raincoat came up from the vestibule. His ink-black hair was wet from the rain. He was carrying a pile of books. He nodded to them with a smile and headed toward his room.

"Chün-yen," Professor Yü called to the young man, "Come and meet Uncle Wu."

Wu Chu-kuo glanced at the young man's handsome, lively face. "Ch'in-lei! The two of you, father and son! why—" Wu Chu-kuo laughed in spite of himself and pointed at Chün-yen. "Chün-yen! If I had seen you first when I came in, I would have thought your father had been restored to his youth! Ch'in-lei, you looked just like Chün-yen here when you were at Peita." The three of them laughed together.

"Uncle Wu is teaching at UC Berkeley. You want to go there to study, don't you? Now you can ask Uncle Wu all about it."

"Uncle Wu, is it easy to get a fellowship in the physics department at Berkeley?" Chün-yen asked eagerly.

"Well . . ." Wu Chu-kuo hesitated a moment. "I don't know that much about it, but of course there are a lot more scholarships in the sciences than in the humanities."

"I hear their physics department often spends a million dollars or so on one experiment alone!" Chün-yen's youthful face gleamed with envy.

"America is indeed a rich and powerful country," Wu Chu-kuo sighed.

Chün-yen stayed for a while; then he excused himself. As he watched the retreating figure of his son, Professor Yü whispered, "These days, all the boys want to go abroad to study engineering or science of some kind."

"Well, that's the trend all right."

"We all went out for 'Mr. Science' in our day, didn't we. And now 'Mr. Science' has practically snatched the food out of our mouths." Professor Yü and Wu Chu-kuo chuckled. Professor Yü stood up to get some fresh tea; quickly Wu Chu-kuo stopped him and stood up himself. "I have to give a lecture tomorrow morning early at Chengchi University; I think I'd better leave now and get some rest." He mused for a moment. "The day after tomorrow, I'm flying to West Germany to attend a conference on Sinology. Look, why don't you save yourself the trouble of seeing me off. Let's say good-bye here."

Professor Yü handed Wu Chu-kuo his overcoat. "Really," he said apologetically, "Now you're back at last, and I haven't even asked you over for dinner. My present wife . . ." Professor Yü gave an embarrassed smile.

"Oh, yes! Where is your wife?" Wu Chu-kuo interrupted. "I'd almost forgotten to ask."

"She's next door." Professor Yü squirmed. "Playing mah-jong."

"Oh, well, then please give her my regards, won't you?" As he spoke, Wu Chu-kuo walked toward the door. Professor Yü slipped into his wooden clogs, opened his tattered oilpaper umbrella and followed behind.

"Don't, don't come out, please." Wu Chu-kuo tried to stop Professor Yü. "It's so hard for you to walk."

"You don't have a hat on. Let me walk you part of the way." Professor Yü held the umbrella over Wu Chu-kuo's head; he put an arm around his shoulder, and they walked toward the mouth of the alley. The alley was steeped in darkness; everywhere the rain blew about endlessly. Leaning on each other, treading through the pools of water in the alley, Professor Yü and Wu Chu-kuo trudged slowly along, halting at every step. As they approached the street, Wu Chu-kuo's voice dropped.

"Ch'in-lei, I'll probably be coming back myself in a little while."

"You're coming back?"

"I'll be retiring in a year."

"Really?"

"I'm all by myself over there now. Ying-fen passed away; it's awfully hard getting along alone. My stomach's giving me trouble all the time; besides—I don't have any children, you see."

"Oh . . ."

"It seems to me the area around Nankang is a rather nice, quiet neighborhood. The Academia Sinica is right there, too."

"Nankang's not at all a bad place to live."

Raindrops trickled through the tear in the umbrella and hit their faces. The two of them hunched their shoulders against the cold. Just then, a taxi drove up; Professor Yü immediately raised his hand to signal it. As the taxi driver pushed open the door, Professor Yü offered his hand to Wu Chu-kuo for a last farewell.

"Chu-kuo." As he held Wu Chu-kuo's hand in his, suddenly his voice shook. "There's something I haven't been able to bring myself to ask."

"Eh?"

"Do you think you could possibly write a recommendation for me? If any American university happens to have an opening, I'd still like to go abroad to teach for a year or two."

"But—I'm afraid they wouldn't want to hire a Chinese to teach English literature."

"Of course, of course." Professor Yü cleared his throat. "I wouldn't go to America to teach Byron—what I mean to say is that if there's a school where they need somebody to teach Chinese or something like that."

"Oh . . ." Wu Chu-kuo hesitated. "Why yes, I'll try."

After Wu Chu-kuo was in the taxi, he reached out and gave Professor Yü a firm handshake.

Professor Yü plodded back home. By now the bottom of his gown was soaked through; wet and cold, it clung to his legs; his right knee had really begun to hurt. He hobbled into the kitchen, got the plaster from the Yü Shan Drug Emporium that had been warming on the stove, and pressed the hot dressing snugly over his knee. As he went back to the living room, he noticed that the window shutter over his writing desk had blown open and was flapping noisily in the wind. He hurried over and bolted it. Through the wooden slats he could see the light was still on in his son's room. Chün-yen was seated at his window studying, his head bent low, his handsome profile framed in the window. Professor Yü was somewhat taken aback; for an instant he thought he was looking at himself as a young man. He had gradually forgotten how he'd looked long ago. He remembered he was only twenty, Chün-yen's age, when he first met Ya-hsing. That time they were together at Pei-hai Park, Ya-hsing had just cut off her braids, and her beautiful hair flew about in the wind. In her dark blue college skirt she stood beside Pei-hai Lake. Her skirt fluttered in the breeze. The evening light in the west set the whole lake on fire and tinged her face with a crimson glow. He had contributed a poem to *New Tide*; it was dedicated to Ya-hsing:

> When you recline on the jade green waves
> the sky's profusion of afterglow
> metamorphoses into myriads of lotus flowers
> that lift you up
> to drift away with the wind
> Hsing Hsing
> you are the Goddess Who Walks on the Waves

Professor Yü shook his very bald head and smiled shame-facedly. He found it had rained in on his desk and wet the pile of books there. He gave them a quick wipe with his sleeve and picked up a book at random, *The Hermit Knight of Willow Lake*. He sat down in the chair under the dim light and turned a page or two before his eyes closed; soon he began to nod and dozed off. Half-asleep, he could vaguely hear the sounds of mah-jong tiles being shuffled and the women laughing and chattering next door.

The winter night in Taipei deepened as the cold rain outside the window continued to fall incessantly.

State Funeral

It was an early morning in December. The sky was somber and overcast, the air raw and piercing, as squall upon squall of cold wind swept past. In front of the Taipei Metropolitan Funeral Hall rows of white wreaths stretched all the way from the gate to the sidewalk. An honor guard, metal helmets shining, stood at order arms in two columns, one on either side of the main entrance. The street had been closed to normal traffic; every now and then one or two black official limousines drove slowly in. An old man, leaning on his staff, walked up to the gate of the funeral hall. The hair on his head was white as snow; even his beard and eyebrows were all white. He had on a Sun Yat-sen tunic of blue serge somewhat the worse for wear and a pair of soft-soled black cloth shoes. Stopping before the memorial arch at the entrance, he raised his head, squinted his eyes and took a look at the plaque on the arch: MEMORIAL CEREMONY FOR THE LATE FOUR-STAR GENERAL LI HAO-JAN. The old man stood there for a moment, then, leaning on his staff, his back bent like a bow, made his way into the hall.

A table stood by the door; on it lay an ink-slab, writing brushes, and a folding guest book. As the old man drew near, from behind the table a young officer in a brand-new uniform quickly motioned to him, inviting him to sign his name.

"I am Ch'in I-fang—Ch'in, the aide-de-camp," said the old man.

Very politely, the young aide handed him an ink-soaked brush.

"I was General Li's old aide-de-camp," Ch'in I-fang insisted, his face solemn, his voice trembling. Without waiting for the young officer's reply, his staff rapping on the floor, he moved on step by step into the hall. There was only a scattering of early mourners inside, all government officials. The walls were covered with memorial scrolls bearing elegiac couplets, many of them so long they trailed down to the floor and fluttered with the wind. In the center of the altar hung a portrait of General Li in full-dress uniform arrayed with medals and decorations; on the wall to the left was spread the green military standard emblematic of a four-star general. The altar was covered with offerings of fruit and fresh flowers, and smoke was already spiraling up from the sandalwood incense in the cylindrical burner. Above the altar hung a horizontal plaque; on it, the huge characters: IN ETERNAL COMMEMORATION OF AN EMINENT HERO. As Ch'in I-fang walked up to the altar and, with great effort, straightened to attention, the Master of Ceremonies stationed to the right of the altar intoned:

"First bow!"

Ignoring the appropriate ritual, Ch'in I-fang threw his staff to the floor, struggled down on his knees, prostrated himself and struck his forehead against the ground several times. Shaking with the effort, he rose to his feet and rested himself on his staff, panting heavily. There he stood and gazed at the late General's portrait; he pulled out his handkerchief, blowing his nose and wiping away his tears. A line of government officials had formed behind him already, waiting their turn to pay tribute to the deceased. A young aide hurried over and gently took Ch'in I-fang by the arm to lead him away. Brusquely Ch'in I-fang wrenched himself free and gave the young fellow a dirty look before withdrawing to one side, his staff thumping. As he stared at those young aides hurrying to and fro about the hall, sleek and clean-cut every one of them, anger flared up inside him like fire in a pan. If you ask me, the General was as good as murdered by these bastards, he growled furiously to himself. Stinking little tortoises, how would *they* know how to take care of him. Only he, Ch'in I-fang—only he who had followed the General all those years knew about his headstrong ways. The moment you asked him, "General, are you sure you're all right?" his face would darken. When he got sick you weren't supposed to ask him about it; the only thing you could do was keep a quiet watch on him from the side. These here sons of tortoises, how would they understand the way it was? The year before last, when the General went to hunt wild boar in Hualien and slipped climbing a mountain and broke his leg, he himself had rushed back from Tainan to see his old chief. There he was, leg in a cast, sitting back on a couch in the living room, all by himself. "General, Sir, at your age, you should take better care of yourself," he had remonstrated with him. You should have seen the way he scowled! You wouldn't believe how grouchy he looked. These years when there were no more battles to fight, he'd go mountain-climbing and hunting. He was well past seventy, but you'd never hear him admit it.

Ch'in I-fang looked up at the General's portrait again. Still the same stubborn look on his face! He sighed, shaking his head. The old man had carried himself like the hero that he was all his life, how could he have given up and lain down like this so easily? But say what you like, he should never have sent his old faithful aide away. "Ch'in I-fang, it's warmer down in Tainan. It'll be better for your health," he had said to him. So he thought he was too old, did he? Grown useless, had he? Or was it because he'd come down with asthma? Since the master had spoken already, how could he still have the face to hang around the Li residence? Ever since the year of the Northern Expedition, when he followed the General with a thermos bottle on his back, fighting their way from Canton in the south to Shanhaikwan in the north, all those many years, who was it but Ch'in I-fang who had stood by him through hell and high water? To think that after all those years of loyal personal service he should have dismissed him with the words—"Ch'in I-fang, it's for your own good!" Just to hear people refer to him as "General Li Hao-jan's aide-de-camp" was enough to make him glow with pride. A fine thing, an old white-haired retainer to be thrown out by his General just like that! Just think about it, is that something you can hold your head up about? When he was in the Veterans Hospital, if anybody asked him about himself and General Li he'd simply ignore them and pretend to be asleep. But that night he saw the Old General clearly with his own eyes, galloping up to him on his black charger, Covered Snow, shouting "Ch'in *Fukuan*! I've lost my commander's sword!" He fell out of bed in his fright, a cold sweat breaking out all over him; it could mean only one thing: the General is done for! Don't think that just because he had led a million troops in battle he should know to take care of himself and keep warm. In those years after Madame passed away, often on winter nights *he* was the one who got up and put the covers back on him. This time, if he, Ch'in I-fang, had still been by the General's side, this would never have happened. He would have seen he wasn't feeling well, he would have seen he was ill, he would have watched over him day and night. These newcomers! Young whippersnappers! Do they feel the same way about their work? People say the night the General suffered a heart attack and fell on the floor, not a soul was around to help him. He didn't get to leave one last word behind.

"Third bow!" the Master of Ceremonies intoned. A bespectacled middle-aged man in the traditional white hemp-woven mourning had appeared and was on his knees by the altar, bowing time and again to acknowledge the condolences of the guests.

"Young Master—" Unsteadily Ch'in I-fang hurried over to the middle-aged man and called to him gently. "Young Master, it's me, Ch'in *Fukuan*."

Suddenly Ch'in I-fang's wizened old face broke into a smile. He remembered the time when Young Master was little when he had helped him into a child-size Army uniform, complete with a pair of jodhpurs and small riding boots, and even fastened his small military cape for him. He had taken him by the hand, and they had dashed to the parade ground. There the General was, mounted on his great black charger, waiting. Behind the horse stood a little white colt. In a flash father and son had galloped off around the grounds. He could see the two of them, father and son, rise and fall on the horses' backs, Young Master's cape flying in the air. When Young Master had shammed ill health and dropped out of the military academy to go off to America, the General was so enraged that his face turned an iron black. Pointing at Young Master, he roared, "After this, don't ever bother to come back and see me!"

"The General—he—" Ch'in I-fang stretched out his hand. He wanted to pat the middle-aged man on the shoulder, he wanted to tell him: Father and son are still father and son, after all. He wanted to tell him: In his last years, the General was not really at peace with himself. He wanted so much to tell him: Once Madame was gone, the General was all by himself in Taiwan; he had felt very lonely. But Ch'in I-fang withdrew his hand; the middle-aged man had raised his head and given him a stare, his face expression-less, as if he had not quite recognized him. A formidable-looking general in full regalia came up to preside over the memorial ceremony. In an instant people thronged the hall. Ch'in I-fang hastily retreated to a corner; he saw rows and rows of generals in the crowd, all standing there at attention, solemn and holding their breath. The presiding general raised the scroll high in both hands and began to pronounce the eulogy in a sonorous Kiangsu-Chekiang-accented voice, reading in rhythmic cadence:

> Titan of warriors! Like a winging eagle.
> He gave his life to the Revolution. Clouds of
> men followed him on the Northern Expedition.
> His command held sway against the Japanese foe.
> Then, pen in hand, he counselled our chief. . . .

With the close of the eulogy, the ceremony began. The first delegation to approach was from the Army Headquarters Command, headed by a three-star general bearing a wreath. Behind him stood three rows of generals in full-dress uniforms all emblazoned with splendorous decorations. His eyes narrowed, Ch'in I-fang took a good look, only to find that among these new generals there wasn't one he recognized. Then followed representatives from the headquarters of the three armed forces, the government ministries, and the legis-lature, who came forward one after another to pay their respects. Ch'in I-fang stood on tiptoe and craned his neck looking all over for old acquaintances in the crowd. Finally he caught sight of two old men walking up side by side. The towering one with the white beard and moustache wearing a dark blue satin robe and mandarin jacket—isn't that Commander Chang? Ch'in I-fang moved forward a step, his eyes narrowed to a thin line. This man has long been living in seclusion in Hong Kong; so he's come, too. Then the one next to him looking so ill and feeble, who keeps wiping his eyes with a handker-chief and is supported by an old orderly, he must be Deputy Com-mander Yeh. He's been bedridden in the Taipei Veterans Hospital for many years, imagine he's still in the land of the living! During the Northern Expedition these were the two stalwarts on the General's staff; everybody called them "Commanders of the Steel Army."*

* "The Steel Army": the Kwangsi Army of the Northern Expedition.

When they fought shoulder to shoulder they were like the Sung Dynasty inseparables Chiao Tsan and Meng Liang,[†] for years they made an invincible team. Just a while ago he had seen their memorial scrolls hanging side by side next to the door:

Pillar of the State! your Genius will be remembered
    a thousand Autumns;
Upon your Strategy Victory followed ever;
Your one Regret: the Yellow Turbans were yet
    to be conquered.

Champion of the Han! a Chu-ke Liang reborn, you swore
    never to share the same Ground with the Enemy;
Lofty in Justice, your Loyalty never failed,
And shall we let your History be burned to Ashes?
                    Chang Chien, in Reverent Memory

In Passes and on Rivers you fought
    a hundred Battles;
Forever shall it live Immortal! your honorable Name;
Too suddenly it rose, the mortal Wu-chang autumn Wind;
The World Entire mourns a True Hero.

Our Country, our Nation is split in two;
How can we bear to see the unending Tragedy and Woe?
When I hear how you went hunting by night,
    like Li Kuang at Pa Ling,
I ask, Was there anyone willing to call back
    the Old General?
                    Yeh Hui, in Reverent Memory*

† Chiao Tsan and Meng Liang: two fierce warriors, who make an invincible team in the popular novel *The Saga of the Yang Family.*

* The memorial scroll, a couplet of parallel construction that follows a set rhyming pattern, is usually couched in extravagant and allusive terms in tribute to the life and work of the deceased.

Here, the first scroll contains historical allusions to the Later Han rebellion of the Yellow Turbans and to the heroic prime minister of Shu Han, Chu-ke Liang.

The second scroll refers, again, to Chu-ke Liang (A.D. 181–234), who died in the midst of a military campaign at Wu-chang Yuan (in present-day Shensi Province), his mission of restoring the Han Dynasty unfulfilled, and to Li Kuang (?–119 B.C.), famous general of the Earlier Han, who distinguished himself defending China's borders against the Huns. During an enforced retirement, Li Kuang spent much of his time hunting. One evening he was coming home late from having a drink in the country and was stopped at the Pa Ling watch station by the drunken station guard.

"This is the former General Li," said Li Kuang's attendant.

"Even an accredited general isn't allowed to go traipsing about after dark," retorted the guard, "much less an ex-general!" And he kept Li Kuang there overnight.

"I've got myself three fierce warriors," the General once said with obvious pride, three fingers raised. "Chang Chien, Yeh Hui, and Liu Hsing-ch'i." But who can this old Buddhist monk be, with such a sorrowful look on his face? Ch'in I-fang, dragging his staff, took a couple of steps forward. The old monk was robed in a black cassock, a pair of straw sandals on his feet; around his neck hung a string of russet-colored rosary beads. Standing before the altar, palms together, he bowed three times, swung round, and walk out.

"General!—" Ch'in I-fang uttered an involuntary cry. He had caught sight of a palm-sized scar, reddish in color, on the back of the old monk's neck. He remembered that wound vividly; during the Northern Expedition, at the battle at Lungt'an against the warlord Sun Ch'uan-fang, Liu Hsing-ch'i got himself a grapeshot wound on the back of his neck. He was taken to the Nanking Sanatorium; the General had sent Ch'in I-fang there specially to take care of him.

You wouldn't believe with what flamboyance Liu Hsing-ch'i carried himself in the old days! He was young, capable, and high in the General's favor; his troops had won virtually every battle they were engaged in. You could say that of all the General's subordinates he was the most successful. 'The Commander of the Iron Forces'*—at the very mention of his nom-de-guerre soldiers would gasp with awe. But what on earth had caused this change in him? Why was he dressed like this? Hobbling with his staff, Ch'in I-fang pushed his way through the crowd and rushed outside after the monk.

"General, it's me, Ch'in I-fang." His back bowed, leaning on his staff, Ch'in I-fang addressed the old monk; he was panting so hard he could scarcely draw a breath.

The old monk halted, surprise written all over his face. For a moment he looked at the man intently, from head to foot. He hesitated.

"Is it really you? Ch'in I-fang?"

"It is Ch'in I-fang, wishing the Lieutenant-General the best of health." He folded his hands in a salute and bowed. Palms together, the old monk quickly returned Ch'in I-fang's salute. That sorrowful

* "The Iron Forces": the Kwangtung Army of the Northern Expedition.

look was slowly reappearing on his face; after a long moment he uttered a sigh.

"Ch'in I-fang—ah, the General—" As he spoke, the old monk's voice choked, and his tears began to fall; hastily he touched the wide sleeve of his cassock to his eyes. Ch'in I-fang pulled out his handkerchief and blew his nose vigorously. How many years it had been since he had seen Liu Hsing-ch'i last! Not since the Lieutenant-General had escaped all alone from Kwangtung to Taiwan. He had just been stripped of his military rank and had come to the Li residence to report to his superior officer. He had been held captive for a year by the Communist Eighth Route Army, and he was unrecognizable: his face looked seared, virtually all his hair had fallen out, and he was so emaciated there was almost nothing left of him but his skeleton. The moment he saw General Li he called out in a trembling voice, "Your Excellency Hao-jan—" then he broke down completely and could not utter another word for sobbing.

"Hsing-ch'i, how you must have suffered. . . ." The General's eyes reddened; he kept patting Liu Hsing-ch'i on the shoulder.

"Your Excellency—I feel so ashamed," Liu Hsing-ch'i swallowed hard, shaking his head.

"The whole situation had gone beyond help; it really could not be blamed on any one person." The General let out a long, deep sigh. The two sat facing each other darkly, at a loss for words.

"When we retreated to Kwangtung, I thought we could put up a last-ditch fight." His voice low and mournful, the General spoke at last. "Chang Chien, Yeh Hui, and you—your divisions were all made up of our own Kwangtung boys; they'd been following me all these years; now that we had returned to Kwangtung we'd be defending our own homes and villages; if we fought to the death, maybe we could still turn the tide. We never dreamed that the end would be such a debacle—" The General's voice shook. "Tens of thousands of our own Kwangtung boys, all lost to the enemy; just to talk about it—ah—makes your heart ache." And at last two streams of tears started to flow down the General's face.

"Your Excellency!—" His own face covered with tears, Liu Hsing-ch'i cried out painfully. "I've followed Your Excellency a good thirty years, ever since we first started out campaigning from our home province—on the Northern Expedition and in the War of

Resistance against Japan—I may say that my troops contributed to our cause in no small measure. And now, the entire force is destroyed. As the commander of a defeated army, I deserve to die ten thousand deaths! And more, I had to suffer all kinds of humiliation at the hands of the enemy. Your Excellency, indeed I cannot bear to face the fathers and elders at home!—"* Abandoning all restraint, Liu Hsing-ch'i let loose a storm of wails.

During the final retreat from the mainland the General, Commander Chang, and Deputy Commander Yeh had waited three days on board the battleship *Pa Kuei* at Lungmen Harbor off Hainan Island for Liu Hsing-ch'i and his troops to withdraw from Kwangtung. Every day the three of them stood side by side on the deck watching and hoping to see him come out. Up to the very last moment when the order was given to sail, the General was still holding his binoculars, peering again and again in the direction of the Bay of Kwangchou. He had gone sleepless for three days and nights; his face was as haggard as if he had aged ten years in an instant.

"The General, to me, he was so—" Shaking his head, the old monk sighed deeply and turned to leave.

"General, Sir, do take care of yourself!" Ch'in I-fang followed him a few steps, calling after him. The old monk didn't even turn his head; his black cassock floating about in the bitter wind soon became no more than a shadow shape vanishing into the distance.

Inside the hall the funeral march sounded; it was time to move the casket. The crowd outside the gate suddenly parted; rifles and bayonets raised, the Army Honor Guard stood to attention; General Li Hao-jan's casket, draped with the Blue Sky and White Sun, was borne from the hall by eight Honor Guard officers. Outside, an Honor Guard jeep was waiting; in it stood a standard-bearer holding aloft the four-star general's banner; behind it stood the hearse, which had General Li's portrait on the front. As soon as the casket was placed in the hearse, all the officials who were to attend the graveside ceremony entered their cars. The long line of official sedans stretched bumper to bumper like a black dragon along the avenue. Both civil

---

* A paraphrase of the famous quotation from Hsiang Yü (232–202 B.C.), the all-conquering general of the Warring States-Ch'in Dynasty periods, who suffered a devastating defeat and ended his own life, too ashamed to face the "Elders East of the River" in his home district.

and military police, their whistles blowing, were busy directing traffic. Ch'in I-fang hastily wrapped a mourning sash of white hemp around his waist; pushing through the crowd with one hand, clutching his staff in the other, he hobbled toward the hearse. Behind the hearse was parked an open-top military ten-wheeler. Several of the young aides had already jumped on and were standing inside the vehicle. Ch'in I-fang went round to the rear and started to climb up, only to be stopped by an MP.

"I am General Li's old aide-de-camp," said Ch'in I-fang agitatedly, and started to climb on again.

"This is a military vehicle." The MP pulled him back down.

"You—you people—" Ch'in I-fang staggered backward, choking with rage; he pounded his staff furiously on the ground.

"When General Li was alive I followed him for thirty years!" he shouted, his voice quivering. "This is the last time I'm seeing him off; how dare you not allow me?"

The captain of the aides ran up to inquire what the matter was, and finally Ch'in I-fang was allowed to board the truck. The old man clambered up, but before he could find his footing the truck pulled off, sending him lurching this way and that until a young aide caught him and helped him to one side. He grabbed the iron railing and hung on, doubled over, panting a long time before he recovered his breath. A chilly gust blew against his face, making him hunch his shoulders. Soon the funeral procession turned onto Nanking East Road; at the intersection stood a giant arch of pine branches; across the top were large characters made up of white chrysanthemums: TRIBUTE TO HIS EXCELLENCY THE LATE GENERAL LI HAO-JAN. As the hearse was proceeding through the arch, an infantry company came marching along one side of the avenue. Seeing the hearse, their commanding officer barked out the order: "Sa-lute!"

The soldiers in the company snappily turned their heads toward the hearse in a military salute.

At the sound of the order Ch'in I-fang, standing in the truck, straightened up in spite of himself, head held high, chin in the air, his face most solemn, his white hair blown erect by the wind. All of a sudden he recalled the year the anti-Japanese war was won and they had moved back to Nanking, the former capital. The General had gone to the Sun Yat-sen Mausoleum at Purple Mountain to pay tribute to the Father of the Country. He himself had never seen so many high-ranking generals together at one time—they were all there, Commander Chang, Deputy Commander Yeh, Lieutenant-General Liu. That day he was the one who served as captain of the General's aides, he with his riding boots, white gloves, a wide belt buckled so tight it held his back straight, and a shiny black revolver strapped to his side. The General was apparelled in a military cape, sword glistening at his side. He was right behind the General, their riding boots clicking jauntily on the marble steps. In front of the Mausoleum the military guard stood in formation, waiting. As they approached, a thunderous chorus burst out:

"Sa—lute—"

Late Winter, the Fifty-ninth Year of
the Republic of China (1970),
California, U.S.A.